Reading
John Milton

Reading
John Milton

HOW

to PERSIST

in TROUBLED TIMES

Stephen B. Dobranski

STANFORD UNIVERSITY PRESS
Stanford, California

STANFORD UNIVERSITY PRESS
Stanford, California

Printed in the United States of America on acid-free, archival-quality paper

Library of Congress Cataloging-in-Publication Data
Names: Dobranski, Stephen B., author.
Title: Reading John Milton : how to persist in troubled times / Stephen B. Dobranski.
Description: Stanford, California : Stanford University Press, 2022. | Includes bibliographical references and index.
Identifiers: LCCN 2022004022 (print) | LCCN 2022004023 (ebook) | ISBN 9781503632707 (cloth) | ISBN 9781503633308 (ebook)
Subjects: LCSH: Milton, John, 1608-1674. | Poets, English—Early modern, 1500-1700—Biography.
Classification: LCC PR3581 .D63 2022 (print) | LCC PR3581 (ebook) | DDC 821/.4 [B]—dc23/eng/20220425
LC record available at https://lccn.loc.gov/2022004022
LC ebook record available at https://lccn.loc.gov/2022004023

Cover design: Rob Ehle
Cover art: Engraving of John Milton, ca. 1887. iStock
Typeset by Elliott Beard in ITC Galliard 10/15

To Shannon and Audrey,
yet once more and always

He above the rest
In shape and gesture proudly eminent
Stood like a tow'r; his form had yet not lost
All her original brightness, nor appeared
Less than Archangel ruined, and th' excess
Of glory obscured: as when the sun new ris'n
Looks through the horizontal misty air
Shorn of his beams, or from behind the moon
In dim eclipse disastrous twilight sheds
On half the nations, and with fear of change
Perplexes monarchs. Darkened so, yet shone
Above them all th' Archangel: but his face
Deep scars of thunder had intrenched, and care
Sat on his faded cheek, but under brows
Of dauntless courage . . .
    —*Paradise Lost*, Book 1, lines 589–603

CONTENTS

LIST OF ILLUSTRATIONS

PRINCIPAL EVENTS IN JOHN MILTON'S LIFE

1608 9 DECEMBER: Milton is born in All Hallows Parish, in London, at 6:30 a.m.

1615 NOVEMBER: Milton's brother Christopher is born at 5:00 a.m.

1620 Milton enters St Paul's School, London, where he meets his best friend, Charles Diodati.

1625 FEBRUARY: Milton is admitted to Christ's College, Cambridge University.

MARCH: Charles I becomes king.

1628 Milton's first poem is printed, a Latin verse, now lost.

1629 JANUARY: Milton receives his BA degree from Christ's College, Cambridge.

MARCH: Charles I disbands Parliament and attempts to rule the nation without a legislature, thus inaugurating his eleven-year "Personal Rule."

DECEMBER: Milton composes "On the Morning of Christ's Nativity."

1630 Milton composes "On Shakespeare."

1632   Milton's "On Shakespeare" is his first English poem to be printed. It appears anonymously at the start of Shakespeare's Second Folio under the title "An Epitaph on the admirable Dramaticke Poet W. Shakespeare."

Milton's family moves to the suburban district of Hammersmith.

JULY: Milton earns his MA degree from Christ's College, Cambridge, and graduates cum laude; he joins his family in Hammersmith.

1634   29 SEPTEMBER: Milton's court drama, *A Masque Presented at Ludlow Castle*, is performed.

1635   Milton moves with his parents to Horton, another suburban district of London.

1637   Court musician Henry Lawes publishes *A Masque Presented at Ludlow Castle* but without Milton's name.

APRIL: Milton's mother dies.

1638   Milton's "Lycidas," an ode about his late university acquaintance Edward King, is published in a collection of commemorative verses, *Justa Edouardo King*.

MAY: Milton leaves England for his Continental journey.

AUGUST: Charles Diodati dies.

1639   JULY: Milton returns to England, much earlier than he had planned.

1640   Milton's commemorative Latin poem to Charles Diodati, "Epitaphium Damonis," is published.

Milton moves to his own house in Aldersgate Street, opens a grammar school, and begins teaching his first two pupils, his nephews, John and Edward Phillips.

5 MAY: The First Civil War begins when Charles I dissolves Parliament after only three weeks.

1641 MAY: Milton's first prose tract opposing the bishops in the Church of England for being corrupt and self-serving is published anonymously, *Of Reformation Touching Church-Discipline in England.*

JUNE: Milton's second prose tract opposing the bishops is published anonymously, *Of Prelatical Episcopacy.*

JULY: Milton's third prose tract opposing the bishops is published anonymously, *Animadversions upon the Remonstrants Defence.*

1642 JANUARY: Milton's fourth prose tract opposing the bishops is published, *The Reason of Church-Government.* This is the first time that his name appears in print.

APRIL: Milton's fifth and final prose tract opposing the bishops is published, *An Apology Against a Pamphlet Called A Modest Confutation.*

2 SEPTEMBER: Parliament closes the theaters for the duration of the civil wars.

JUNE: Milton travels to Oxfordshire and visits the Powell family.

JULY: Milton marries seventeen-year-old Mary Powell; he is thirty-three.

AUGUST: Mary Powell returns home to her family in Oxfordshire.

NOVEMBER: Milton composes Sonnet 8 ("O Captain or colonel") and hangs it on his door as London braces for a military attack.

1643 Milton's sight begins to worsen around this time.

AUGUST: Milton publishes his first prose tract defending divorce in cases of emotional incompatibility, *The Doctrine and Discipline of Divorce.*

1644 FEBRUARY: Milton publishes a revised and expanded second edition of *The Doctrine and Discipline of Divorce.*

JUNE: Milton publishes a tract on pedagogy, *Of Education.*

AUGUST: Milton publishes his second prose tract defending divorce, *The Judgment of Martin Bucer.*

NOVEMBER: Milton publishes *Areopagitica,* a prose tract opposing prepublication censorship.

1645 Mary Powell Milton returns to her husband in London after an almost four-year absence.

MARCH: Milton publishes his final two prose tracts defending divorce, *Colasterion* and *Tetrachordon.*

JUNE: Oliver Cromwell is appointed Lieutenant-General of the New Model Army.

14 JUNE: The Battle of Naseby is fought, a decisive military victory for Parliament's New Model Army.

SEPTEMBER: Milton moves to a house in Barbican Street.

NOVEMBER: William Marshall draws and engraves a portrait of Milton to appear on the frontispiece of *Poems of Mr. John Milton.*

1646 JANUARY: Milton's first collection of poetry is published, *Poems of Mr. John Milton, both English and Latin, Compos'd at Several Times* (dated 1645 because the new year then began in March).

5 MAY: Charles I surrenders to the Scottish army (marking the end of the First Civil War).

JULY: Milton's first daughter, Anne, is born.

1647 30 JANUARY: The Scottish army hands over Charles I to Parliament (marking the start of the Second Civil War).

MARCH: Milton's father dies.

1648 OCTOBER: Milton's daughter Mary is born.

1649 JANUARY: King Charles I is tried, found guilty, and executed (marking the end of the Second Civil War).

13 FEBRUARY: Milton publishes a tract arguing against the divine right of kings, *The Tenure of Kings and Magistrates*; the next day,

Parliament establishes the Council of State to rule in place of
the monarch and the House of Lords (marking the start of the
Third Civil War). A revised, second edition of *Tenure* appears in
September.

MARCH: Milton is appointed Secretary for Foreign Tongues under
the new government.

MAY: Milton publishes his first tract for the new government,
Observations on the Articles of Peace, a formal response to a treaty
by which Ireland was granted political independence and Irish
Catholics were given religious freedom in exchange for their
support of the Royalist cause in the British civil wars.

OCTOBER: Milton publishes his second government tract,
Eikonoklastes, in response to a best-selling book that allegedly
contained Charles I's private meditations while in prison awaiting
trial.

1650 JUNE: A revised second edition of *Eikonoklastes* is published.

1651 FEBRUARY: Milton publishes *Pro Populo Anglicano Defensio*
(*Defense of the English People*), a tract commissioned by the new
government in response to the celebrated European scholar
Claudius Salmasius. Milton's tract contains a detailed, moral
justification for deposing a tyrant.

MARCH: Milton's only son, John, is born.

3 SEPTEMBER: Battle of Worcester: Cromwell defeats Charles I's
son (the future Charles II), who is in league with the Scots.

1652 Milton becomes completely blind.

FEBRUARY: Parliament questions Milton about officially approving
the publication of a heretical book, *The Racovian Catechism*.

MAY: Milton's third daughter, Deborah, is born.

MAY: Milton's first wife, Mary Powell, dies.

JUNE: Milton's only son, John, dies.

1653   DECEMBER: Oliver Cromwell is established as Lord Protector. Milton is hampered by blindness and ill health; most of his responsibilities as Secretary for Foreign Tongues pass to John Thurloe, Secretary of State.

1654   MAY: Milton publishes *Pro Populo Anglicano Defensio Secunda* (*Second Defense of the English People*), a prose tract commissioned by the Council of State in which he defends the new government and responds to a personal attack on his character published in a Latin treatise that sharply criticized Parliament and the Army, *Regii Sanguinis Clamor* (*The Cry of the Royal Blood*).

1655   AUGUST: Milton as a private citizen publishes *Pro Se Defensio* (*Defense of Himself*) in an attempt to defend his rhetorical strategy in his *Second Defense*; here he continues to treat the Protestant cleric Alexander More as the author of *Regii Sanguinis Clamor* despite new evidence that Milton had received to the contrary. More wrote only a preface to *Clamor* and supervised and corrected the press work.

1656   NOVEMBER: Milton marries his second wife, Katherine Woodcock.

1657   OCTOBER: Milton's daughter Katherine is born.

1658   Milton probably begins writing *Paradise Lost*.

FEBRUARY: Milton's second wife, Katherine Woodcock, dies.

MARCH: Milton's daughter Katherine dies.

SEPTEMBER: Oliver Cromwell dies; his son Richard is installed as Lord Protector.

OCTOBER: A revised second edition of *Pro Populo Anglicano Defensio* is published.

1659   FEBRUARY: Milton publishes *A Treatise of Civil Power*, a prose tract in which he argues that neither civil government nor ecclesiastical authorities should control believers' inward faith and conscience.

MAY: Richard Cromwell resigns, and royalist members of Parliament are able to return to the legislature, leaving a clear path for the nation to return to monarchy.

AUGUST: Milton publishes a tract opposing tithes and paid ministers entitled *Considerations Touching the Likeliest Means to Remove Hirelings out of the Church*.

OCTOBER: Milton writes *Letter to a Friend Concerning the Ruptures of the Commonwealth*, a tract about the government's civil and ecclesiastical problems (first published in 1698).

NOVEMBER: Milton writes *Proposals of Certain Expedients*, another tract about resisting a return to monarchy (first published in 1938; there might have been an earlier edition published in 1659 or 1660, but if so, it is now lost).

1660 FEBRUARY: Milton publishes a prose tract, *The Readie and Easie Way to Establish a Free Commonwealth*, in an effort to preserve England's republican government and avoid a return to monarchy (a revised second edition appears in April).

MARCH: Milton writes another tract to forestall the country's return to monarchy, *The Present Means . . . of a Free Commonwealth* (first published in 1698).

APRIL: Milton publishes *Brief Notes upon a Late Sermon* in response to a royalist minister who lauded Charles II.

MAY: Charles II returns triumphantly to London, and monarchy is restored in England. Milton goes into hiding in the house of an unknown friend in Bartholomew Close in London.

JUNE: Milton's arrest is ordered by Parliament, and *Eikonoklastes* and *Defense of the English People* are ordered to be burned publicly.

OCTOBER: Milton is arrested; he is briefly imprisoned and fined for his opposition to monarchy and his support of Charles I's trial and execution. The exact dates and the specific circumstances of his capture and release are unknown.

1661 Milton moves to a new house in Jewin Street, where he will live until his third marriage.

1663 FEBRUARY: Milton marries his third wife, Elizabeth Minshull; the couple moves to a home in Artillery Walk.

1665 JULY: Milton and his family move temporarily outside of the city to a cottage in Chalfont St. Giles as London's death toll climbs because of the Great Plague.

1666 SEPTEMBER: The Great Fire of London breaks out in a bakery, and the city burns for four days.

1667 NOVEMBER: Milton publishes *Paradise Lost* as a ten-book poem.

1669 JUNE: Milton publishes a Latin textbook, *Accedence Commenc't Grammar*.

1670 NOVEMBER: Milton publishes *The History of Britain*.

1671 Milton publishes *Paradise Regained* and *Samson Agonistes* as a twin book.

1672 Milton publishes a textbook, *Artis Logicae* (*Art of Logic*).

1673 BEFORE MAY: Milton publishes *Of True Religion, Heresie, Schism, Toleration*.

NOVEMBER: Milton publishes a second edition of his collected shorter poetry entitled *Poems, &c. upon Several Occasions*; it includes the prose tract *Of Education*.

1674 Milton publishes a revised second edition of *Paradise Lost*, in which he divides the original ten books into twelve.

MAY: Milton's *Epistolarum Familiarium* (*Familiar Letters*) is published, which also contains some of his college exercises.

JULY: Milton's translation of *A Declaration or Letters Patent* is published.

9 OR 10 NOVEMBER: Milton dies at age sixty-five. He is buried a few days later on 12 November in St. Giles Church in Cripplegate, London.

1676   Milton's *Literae Pseudo-Senatus Anglicani* (*Letters of State*) is published.

1681   Milton's *Character of the Long Parliament* (sometimes called "The Digression") is published. It is a previously omitted passage from *The History of Britain* (pub. 1670) in which Milton compares the current state of corruption in England with the evils that were rampant after the ancient Romans departed.

1682   Milton's *A Brief History of Moscovia* is published.

1694   An English translation of Milton's *Letters of State* is published, including his previously unpublished sonnets to Oliver Cromwell, Thomas Fairfax, and a former student, Cyriack Skinner. Also included is a sonnet to Henry Vane, printed previously in 1662 without Milton's name.

1823   The manuscript of Milton's heterodox theology, *De Doctrina Christiana* (*Christian Doctrine*), is discovered in the State Papers Office in London (and is published two years later in 1825). ·

1874   Milton's commonplace book is discovered at Netherby Hall, Cumberland (and is published two years later in 1876).

Reading
John Milton

Introduction

WHEN JOHN MILTON WAS TEN, his parents had him sit for a portrait. It is the earliest known record of the author's existence after his baptism. He wrote in the front of his family Bible that he was born at 6:30 in the morning on Friday, 9 December 1608; parish records show that he was baptized eleven days later in the church of All Hallows, in Bread Street, in the heart of London, not far from the tenement, the Spread Eagle, where he most likely entered the world.

The painting of Milton at age ten is small—it measures only 20 × 16 inches—but the canvas reveals a good deal about the young poet. He looks pale and earnest, a little timid, with fine, almost feminine features. His hair is auburn, and he wears it closely cropped, a style suggesting an early religious zeal, perhaps a youthful call to pursue a higher moral purpose. Short hair at that time was mostly associated with Puritans, a wide-ranging group of devout Protestants who were not formally organized—there was no "Puritan Church"—but who generally agreed on the need for doctrinal and clerical reform. They advocated personal interpretation of the scripture and opposed the English church's emphasis on ceremony, two positions that Milton would later passionately espouse.

FIGURE 1. Portrait of John Milton (at age ten)

Source: Robert J. Wickenheiser Collection of John Milton, Irvin Department of Rare Books and Special Collections, University of South Carolina Libraries, Columbia, S.C.

Yet, the hairstyle in the painting was probably not of Milton's choosing. According to his widow, his tutor had cut it short.[1] This was most likely Thomas Young, the devout Presbyterian who taught Milton for about a two-year period, beginning in 1618, before Milton began at St. Paul's grammar school.

Milton's clothes in the portrait were also probably not his choice. He wears aristocratic attire: a gold-trimmed doublet with a collar of lace frill. Many of the prosperous merchants who lived in the same parish as Milton's family had boys who were the first in their families to attend Cambridge or Oxford, and Milton's parents clearly had lofty aspirations for their child at a young age. Milton's clothes—almost a costume—are not the outfit of a mere Scrivener's son. The reputed artist, Cornelius Jansen, would also not have come cheaply; he went on to paint James I, his children, and various aristocrats at the courts of both James and Charles I.

Milton had an older sister, Anne, and his younger brother Christopher was born seven years after him. But his parents, Sara and John Milton, had lost a child in infancy in their first years of marriage, and before John turned seven, they suffered the infant deaths of two more girls, Sara and Tabitha. Maybe the couple was investing so much in young John, their first boy, because they had already lost so much. Or, if the couple had great expectations for their middle child, perhaps Milton's musician father had begun to glimpse his son's creative potential. Milton wrote that his family and friends expected him early on to become a priest, but he had a good singing voice, and around this same time, at age ten, he had started to write his first poetry. Perhaps his parents already realized that this would not be just a painting of a boy; it was a portrait of an artist.

———

And what an artist he would become. To many, Milton's *Paradise Lost* is the greatest single poem ever written in English, and Milton himself is arguably the greatest poet of all time, in any language. Alfred, Lord Tennyson praised Milton as that "mighty-mouthed inventor of harmonies," the "God-gifted organ voice of England."[2] Ralph Waldo Emerson said that Milton was "the sublimest bard of all, . . . born for the exaltation of mankind," and Margaret Fuller, a pioneer for women's rights who first encountered Milton at age fourteen, concluded more simply that he was "absolutely the greatest of human beings."[3]

For the music of his verse, the breadth of his learning, and the force of his convictions—Milton is unrivaled. He wrote grand, soaring poems about heroic subjects, penned deeply felt lyrics about personal loss and ambition, and created vast, complex mythologies in a bold attempt to supplement the world's religions and surpass antiquity's greatest epics.

And yet, despite Milton's undisputed brilliance, despite the enormity of his poetic achievement, few readers today would describe themselves as his fans. The Milton who emerges from the several excellent biographies that have been published in the past fifty years sometimes seems more remote than relevant, a dour and devout scholar, tailor-made for a scholarly monograph or graduate seminar but removed from our cares and concerns. Readers today, if they think of him at all, may imagine a blind, sullen pedant, warming himself by the fire, while his three daughters sit at a distance, hunched over a table and ready to take down his verses.

This book sets out to see beyond Milton's academic standing—to correct the popular misperception of a censorious purist—and reveal the ongoing power of his writings, their intelligence and emotional depth as well as their impact and prescience. The intended audience is general readers who care about language and literature but who might be reluctant to read a seventeenth-century British poet who mostly seems enmeshed in arcane philosophical debates. I want to show how, some 400 years later, Milton's poetry and prose remain vital and inspiring. His richly imagined scenes, complex and compelling characters, beautifully expressed principles and beliefs—all of these qualities help Milton to transcend the period in which he lived.

But instead of following the well-trod path of a strict chronology or a greatest-hits overview, this book traces some of the major themes in Milton's life and writings—fundamental human concerns—that help us to see the author anew and to discover his continuing relevance. Each of the ten chapters focuses on a central theme that he explored—language, loss, injustice, suffering, liberty, pride, forgiveness, temptation, doubt, and fortitude.

The larger story that these ten chapters tells is about grit as much as great writing. Milton's unyielding commitment to the pursuit of truth and religious freedom—sometimes at great personal cost—set him apart from his contemporaries, and he repeatedly turned to words, in both poetry and prose, as the best way of fighting for these ideals. Plato was one of the first writers to suggest that courage is not an absence of uncertainty or fear but instead a refusal to relent; it is the will to press forward with an awareness of life's hazards and hardships.[4] This is the quality that Milton celebrated in his writings and that, at key moments in his own life, he personally evinced. He could be arrogant and acrimonious, and was as prone to weakness and error as any of us, and yet he distinguished himself by his decision to "bear up and steer / Right onward," as he put it in a sonnet on his blindness, and by his insistent depiction of characters struggling to do the same.[5]

The defining event of Milton's lifetime was the British civil wars and the execution of King Charles I. In 1642, when Milton was thirty-three, the nation became embroiled in an eleven-year political and religious conflict that ultimately killed some 62,000 soldiers, likely a larger proportion of the nation's population than died in World War I.[6] The civil wars were fought over the king's efforts to curb Parliament's authority, and in particular his attempt to limit religious freedom and enforce a uniform practice of worship across England, Wales, Ireland, and Scotland. Milton so believed in the revolution and its military-leader-turned-statesman, Oliver Cromwell, that he sacrificed his sight, ignoring doctors' warnings, putting aside his pain, and writing tirelessly in defense of the rebellion against the king. When, in January 1649, Charles I was tried, found guilty of high treason, and publicly beheaded, his supporters wept openly. Some, hearing news of the king's death, fell to their knees in the street. Milton instead thought that justice had been served. He began working for the new government and soon moved into sumptuous new lodgings in the Palace of Whitehall, formerly occupied by the king.

Reports of the death of monarchy were greatly exaggerated, however, and on 29 May 1660 Charles II donned a cloak with gold lace to lead a grand, military procession through the streets of London as he reclaimed the throne that his father had held before him. It is this later period that is especially important for Milton—after the revolution failed, after the return of a king, when Milton went to prison and then witnessed the capture and execution of many of his friends. That in 1649 he had published a tract in support of deposing and punishing the monarch was sufficient grounds for his execution or life imprisonment; "compassing or imagining the King's death" remained a capital offense.[7] With the restoration of monarchy, he had to go into hiding, and his three young daughters had to be taken away, probably to live with their grandmother.[8] The social author temporarily found himself isolated, shut up in an anonymous house in the London parish of Bartholomew Close—"fall'n on evil days," as he describes his predicament in *Paradise Lost*, blind and afraid, in danger and in darkness.[9] He must have listened anxiously as supporters of the newly restored king celebrated, firing guns, lighting bonfires, and singing and shouting in the streets.

But this was also the period of Milton's greatest literary achievements. If hardship makes the man, then Milton was made in his forties and fifties, after his political ideals were crushed by the Restoration, after losing his sight, and after the deaths of two wives and two children. He continued to defend political liberty and religious toleration, and he went on to write and publish *Paradise Lost*, his masterpiece. If Dante is the author of the afterlife, and Montaigne the writer of the self, Milton is the poet of resilience. He has more to say about the cost of human frailty, the experience of defeat, and the way to persevere—to go on and rise above—than any other writer in English. He wrote about the fall of Adam and Eve, Satan's inglorious rebellion, and Samson's agony among the Philistines. In his writing and in his example, Milton repeatedly suggests how to overcome loss, whether dealing with a failed marriage, the loss of free expression, a crumbling republic, the tragedy of religious violence, or the very first human sin in the Garden of Eden. He is, after all, the author who coined the notion that every "sable cloud" has a "silver lining," who followed *Paradise Lost* with *Paradise Regained*, and who, despite his devout belief in a divine power, focused less on heavenly reward than on each person's finding answers within.[10] Faced with devastating loss, both personal and political, Milton was undeterred, not just enduring but continuing to write, insistently finding a reason to believe—in himself, his country, and a better world.

For readers today, living in an age of almost incessant information—of endless blogs, posts, tweets, and updates—Milton is especially well suited. He was writing during a period of print overload. The London book trade exploded during the middle of the seventeenth century, as more and more books and tracts were published, and politicians, clergy, and laypeople—both before and after the war years—quarreled with and attacked each other in quickly printed ballads, newsbooks, and pamphlets. It was an age when deep political divisions were a constant and when an autocratic style of rule—the king adamantly refused to abide criticism or accept compromise—deepened the nation's political and religious fractures.

Milton's commitments speak to our times. He himself was not always above the fray—not above wading into the mire of petty grievances and grudges—but his works repeatedly offer insight and hope for charting a course above the mess of opinions, prejudices, and half-truths to address some of the most pressing concerns and problems of his day and ours:

censorship, intolerance, greed, tyranny, and corruption. Of course, the seventeenth century should not be equated with the modern world, and Milton should not be made a spokesperson for any side of our present-day culture wars. Nor should Milton be treated as a hero. Irascible when criticized, sometimes mean to his daughters, preoccupied with his own poetic ambition, and blinkered at times by his biases—he wore his shortcomings on his sleeve. But, instead of being canceled or dismissed for his limitations, John Milton deserves to be read today for his poetry's extraordinary majesty and subtlety and for his keen understanding. Especially in his mature writings—complex, dynamic poems and vivid, impassioned prose works—he shows us how to remain steadfast in the face of uncertainty, temptation, and the inevitable missteps that come with being human. He shows us how to be dauntless.

ONE

The Power of Language

"These defenseless doors"

WHEN IN AUTUMN 1642, near the start of the civil war, Robert Devereux, the 3rd Earl of Essex, assumed command of Parliament's forces, Londoners lined the streets to cheer him on as he mounted his horse at Temple Bar and rode out of the city.[1] Devereux—slim, dark-haired, fashionably goateed—cut an imposing figure in his breastplate and leather buff coat as he waved to the crowds and led a large group of lords, soldiers, and gentlemen. Here was a battle-tested captain, a man who had no difficulty recruiting volunteers to serve under his command. He planned to lead an attack on Charles I's troops outside of Worcester in the hope of catching the royalist army unawares. As the two sides—the armies of Parliament and the king—steeled themselves for battle, the earl hoped that Britain's civil wars might be over before they really began.

Devereux's flaw, though, was his caution. He rushed away from London, but then commanded his men to wait: he wanted the royalist army to leave its headquarters at Shrewsbury so that they would be completely exposed before he attacked. It was only after Charles began marching in the other

FIGURE 2. Robert Devereux

Source: *Cassell's Illustrated History of England* (London: Cassell, Petter, and Galpin, 1865), volume 3. Photograph by Lori Howard, Georgia State University.

direction, east toward London, that the earl realized his tactical mistake. He had left the road to London completely exposed.

In the ensuing days, as Devereux hurried back to the city to cut off the king's men, Londoners braced for a royalist attack. Trained bands were hastily called out to reinforce the few generals and soldiers who had remained behind, and the citizenry—men, women, and children— frantically dug trenches, built ramparts, and rounded up anyone suspected of being loyal to the king. Ordnance stored in the Tower of London was dispersed across the capital, and each parish set up its own volunteer guard to arrest suspicious persons and stand watch around the clock. On 25 October, Parliament went so far as to order the closing of all shops so that tradesmen could devote their time to fortifying London and helping to defend its roads and ports.[2]

John Milton's response was to write a poem.

According to a note in the author's hand, he composed Sonnet 8 "when the assault was intended to the Citty"; a note in another hand in the same copy adds that the poem was hung "on his dore."[3] But even without these manuscript details, the opening lines of the sonnet indicate its immediate purpose:

> Captain or colonel, or knight in arms,
> Whose chance on these defenseless doors may seize,
> If deed of honor did thee ever please,
> Guard them, and him within protect from harms.
> (lines 1–4)

Milton begins by directly beseeching any military leader who might happen upon his poem; he was not sure who would be leading the royalist forces and so casts a wide net, addressing broadly any "captain or colonel, or knight." He wants this armed leader to guard his "defenseless doors" and to spare his home—and himself—from violence and plunder. In exchange, he offers to spread the name of the would-be marauder "o'er lands and seas" (line 7).

The sonnet's tone may be poised between the serious and the smiling, but the thrust of the ancient examples that follow the opening lines conveys confidence, not naiveté. Milton recalls that in the sacking of Thebes, Alexander the Great preserved a home because the Greek poet Pindar had once lived there, and he alludes to an unnamed man during the Peloponnesian War who sang the first chorus of Euripides's *Electra* to plead that the walls of the dramatist's city, Athens, would be spared from an army of Spartans, Corinthians, and Thebans. Milton in 1642 was, of course, no Pindar or Euripides—not yet—but the sonnet finds the author in the middle of his life, at age thirty-three, taking seriously the notion that the pen is mightier than the sword. In the process, he was taking a mode of writing mostly associated with romantic love and remaking it into an explicitly political form.

The door to which Milton tacked his fourteen lines would have been his home in Aldersgate Street, in St. Botolph's parish, just outside London's crumbling medieval wall (a few sections are still visible today), an area known at the time for its religious and political radicals.[4] One group, called Ranters, believed that grace released believers from having to obey the Ten Commandments, while another, the Levellers, insisted that even a monarchical government is sustained only by its people's consent. The nonconformist Milton would have comfortably fit in. He had returned to his native city three years earlier, armed with an MA from Cambridge University, fresh from a highly successful tour of the Continent, and eager to establish himself in a career, at last. Milton already planned to write something grand and enduring, but when he saw how the king was attempting to increase the power of bishops and enforce a more consistent form of worship that superseded the authority of individual parishes, he could not keep quiet. How could Charles interfere with one of the central tenets of the Reformation, the right of individuals to worship according to their private, enlightened conscience? Also, England's bishops, Milton was convinced, were shamelessly inept and self-serving. He decided to put his literary plans on hold and soon became embroiled in the controversy about the best way to govern the Church of England—what he derisively called a "troubl'd sea of noises and hoarse disputes"—a disagreement, we will see in a later chapter, that contributed decisively to the start of the civil war (YP I: 821).[5]

The London to which Milton returned in 1639 comprised a vast range of crowded neighborhoods. The inner city—the rectangular area fronting the River Thames to the south and surrounded by walls of Kentish ragstone on the west, east, and north—was especially packed. Innumerable small houses, most of them half-timbered structures, had been built there along with more than 50 guild halls, 109 parish churches, and thousands of shops.[6] In Milton's lifetime, the capital was expanding rapidly; its population more than doubled from 200,000 to 500,000 as the economy boomed and merchants moved to the metropolis to earn sums that dwarfed the income of land-holding aristocrats.[7] But it was mainly the districts surrounding the city proper, like the one where Milton moved in 1640, that continued to swell and flourish. Each of these areas, outside London's ancient wall, developed its own reputation and character, but generally they had a lower cost of living and early on earned a reputation for iniquity. Lying beyond the scrutiny of the London magistrate, the suburbs housed most of the theaters and almost all of the brothels.

Milton probably moved to St. Botolph's parish so that he could concentrate on his writing and teaching. Aldersgate Street was known as one of the quietest spots in London.[8] But even just outside the city's wall, Milton must have coped with a great deal of daily tumult. Visitors routinely commented on how loud the city was. Street vendors shouted out their wares, each trade adopting its own, readily distinguishable sound—its own timbre and rhythm—so that experienced city dwellers could tell them apart.[9] Meanwhile, coaches and hackney carriages clambered along roads made of stone or rubble, and a crush of pedestrians bustled or traipsed along winding passageways, their voices and treads often echoing off the surrounding structures and cramped streets.[10] With the exception of Cheapside and Cornhill, two sections in the city's social center, many streets were so narrow that a person standing in the middle could touch the buildings on either side.[11] Carts jostled for space with tradesmen, water carriers, beggars, peddlers, courtiers, clergy, and horses. On windy days, the brightly painted wooden signboards hanging over the many shops creaked dangerously overhead.[12] Adding to the din were the wooden lifts called pattens that some women affixed to the soles of their shoes to raise their skirts out of the inevitable puddles and mud.

The possibility of an imminent military strike in 1642, when Devereux left the city unguarded, threatened to bring all of this activity—all of this liveliness—to a halt. Londoners that autumn felt uneasy, going to bed each night wondering whether they would awaken to a full-scale war and worried that their hastily built defenses would fall short. Milton no doubt shared their dread: he had started working as a teacher just a few years earlier, and his first students were his sister's two sons, John Phillips (age nine), who moved in with his uncle, and Edward (age ten), who was at first a day student.[13] Milton was by all accounts a good teacher—Edward said he and his brother were fluent in Latin within the year[14]—and the poet felt an avuncular, maybe even fatherly affection for the boys: they continued to visit him in his later years, sometimes seeking his assistance with their own prose and also helping him with his writing after he lost his sight. While living in Aldersgate Street, Milton probably composed his Latin grammar (published in 1669), his treatise on logic (published in 1672), and his Latin and Greek thesauruses (now lost).[15] All of these textbooks—along with a brief treatise he published on educational reform in 1644—suggest that he had high hopes for his teaching. He may not have aspired to teach most of the boys in St. Botolph's parish, but if the civil wars had not intervened, he had expected to expand and formalize his school.[16] The threat of violent attack in 1642 changed all of these plans.

But for Milton to nail the sonnet on his door must have seemed strange, even foolish to neighbors and passersby as the rest of the city took more drastic, practical precautions against an imminent military strike. In times of peace, notices were regularly posted around the city; each Saturday night, printed copies of title pages were hung from windows, doors, and posts for books that would be put on sale in the coming week.[17] Milton's small, handwritten poem must have appeared especially vulnerable at the start of the war. He was promising its reader immortality, but it was just one among hundreds of leaves of paper tacked around the city that, flapping in the wind, gradually faded, curled, and tore.

Still, if the sheet of paper that Milton used was only a gust away from taking flight or being destroyed, he believed in the transcendence of his words and the endurance of verse. He already assumed that he could compose something great enough to outlive a military leader, the anonymous colonel or captain to whom he addressed the sonnet, and he did not doubt that the king's cause would ultimately fail because it was dishonest and unjust. Clearly, he was presenting the poem's royalist reader with a moral choice: to commit senseless destruction, or to find life and grace through art. Maybe, as a newly established schoolmaster, Milton also hung the sonnet on his door to teach his first students a lesson about the preservative power of righteous expression in the face of overwhelming odds, to show them that inspired words will always triumph and that for defeating evil what they needed most was the truth.

Milton's insistence in the power of words was one of his distinguishing beliefs. Later chapters will show that he embraced this ideal in his polemical prose, in his specific opposition to Parliament's censorship, and in the many powerful exchanges in his three major poems—between Adam and Eve, Satan and Eve, Samson and Dalila, and Jesus and Satan. The belief probably emerged early on as part of the language training that dominated Milton's school years, although initially the words that fascinated him would not have been English. Throughout the seventeenth century, Latin remained the language of not only statecraft but also scholarship and all serious literature; well-wrought Latin, in poetry or prose, represented the crowning achievement of humanistic learning. If Milton truly wanted to write something lasting, he should have chosen Latin so that he could reach an international audience.

Milton already knew Latin when, two decades before the start of the civil war, he began attending St. Paul's grammar school in the center of London. Education at the time still focused on the study of classical texts; just to be admitted to St. Paul's, students had to demonstrate their ability to read and write both English and Latin.[18] In the first year, boys were then expected to master Latin grammar; in the following years, they proceeded to study a range of classical authors—Justinus, Ovid, and Terence, then advancing to Cicero, Horace, and Virgil. The study of Greek literature began a little later, once again starting with grammar, then progressing to the New Testament, then to Hesiod and Theocritus, and finally to Euripides, Isocrates, and Homer. The practice of requiring students to copy and imitate the works of these authors helps to account for the preponderance of classical ideas and allusions in poems and pamphlets by early modern writers. Homer and Virgil were in these writers' blood.

St. Paul's comprised a single room, but that room was spacious, and the school was one of the city's most highly regarded. Each year it enrolled exactly 153 boys, the number of fish that Simon Peter caught after following Jesus's advice (John 21:11). The motto painted on the glass of each window was blunt, "Aut doce, aut disce, aut discede" (Either teach, or learn, or leave). Whipping remained a widely accepted practice in grammar school, almost a rite of passage. Severe teachers were thought to be good teachers, and even the best students would not have escaped their share of floggings.

Milton apparently thrived there. He formed life-long bonds with some of his fellow students—most notably, Charles Diodati, his best friend, and Alexander Gill, the schoolmaster's son—while Milton's ability and doggedness must have set him apart from his peers. In one of his letters, he contrasts Diodati's reading habits with his own:

> I know your method of studying to be so arranged that you frequently take breath in the middle, visit your friends, write much, sometimes make a journey, whereas my genius is such that no delay, no rest, no care or thought almost of anything, holds me aside until I reach the end I am making for, and round off, as it were, some great period of my studies.[19]

Milton's younger brother also reported that the poet-to-be studied "very hard," working by candlelight, poring over his books, and staying up until midnight or 1 a.m. Milton's ever-attentive father asked the maid to sit up with him.[20]

It would have been dark each morning and many nights as Milton walked to school and then home; classes began promptly with prayers at 6:00 a.m. (7:00 a.m. in the winter) and stretched until 5:00 (4:00 p.m. in the winter). In the middle of the day, boys usually had two hours for lunch.[21] What did the teenage Milton think about as he sleepily made his way back and forth through the city? Was he practicing his conjugations and declensions, musing on the pretty girls he passed—in one early poem he described them as "stars breathing forth seductive flames"[22]—or was he already starting to formulate his literary plans? This much is certain: the experience of translating, paraphrasing, and analyzing Latin and Greek literature—day after day, term after term—provided the crucial technical preparation that was the foundation for his later becoming a great poet.

Milton probably began writing poetry at age ten, even before enrolling at St. Paul's. So reports the usually reliable John Aubrey, a contemporary of Milton's, an avid antiquarian and natural philosopher, and one of the first English writers of biography.[23] Milton's earliest surviving compositions, though, come from five years later, when he wrote English translations of Psalms 114 and 136. These poems reveal a youthful religious

enthusiasm, a Protestant emphasis on Bible-reading, and perhaps his father's special fondness for the Psalter. Two years prior, Milton's father, an
amateur composer and musician, had written and contributed six musical
settings to Thomas Ravenscroft's *The Whole Book of Psalms* (1621).

Milton's psalm translations also suggest his early enthusiasm for English. Instead of aspiring to devote himself to Latin and follow in Virgil's
footsteps, he decided to forge his own path. He would write for his own
country's honor and moral instruction:

> For which cause, and not only for that I knew it would be hard to
> arrive at the second rank among the Latins, I applied myself to that
> resolution . . . to fix all the industry and art I could unite to the
> adorning of my native tongue; not to make verbal curiosities the
> end, that were a toilsome vanity, but to be an interpreter & relater
> of the best and sagest things among mine own Citizens through-
> out this Island in the mother dialect.[24]

This was a brazen choice. Here is Milton—before the sun had fully risen
on the British empire—committing himself to a language mostly spoken
on one island, and even there it competed with Irish Gaelic, Scottish
Gaelic, Cornish, and Welsh. Milton did compose more than two dozen
Latin poems, no doubt a reflection of his classics-based education and
the prestige still associated with the ancient tongue. The date of most of
these poems is uncertain, but they were probably composed in the 1620s,
sometime when he was between age fifteen and twenty-one. Later, inspired by his trip to the Continent, Milton would turn again to Latin for
a few exquisite, personal poems—to his father, to his best friend Charles
Diodati, and to the Italian patron Giovanni Battista Manso—and afterward, in his role as secretary for Cromwell's government, he would be
tasked with reaching an international audience by writing whole treatises
in consummate Latin prose. Yet, for his greatest works, Milton consistently preferred his native English. He refused to come in second, to
stand in anyone's shadow; he wanted to be the best English author and
to convey the loftiest truths for his country's moral improvement, even
if doing so meant reaching a much smaller readership—what many years

later in *Paradise Lost* he would describe as a "fit audience . . . though few" (Book 7, line 31).

It is not surprising, then, that the sonnet Milton hung on his door in the fall of 1642 was in English. Carriers, drapers, lace makers, and merchants—people from all professions and backgrounds wanted their sons to learn the Roman tongue, both as a sign of respectability and a means of advancement. But still more Londoners could understand English, and Milton in 1642 wanted to reach as many of his fellow citizens as possible. Most important, he was writing about the British civil wars, not some international conflict. His promise—in English—to immortalize any colonel or captain who happened upon his sonnet, to spread his name "o'er lands and seas, / Whatever clime the sun's bright circle warms" (lines 7–8), was not just a bold declaration for the power of his poetic ability. It was a bold declaration about his nation's language.

Almost eight years before tacking the handwritten poem on his door in Aldersgate Street, Milton was already committed to the moral power of true expression to save lives and defeat evil. In *A Masque Presented at Ludlow Castle*, he depicts a virtuous young woman who stares down a sorcerer named Comus by relying on her words and her wits. Milton was commissioned to write the drama by John Egerton, the Earl of Bridgewater, a dashing lawyer and politician, well known for his intelligence and fair-mindedness at the court of Charles I.

The earl wanted the piece to commemorate his formal installation as Lord President of the Council of Wales and the feast of Michaelmas on 29 September 1634. The latter, in honor of St. Michael, was not one of the church's major feast days. People might hold games or attend a procession; mostly the feast was used to signify one of the quarterly dates for collecting rents. But the earl's new position deserved special celebration: he now had authority over seventeen western counties and reported directly to the king. An expensive performance was needed, not just a fine meal—something to make a splash, to establish without doubt the stature and dignity of Ludlow Castle's new residents.

How the thoroughly middle-class Milton came to write for one of England's most prominent and accomplished aristocratic families is not clear. The best musicians, architects, and poets were usually hired to carry off these shows, while all of the performers were amateurs from the court. The performers—not really "actors"—had few or no lines and wore masks until the concluding dance, although their true identities in many cases must have been easily guessed. The wearing of disguises is the reason that such court entertainments were called *masques*. They did not have the clever plotting or psychological realism that characterizes the best-known Renaissance plays; instead, masques emphasized special effects— "spectacle," as it was then called, including expensive costumes and lavish sets. According to the few records that survive, a masque written by Ben Jonson and performed the same year that Milton was born cost more than £4,000, an astronomical sum for a one-night show.[25]

Did the Earl of Bridgewater turn to the young, untested Milton because the earl thought he could exert more influence and get the entertainment that he wanted? A recent graduate from Cambridge in his early twenties, Milton did not have much of a résumé. He had one printed English poem to his credit ("On Shakespeare"), and he had undertaken his only previous aristocratic work two years earlier when he wrote a small part of another royal entertainment entitled *Arcades*, performed by the earl's children in honor of his stepmother, the Dowager Countess of Derby, probably to celebrate her seventy-fifth birthday. The success of this earlier piece no doubt led to Milton's second, larger, and more prestigious commission, although how he got his foot in the door for the first performance is still a mystery. Most likely, Henry Lawes, the music tutor to the earl's children, somehow discovered Milton's talent and convinced the Egerton family to hire his friend for both events. Lawes was twelve years Milton's senior, an accomplished singer and the most famous songwriter of his day. He would compose all of the songs for the performance in Ludlow, and Milton would later write a sonnet in praise of Lawes and his "tuneful and well-measured song" (line 1); eleven years after the masque, Lawes's name and position would be featured prominently on the title page of Milton's first collection of poetry, like a celebrity endorsement.[26]

Milton's masque was his first big break. Of course, he was writing for the earl on demand, not pursuing his own muse, and so had to follow orders. Yet the drama he composed is thoroughly Miltonic; other writers featured marriage and fidelity in court entertainments, but it is hard to imagine anyone else who would have chosen to place the themes of chastity and virginity at the heart of such a work.

Milton's masque is also remarkable for its wordiness. Just that his own writing dominates the drama's spectacle suggests the case he was making for the power of language. The occasion's limitations and constraints seem to have inspired him. Write a story about the earl's three young children? Milton devised a simple narrative of two brothers becoming separated from their older sister in the Welsh woods. Write about the Egerton family's reunion? The masque concludes with the three children emerging unscathed and victorious and being presented to their proud parents. Milton even added a flattering part for his friend, Lawes, who as the Attendant Spirit guides the action and helps the children escape the clutches of the evil tempter, Comus. Likely one of the earl's older daughters performed in the drama's other major role of Sabrina, a water deity, but there is no record of who played Comus. Authors sometimes took part in the performances that they wrote. Could Comus have been Milton? Scholars like to speculate that the ambitious young poet could not resist, that he saved for himself the best role, donning a mask and joining in the fun. Also, as the villain, he could have channeled into his performance any frustration he felt in having to follow closely the earl's orders. It is Comus who threatens (but of course fails) to ruin the Egerton family.

Milton's masque was staged in the town of Ludlow, the official headquarters for the Lord President, in Shropshire, a county dominated by breathtaking scenery, a patchwork of fields, hedges, and pastures spread over rolling green hills. The audience on the night of Milton's entertainment would have entered the ancient stone castle by crossing its massive drawbridge, past the keep (one of the castle's oldest parts, probably dating back to the eleventh century), and through a grassy inner court. Worries about Welsh resistance to the English crown had long subsided by the time of Milton, and the country's magnificent castles—including

FIGURE 3. Ludlow Castle, the Round Chapel

Ludlow, the grandest—had become merely ceremonial residences. The earl would have held court at Ludlow, but several of its structures were already prized more for their antiquarian value than their usefulness.[27]

The audience on that cool fall evening in 1634 consisted of members of the Lord President's council, with their spouses, as well as dignitaries, judges, and knights from Shropshire and the vicinity. These aristocratic and high-ranking guests must have been surprised by the drama's sobering lesson. The guests that night—enjoying their luxurious surroundings, decked in their finest doublets and gowns, feasting and drinking from the earl's richly laid table—would not have expected to hear the Lady rail against indulgence. She denounces both "swinish gluttony" that crams itself at the "gorgeous feast" and "lewdly-pampered Luxury" that "heaps upon some few with vast excess" gifts that should be widely shared (lines 770–79).

Sometime after dinner, the performance began, opening with a dark stage to indicate that it was night as the Spirit walks out alone to deliver his soliloquy, announcing the plot and setting the mythical mood. "The first scene discovers a wild wood," reads the initial stage direction, and the Spirit might have entered among an array of glimmering tapers meant to stand for stars, or he might have held a single flickering torch that cast spindly shadows, hinting at the danger and moral murkiness of things to come. Milton's story is literally about three lost children, but the drama clearly suggests their life journey—their battle with temptation and evil, and their efforts to find a righteous path out of the moral tangles symbolized by the wild woods.

The Lady enters, bejeweled, masked, probably balancing an elaborate headdress. Played by Alice Egerton, the earl's fifteen-year-old daughter—blonde, blue-eyed, and with a high, regal forehead—she is already separated from her two younger brothers, who wandered off to fetch some berries and never returned. She has now heard something threatening, "of riot and ill-managed merriment" (line 172), and she is worried, but not so anxious that she doubts God will protect her. The Lady is alone, but not lost.

The evil enchanter Comus steps forward and offers to help. Milton dramatizes the abrupt shift in mood when the tempter first enters by changing to brisk, rhyming couplets. Comus celebrates an enchanted world of magic and mirth:

> And on the tawny sands and shelves,
> Trip the pert fairies and the dapper elves,
> By dimpled brook and fountain brim,
> The wood-nymphs decked with daises trim
> Their merry wakes and pastimes keep:
> What hath night to do with sleep? (lines 117–22)

Comus as a tempter of virtue is clearly an early version of Milton's Satan. Comus lacks the archfiend's psychological complexity and biblical stature, but his effect is similarly ambivalent: like Satan, Comus is both a force of unremitting malice and a figure whose intelligence and energy are undeniably compelling. Nightly, he haunts the woods with his monstrous rout—roaring like rapacious tigers, howling like stabled wolves (lines 533–34). When he first spies the Lady and hears her beautiful song, he is

FIGURE 4. Engraved title page of *Comus: A Mask* by John Milton (1791)

reminded of the "sweet madness" of a song sung by his mother (line 261), the sorceress Circe, who most famously beguiled Odysseus and transformed his men into pigs. Comus decides that he must have the Lady. He disguises himself as a courteous villager and offers to help. If he fails to find the Lady's brothers, he will take her to a safe cottage. She agrees to go with him.

Here Milton could not resist needling the aristocrats who had assembled at Ludlow. The Lady proclaims that she accepts Comus's "honest offered courtesy" because it "oft is sooner found in lowly sheds / With smoky rafters, than in tap'stry halls / And courts of princes" (lines 322–25). Comus, of course, only pretends to be a lowly shepherd, and he is certainly not to be trusted. The Lady is wrong in an important way, and the irony of her pronouncement might have been met with polite laughter in 1634. But even as the moment passes quickly, Milton was already finding a way to speak truth to power. Years before he would become a full-fledged radical and stridently oppose the monarch, he was hinting that the tapestry hall in which the nobility had gathered to watch his masque might lack genuine civility and kindness.

The next scene depicts the Lady's two brothers searching in vain for their sister and arguing about her safety and strength. The Elder Brother (portrayed by the earl's middle child, Lord Brackley, age eleven) insists that their virtuous sister will prevail, but the Second Brother (portrayed by the earl's youngest child, Thomas, age nine) fears that she may be the victim "of savage hunger, or of savage heat" (line 358). It might have surprised the audience at Ludlow that the brothers were casting the threat to their sister in such clearly sexual terms—the Second Brother, for example, also worries suggestively about her being pricked with "rude burs and thistles" (line 352), and the Elder Brother explains that the Lady's strength lies in her chastity. "She that has that," he concludes, "is clad in complete steel" (line 421).

The virtue of chastity was personally important to Milton. As a young man, he claimed to have taken his own vow of remaining pure, based on his interpretation of St. Paul's letter to the Corinthians, "the body is for the Lord and the Lord for the body" (6:13). Milton said he was also inspired by the chivalric romances he first read as a boy, although there chastity was expressly associated with women:

> I read it in the oath of every Knight, that he should defend to the expense of his best blood, or of his life, if it so befell him, the honor and chastity of Virgin or Matron. From whence . . . I learnt what a noble virtue chastity sure must be, to the defense of which so many worthies by such a dear adventure of themselves had sworn. (YP I: 891)

If chastity is important for women, Milton then went on to reason, it should be even more important for men.

Comus in his second scene with the Lady openly poses a sexual threat. By this point, he has sloughed off his disguise and bound the Lady to a chair. He holds out his glass goblet and tries to coax her to drink a potion that will turn her into one of his riotous acolytes. Travelers who give into temptation and taste his sparkling liquid will have their heads magically changed into those of wild animals (a wolf, bear, lynx, tiger, hog, or goat), a symbol for giving in to passion and giving up all restraint: Comus's followers think that they have become more beautiful and will forget about their friends, family, and homes. In the temptation scene, the stage direction anticipates the setting of Ludlow Castle, a "stately palace, set out with all manner of deliciousness: soft music, tables spread with all dainties." Dancing around the scene is Comus's hideous, animal-headed crew, their mere presence enhancing the tempter's malevolence and warning the Lady of the danger of indulgence.

The masque's main action is an extended argument between the Lady and Comus about giving into temptation: he's for it, she's against. He argues that not using nature's gifts—birds, fish, and flocks—offends God; she counters that nature should not be used recklessly but conserved, anticipating one branch of today's environmentalist movement but on moral (as opposed to ethical) grounds. Yet, if Comus and the Lady seem to be arguing merely about hunting and husbandry, Comus's speech echoes the conversation between her brothers; Comus is implying that the Lady, in all of her natural beauty, should also be enjoyed and consumed. "Beauty

FIGURE 5. William Blake, Illustration 1 to Milton's *A Masque*:
Comus and His Revellers (c 1801). Pen and watercolor.

Source: Huntington Art Museum, San Marino, California.

is nature's coin, must not be hoarded," Comus asserts, in language that
commodifies the Lady's appearance and may pun on the label of *whore*, a
consequence of accepting Comus's perverted communion cup (line 739).
When he urges the Lady to indulge in "mutual and partaken bliss," he
seems to be encouraging not just a sip of his magic potion but partaking
in all sensual pleasures (line 741). The Lady's rejoinder is that nature's
gifts—even her own beauty—must be enjoyed soberly, according to the
"holy dictate of spare Temperance" (line 767). She is not drinking his
drink, and she is not giving in to his taunts.

The power that the Lady wields in the exchange stems from her purity
and virtue—what she calls the "sun-clad power of Chastity" and, as she
becomes more adamant, the "serious doctrine of Virginity" (lines 782,
787). The Lady is confident in her self-determination: "Fool," she tells

the foul sorcerer, "Thou canst not touch the freedom of my mind" (lines 663–64). But as these strongly worded pronouncements suggest, the Lady in Milton's drama also relies on her reason and rhetoric to defeat the demon, and in this regard she is much more powerful than even her brothers realize. She not only rejects Comus's temptation but threatens to destroy him, concluding a long rebuttal of Comus's argument for drinking his potion by appealing to her own innate authority:

> Thou are not fit to hear thyself convinced;
> Yet should I try, the uncontrollèd worth
> Of this pure cause would kindle my rapt spirits
> To such a flame of sacred vehemence
> That dumb things would be moved to sympathize,
> And the brute earth would lend her nerves and shake,
> Till all thy magic structures reared so high
> Were shattered into heaps o'er thy false head.
>   (lines 792–99)

Here the Lady declares that her words have supernatural powers. She had intended to stay silent in protest, but she decides that Comus's iniquity and imposture demand a full-throated response. She tells him her vehemence can even cause an earthquake, and Comus realizes that she is not kidding. He feels panicked:

> She fables not, I feel that I do fear
> Her words set off by some superior power;
> And though not mortal, yet a cold shudd'ring dew
> Dips me all o'er. (lines 800–803)

Like Milton's promise in the sonnet that he would tack on his door at the start of the civil wars, the Lady's words—true ones, inspired by "some superior power" or a "pure cause"—can effect change and disarm villainy. Her "sacred vehemence" can topple monsters, and even the immortal Comus breaks out in a sweat.

But before the Lady can unleash the full force of her linguistic might and vanquish the demon, her brothers rush in with brandished swords and shatter Comus's glass. The Spirit has instructed them how to see through Comus's deception (they must carry a special root), but they fail to grab his wand, and Comus escapes. Here is the plot's single twist: the brothers, even with the Spirit's aid, cannot release their sister from the spell that binds her to the seat. Instead, they must call on Sabrina, a goddess of the region's river who assists young women in need but only if she is correctly invoked. Sabrina has a small role, but it is her powerful song and healing waters that ultimately free the Lady:

> Drops that from my fountain pure,
> I have kept of precious cure;
> Thrice upon thy finger's tip,
> Thrice upon thy rubied lip. (lines 912–15)

Sabrina's pivotal role as a personified purifying river suggests that Milton might have also been trying to teach his aristocratic audience a lesson about the most effective way to rule: just as the Lady argues with Comus about using nature wisely, Sabrina's symbolic, life-saving presence could have reminded the earl's guests that they needed to respect the value of the region's natural resources. That she also died a virgin and now comes to the rescue in cases of "ensnarèd chastity" (line 909) continues the theme of chastity as the most powerful way to defy evil and put down sexual threats.

The drama then concludes as the Spirit guides the three children to their parents' house; Lawes would have probably walked them hand-in-hand across the great hall to their parents' table on the dais. The final scene is staged in traditional fashion with the lifting of masks and a lively dance that brings together the performers and audience.

Of course, Milton's masque in the end celebrates the children's virtue. He had to compliment the earl and his family. When the Spirit hands over the children to their parents before the final song, he praises their faith, patience, and truth; he pronounces that they are "so goodly grown / Three fair branches of your own" (lines 968–69). But more striking is how the Lady and her brothers escape Comus's clutches. They need more than their virtue and depend on powerful words, as spoken by the Lady, the Spirit, and then the goddess Sabrina. Especially notable is the importance attached to poetry and religion. The person who gives the boys the special root to see through Comus's dissembling is described as a type of the humble, true minister, and the person who informed the Spirit about Sabrina's powers was a wise artist figure named Meliboeus. Milton was reminding his aristocratic audience about the values of temperance and chastity. But in emphasizing the power of words he was also telling the high-born guests that they need help—specifically, moral guidance from poets and pastors—if they wish to see their way through the dangers that the dark woods symbolize.

A *Masque Presented at Ludlow Castle* saw only one performance in Milton's lifetime, but it had a long shelf life. So many of Lawes's friends requested a copy that he grew tired of writing it out by hand and had a version printed three years afterward. Milton's name was not included in the book, but today in the Harry Ransom Center in Austin, Texas, sits a single copy of the 1637 publication with a few of the author's neat, handwritten revisions jotted in the margins.[28] Clearly, Milton continued to care about the work. He would publish it two more times, in 1645 and 1673, now with his name.

Still, for whatever reason, no subsequent aristocratic commissions followed for Milton. Most likely, given his growing opposition to Charles I's monarchy as the nation inched closer to civil war, he did not seek any. Instead, Milton embraced the role of polemicist, publishing five tracts criticizing the Church of England's top-down organization—specifically, its corrupt spiritual leaders, the bishops—in an eleven-month span before the start of the military conflict.[29] If words had moral value, then naturally he wished to try his hand at a more direct approach, like the one he then used again in the sonnet he tacked on his door and addressed to a "captain or colonel, or knight in arms."

Decades later, Milton would revisit the Lady's moral dilemma and Comus's threat in another, more famous temptation scene. But, in *Paradise Lost*'s climactic confrontation, he had to follow his scriptural source text, so Eve ultimately succumbs to Satan's wiles and eats the Forbidden Fruit. In *A Masque*, left to his own imagination, Milton created a victorious and forceful heroine. He was not, at this point in his life, apparently

FIGURE 6. Portrait of Milton at age twenty-one after George Vertue, 1725

Source: Robert J. Wickenheiser Collection of John Milton, Irvin Department of Rare Books
and Special Collections, University of South Carolina Libraries, Columbia, S.C.

able to envision the Lady as a fully complicated and free character, as (we
will see) he does with Eve. The Lady is, above all, defined as a virgin, and
despite all of her power, spends most of the drama stuck to a chair. Based
on Milton's other writings, he believed in a hierarchy of the sexes like the
one that informs the exchange between the Lady's brothers. And yet in
A Masque the female character that he puts at the center is redoubtable.
The Lady stands fast and rejects utterly Comus and his bestial drink. If
in the end she needs rescuing, it is by another woman, a goddess, not her
brothers, father, or the male Spirit.

That a few years before the Ludlow performance Milton's friends at
Christ's College, Cambridge, had jokingly called the young author by the
nickname "the Lady" suggests that on some level Milton identified with
the masque's eloquent but chair-bound protagonist.[30] The origin of Milton's feminine sobriquet is unknown. Perhaps his classmates were poking
fun at his delicate voice;[31] his fair, almost ladylike features; or his strik-
ingly long hair (parted in the middle, just reaching his collar). Certainly

Milton and the Lady in his masque shared a belief in chastity and, more important, in sacred vehemence. In his works, he frequently allies himself with prophets—not in the modern sense of a seer foretelling the future but as a person interpreting scripture and applying it to contemporary life. He counted himself among God's messengers, the "selected heralds of peace, and dispensers of treasure inestimable" (YP I: 802).

———

Ultimately, Charles I and his men never invaded London. On 12 November 1642, the king's forces under the command of his nephew, Prince Rupert, advanced only so far as Brentford, about nine miles away from the inner city. The king's army, it turned out, was too slow, and Essex had reached the capital in time to help with its defenses. The zealous, twenty-three-year-old Rupert urged his uncle to press on to London—Brentford had been a decisive royalist victory, including the capture of 500 parliamentarian prisoners and fifteen of their guns—but the king favored retreat to Oxford when confronted with the larger, formidable forces that Robert Devereux now commanded. The civil war, everyone concluded, was not going to be a short one.

Milton that fall may have taken down the paper with his sonnet as the immediate danger passed, or perhaps the autumn rains eventually blurred his inky words and the poem's audacious offer was lost and temporarily forgotten. But as the war years unspooled, he continued to put his trust in the moral power of language, even as his religious allies—and the English citizenry in general—betrayed his political ideals. Like the Lady in *A Masque*, he would travel through his own dark woods in the coming years, and face off against his own fears and dangers. Also like his chair-bound heroine, he would threaten to topple monsters and, like the Lady, discover that he needed help.

TWO

Personal Loss

"Weep no more"

ONE OF THE MOST IMPORTANT voices on which Milton came to depend belonged to his best friend Charles Diodati, but that friendship would be cut tragically short. The two met at St. Paul's grammar school when they were probably twelve. The boys were almost the same age—Diodati, born in 1609, was a few months younger—but they were not in the same class. Diodati had started school when he was very young, and in 1623 he went off to study at Oxford University; Milton would not begin at Cambridge until two years later.

But while the boys overlapped at St. Paul's for only a year or two, they had much in common. Both of their families were middle class and devoutly Protestant; Diodati's father was a physician, and Milton's father a Scrivener, a profession that combined the services of a financial broker with a public notary.[1] Both boys were also passionate about learning and literature, although Diodati published only one poem, a Latin verse on the death of the historian William Camden.[2] Diodati's only other surviving writings are two affectionate letters to Milton. He wrote to Milton in Greek; Milton's letters to Diodati are in Latin.

The correspondence reveals two young men who, above all, cherished each other's company. Their letters are filled with typical epistolary endearments—wishes for good health, requests for news, regrets to be living apart, and plans to meet each other during an upcoming vacation. But underlying all of these expressions is a bond that was lasting and intense. In one letter, Diodati lingers on the pleasures of life in the country—"the scenery blooming beautifully with flowers, . . . on every branch a nightingale or goldfinch"—but he laments that he cannot share these experiences with his boyhood companion, his "kindred spirit."[3] In another letter, Milton tells his friend that when he heard he might be visiting his family's home in London, he raced to see him—"straight away and as if by storm"—riding some seventeen miles from his own parents' home in Horton. He was crushed to discover that Diodati was not there.[4]

The letters also point up the boys' different dispositions. The bright, affable Diodati seems to have been the more outgoing of the two. In his first missive, he is looking forward to Milton's upcoming visit and enthusiastically maps out all the plans he has made. He urges his friend to get ready to "put on a holiday frame of mind" and to expect long walks, much dancing, and much laughing. Milton, as seen through his friend's eyes, seems comparatively shy and studious. In one letter, Diodati playfully rebukes his companion:

> Why do you persist inexcusably in hanging all night and all day over books and literary exercises? Live, laugh, enjoy youth and the hours as they pass, and desist from those researches of yours into the pursuits, and leisures, and indolences of the wise men of old, yourself a martyr to overwork all the while.[5]

But, as in all friendships, the two boys were able to overlook each other's shortcomings. If Diodati could put up with his friend's sometimes avid study habits, Milton could forgive Charles for occasionally being a slow correspondent:

> For I would not have true friendship (*verti amicitiam*) turn on balances of letters and salutations, all which may be false, but that it

should rest on both sides in the deep roots of the mind and sustain itself there, and that, once begun on sincere and sacred grounds, it should, though mutual good offices should cease, yet be free from suspicion and blame all life long.[6]

This seems to be the classical ideal that inspired both boys and kept alive their relationship long after their university years separated them. The expression "deep roots of the mind" ("altis animi radicibus niti utrinque") suggests the profundity of their connection and its origin in their intellectual compatibility. All virtuous and educated young men, according to Aristotle and Cicero, should seek out a similarly intelligent, self-sufficient companion for discussing philosophy and pursuing life's higher truths.[7]

Milton tells Diodati in one poem "I return your love and am devoted to you" ("quam te redamemque colamque," Elegy 6, line 5), and in another he says his friend has "a so loving heart, and a so faithful head" ("Pectus amans nostril, tamque fidele caput," Elegy 1, line 6). This type of impassioned language did not mean that the two boys felt romantic desire. This was a time when men publicly embraced, exchanged kisses, and expressed their friendship like infatuated teenagers. Such intimate same-sex friendships were separate from and sometimes viewed as even the basis for a future heterosexual marriage. Milton in his poetry and letters repeatedly praised his friend's virtue and innocence, and in his own early works he talked about a personal commitment to virtue, like the Lady in *A Masque Presented at Ludlow Castle*. Most often, Milton described his affection for Diodati in terms of a Platonic ideal of beauty so that, to take one example, he tells his friend, "I cannot help loving people like you. For though I do not know what else God may have decreed for me, this certainly is true: He has instilled into me, if into anyone, a vehement love of the beautiful" (YP I: 326).

A crucial part of Milton and Diodati's friendship was helping each other with their poetry. In Elegy 6, Milton mentions a few recent poems that he had composed; he looks forward to sharing them with his friend: "You to whom I recite them will be as it were my judge" (line 90). And Diodati, after sending along some of his poems to Milton, hoped his friend would reciprocate. Milton responded with another affectionate, newsy poem in Latin elegiacs, what he calls a "small gift from a loyal friend" (Elegy 1, line 91).[8]

Diodati grew up in the parish of Little St. Bartholomew, close to the massive Bartholomew's Hospital in the inner city, no doubt a convenient location for the practice of his physician father. (Charles would later pursue the same profession after graduating from Oxford.) Milton in these years lived a few blocks farther south, closer to their school, in All Hallows, another prosperous parish in the inner city inhabited mostly by wealthy merchants.[9] Milton's family home was a six-story tenement occupied by at least seven other families, a building called the Spread Eagle on the north end of Bread Street.[10]

London during this time was a city of strong aromas. The two boys, as they walked to and from school, must have grown accustomed to not just the open produce market in Cheapside, a few yards from Milton's family home, but also the nearby cluster of bakeries which gave the name Bread Street to the lane where Milton was born. The surrounding warren of streets as the boys made their way to St. Paul's would have been filled each morning with a wonderful yeasty scent. Perhaps most important, growing up in All Hallows, Milton lived within a few minutes of the center of the English book trade near St. Paul's Cathedral. Milton and Diodati would have passed daily rows of book shops and printing houses to get to their classes at the churchyard's east end.

The Milton family home was also only a short walk to the Mermaid Tavern, on the corner of Friday Street and Bread. On humid nights the heady perfume of English ale would have wafted toward Milton's house as the tavern's most devoted patrons noisily made their way home. On the first Friday of each month, the poet-actor-playwright Ben Jonson met there with like-minded writers, holding forth on poetry and politics, and cultivating a large group of disciples known as the "Tribe of Ben." Jonson and his fellow writers had to pass directly in front of Milton's tenement to get to the nearest bridge over the River Thames. Did the young Milton ever glimpse the corpulent Jonson, arm-in-arm with some poetic compatriot? Did he ever work up the nerve to talk to the esteemed author—or one of Jonson's fellow drinkers and friends—as the group ambled to and from the Mermaid?

Here, at a formative age, right outside his house, Milton could have had his first contact with poetic ambition and fame, with writers who expected their works to live on long after they were dead. Maybe in these early years he began to formulate his own lofty plans to write something great, something permanent. Maybe he could create his own livelong monument that would triumph over time and death.

But mostly during these early years Milton and Diodati had their heads buried in Greek and Roman literature. The boys would have lingered in the bookshops of St. Paul's Churchyard, wandering among the stalls at their leisure, poring over famous works, paging through new and old books, and sharing the joys of Virgil, Ovid, and Homer.

———

These are the writers to whom Milton would turn sixteen years later as he struggled to confront and cope with Diodati's sudden death. What caused Diodati to die in late August 1638 is not known, but for him to have passed away so young, at age twenty-nine, a little more than two weeks after his younger sister, Philadelphia, suggests that the siblings were stricken with an infectious illness, maybe the plague.[11]

Diodati's final weeks must have been especially hard because his best friend was hundreds of miles away when he first took ill and as his condition worsened. Milton probably did not hear news of his friend's death until many weeks afterward, in the midst of his thirteen-month Grand Tour through France and Italy. Carrying letters of introduction and accompanied by a single servant, he had embarked in May 1638, crossing the channel and traveling through France before continuing on to Italy with the hope of taking a boat and going as far south as Sicily and as far east as Athens. Continental trips were common for mature English students of Milton's social standing, although at age twenty-nine he was a little older and better read than the typical gentleman abroad. He took the route most traveled by other privileged Englishmen, crossing the channel at Dover, then heading from Calais to Paris, his first significant stop. But in the case of Milton, the trip was not just the culmination of his learning; it was a poetic pilgrimage, an opportunity to see the cities of Dante, Tasso, and Petrarch.

Milton must have felt Diodati's presence acutely during his Italian travels—even before news of his friend's tragic death reached him—as he was surrounded everywhere by reminders of Diodati's ancestry. Charles's salutary influence can also be seen in Milton's decision just to go abroad, to forgo the intensity of his studies—"to know a measure in [his] labors," as Diodati put it[12]—and to set off in search of new experiences. Diodati's sway in this regard seems to have been lasting. In later years, Milton, though still bookish, was no bookworm. His nephew recalled that his uncle frequently enjoyed socializing and once every few weeks liked to go out drinking.[13] Milton's youngest daughter, Deborah, also described her father as "Delightful Company, the Life of the Conversation." Another of Milton's friends, the diplomat Henry Wotton, chose a gustatory metaphor to praise the author's company. Wotton commented that after the "first taste" of his friend's conversation, he came to feel "an extreme thirst" and wished to talk again with Milton.[14]

On 27 February 1639, at the comic opera *Chi Soffre, Speri* ("Let He Who Suffers, Hope"), Milton was greeted by the dapper Cardinal Francesco Barberini, who clasped him by the hand.[15] The opera was a lavish public spectacle, designed and staged by a small army of craftsmen and intended to celebrate the completion of the Barberini family's palazzo; the performance was held in Rome's largest theater before an audience of some 3,000 citizens. It was an honor for the cardinal to have singled out Milton from so great a throng.[16] The two men met again the next day, one-on-one. No account survives of their private conversation, but they shared an interest in poetry. Barberini, a celebrated patron of the arts, helped to oversee the decoration of his family's palazzo; perhaps he showed Milton the vast library he had founded or some of the tapestries and paintings he commissioned, including the nearly complete *Allegory of Divine Providence*, a huge baroque fresco by Pietro da Cortona in the ceiling of the grand salon. Barberini, like Milton, also cared deeply about free expression. At the time, he was Prime Minister of Rome and the primary adviser to his uncle, Pope Urban VII; he was one of three members of the Inquisition Tribunal who did not condemn Galileo.

Milton also met Galileo. The physicist and astronomer was already living under house arrest outside of Florence, in Arcetri, a sunny, vine-covered hill south of the city. Galileo was a charming, genial host, and a select group of devoted students lived at his villa and continued to tend to their teacher and help his many guests. Galileo would entertain visitors by playing his own music on the lute and reciting poetry, either his own or works by his favorite Latin and Italian writers. Whether Galileo and Milton shared their poetry with each other is unknown; neither man recorded details of their meeting. Did the blind, seventy-four-year-old scientist talk to his young English visitor about religion? About censorship? About the stars?

Years later, Galileo would be the only contemporary of Milton's mentioned by name in *Paradise Lost*—Galileo's vision through his telescope is compared with the archangel Raphael's perspective—and, more important, the astronomer's stellar, galactic, and lunar discoveries inform the celestial imagery in Milton's epic poem.[17] When Adam asks the angel Raphael whether the earth or sun is at the center of the cosmos—in scientific terms, whether the Ptolemaic or Copernican model is accurate—the angel refuses to give a definitive answer and explains that God has left some things open to humanity's conjecture. Yet Milton himself, like most of his seventeenth-century readers, accepted Copernicus's model of a helio-centered cosmos, a theory that Galileo's telescopic findings unequivocally supported. Thus, when Satan disguises himself as a cherub and asks for directions to Earth, the archangel Uriel relegates our planet to the status of a satellite, reflecting the sun's light:

> Look downward on that globe whose hither side
> With light from hence, though but reflected, shines;
> That place is Earth the seat of man, that light
> His day, which else as th' other hemisphere
> Night would invade, but there the neighboring moon
> (So call that opposite fair star) her aid
> Timely interposes. (Book 3, lines 722–28)

If any doubt remains about the epic's astronomical configuration, when
Satan in a later scene sits alone, soliloquizing to the earth, he incorrectly
reasons that the home of humanity must be at the center of the cosmos.
The devil's wrong-headedness is striking: he tells the earth, "as God in
Heav'n / Is center, yet extends to all, so thou / Cent'ring receive'st from
all those orbs" (Book 9, lines 107–109). Raphael's earlier refusal to con-
firm whether the earth revolves around the sun (or vice versa) seems an
attempt by Milton to emphasize that human knowledge is always limited.
But, more immediately, Adam's doubt and Raphael's demurral highlight
Satan's error and presumption.

Milton alludes to Galileo in connection with Satan one other time in
the epic, as the devil lumbers off the burning lake, just before addressing
the other fallen angels:

> the superior fiend
> Was moving toward the shore; his ponderous shield
> Ethereal temper, massy, large and round,
> Behind him cast; the broad circumference
> Hung on his shoulders like the moon, whose orb
> Through optic glass the Tuscan artist views
> At evening from the top of Fesole,
> Or in Valdarno, to descry new lands,
> Rivers or mountains in her spotty globe. (Book 1,
>   lines 283–91)

Galileo is here the "Tuscan artist," peering at the moon from Fesole, a
town overlooking the Arno river valley (thus, "Valdarno"). The sudden
appearance of a contemporary astronomer in the middle of an epic simile
describing the devil's armament is surprising, but it helps to measure the
distance between Satan's inflated self-importance and diminished stature: the devil looks huge and threatening but only when he is magnified
through a man-made device. Readers will later learn that in heaven Satan's
shield had resembled a sun (Book 6, line 305); now, in hell, it still casts
reflected light as a moon, but it has lost its heroic luster and become a
"spotty globe."

The bitter irony would not have been lost on Milton that, even as he experienced unlooked-for success on the Continent—even as he made so many new friends—he lost his dearest companion back in England. Learning of his best friend's death while still in Naples, Milton came to a halt, devastated and shocked. He seems to have given up all plans to continue and stayed in southern Italy for four months, overcome with grief and grasping at the possibility that there might be some mistake.[18] Why hadn't he been there for Charles? How much had his friend suffered? Milton knew he had to cut short his European journey and relinquish his plans to travel to Sicily and Greece. (He would never get there.) Perhaps it was during these months in Naples that he began to write something to commemorate Diodati and to say all of the things that he had been unable to share with him in the end.

Yet if Milton returned home prematurely, his journey was still deliberate: he decided to honor his best friend by making a last pilgrimage across northern Italy. He traveled back to England via Florence (the city from where Diodati's family hailed), Lucca (the birthplace of Diodati's father), and Geneva (home to Diodati's uncle, Giovanni).[19] More than a decade later, Milton was still thinking about Charles; their friendship resonates in several of his later works—most notably in the description of Samson's friends who try to comfort him in his last hours and in the genial sonnets that Milton addressed to his former students, highlighting the pleasures of their conversation and company. As he tells one of his friends, Cyriack Skinner,

> Today deep thoughts resolve with me to drench
> In mirth, that after no repenting draws;
> Let Euclid rest and Archimedes pause,
> And what the Swede intend, and what the French.
>   (lines 5–8)

Milton is asking Skinner to put aside not only math and learning (represented by the famous Greek mathematicians, Euclid and Archimedes) but all talk of current events such as the invasion of Poland by Charles X of Sweden or the ongoing war between Spain and France. The desire to "drench" such thoughts might be a specific call to distract themselves with drinking, but it more generally reflects the energy of the young Diodati, Milton's lost *primo amico*. Later, in *Paradise Lost*, as the archangel Raphael lunches and converses with Adam, readers may again detect the poet's nostalgia for his dear childhood friend. Raphael, literally "Medicine of God," seems a furtive surrogate for the physician Diodati.[20] The rapport and wide-ranging conversation that the angel and unfallen man enjoy in Paradise conjure images of Milton and Diodati's boyhood days, of their innocent exuberance and intelligence.

The long, moving epitaph for Diodati that Milton wrote and later published in either 1639 or 1640, "Epitaphium Damonis," offers his most poignant expression of his abiding affection for his friend. It is one of Milton's greatest poems for its erudition, intense feelings, and precise rhythms. Yet, modern readers sometimes overlook its achievement because Milton decided to write about his late friend in Latin, likely a nod to the classical languages and authors who were so much a part of the boys' time together. Milton probably had the poem printed to give as a gift-text to Diodati's family and other friends, and may have also chosen Latin to reach a wider, Continental audience. In the poem, he takes comfort in the idea that his writing can memorialize Charles: "You will not wither in an unlamented tomb, and your honor will survive for you, and will long flourish" (lines 27–28). Milton wanted to make sure that future readers also knew about his friend's goodness and brilliance. He had previously been thinking about his own poetic fame, but now he hoped the epitaph would make his friend immortal.

One way that Milton tried to accomplish this was by reaching back to antiquity. After openly praising Diodati as "an extraordinary young man for talent, learning, and other most distinguished virtues,"[21] he expresses his affection for his friend in classical images of fields and sheep, drawing on the Greek and Roman tropes that had been so much a part of the works he and Charles discovered together in grammar school. Milton specifically casts himself as the shepherd Thyrsis and imagines a long procession of nature-minded figures who mourn the death of a shepherd named Damon. Modern readers might find this pastoral imagery strange, but Milton was evidently consoled by the sense of continuity that it conveys. Repetition and patterns provide comfort in his grief. He was writing within a tradition and finding solace that other poets—other people—were able to endure the same devastating sadness. He had lost his best friend, but he was not alone.

Milton knew well that he improved in Diodati's company, and the epitaph is also a tribute to his friend's good influence: "Who will teach me to soften biting cares, who to cheat the long night with sweet conversation while a soft pear hisses before the welcome fire?" (lines 45–49). He misses his friend's laughter and wit and the sophisticated pleasures they shared (lines 55–56). He also misses confiding in his friend: "To whom will I entrust my heart?" he plaintively wonders (line 45), worrying that he will never feel as close to anyone else:

> Each finds scarcely one partner in a thousand, or if a fortune not hostile to our prayers finally gives us one, the unexpected day, the hour for which you had not hoped, snatches him away, leaving eternal loss for all time. (lines 108–11)

The thrum of the poem's refrain, describing painful neglect and unfulfillment—"Go home unfed, lambs; your master has no time for you now"—underscores how wrecked Milton was feeling. He repeats these lines seventeen times.

In part, Milton was working through his guilt in writing the epitaph. He berates himself for having selfishly gone to Italy and having missed the chance to say farewell: "Was it so important to have seen Rome," to have traveled so far and "interposed so many deep seas, so many mountains, so many forests, so many rocks, so many sounding rivers?" (lines 115–20). The list of these many topographical intrusions dramatizes the distance between the young men. He wishes he could have just touched Charles's hand at the end and assured his friend that he would be joining the stars in heaven. The act of writing brings some relief: he can provide a fittingly happy ending for the joyful, easygoing Diodati. By the final lines, he imagines his friend, forever young, at a wedding feast, in heaven, wearing a shining crown and overcome with singing and dancing (lines 215–19).

Milton also finds a measure of peace by looking to the future. Again, his thoughts turn to the Greek and Roman writers whom he and Diodati enjoyed, and he tries again to take comfort in continuity. He now decides to move on to the more ambitious genre of epic and announces his hope to write a heroic poem about King Arthur and Britain's mythic past. (He never would.) It is a striking irony that he states in Latin his plan to one day write an English heroic poem; he seems to be bidding farewell to not just his companion but also the language that had energized them as boys. Yet, Milton acknowledges with sadness, even these aspirations are diminished because he can no longer share them with his late friend, as he had intended to do at their next visit. In *Paradise Lost*, Milton imagines his epic's ideal readership as "fit . . . though few" (Book 7, line 31); in the epitaph, he recognizes that with Diodati's death—with the loss of the friend who had helped to ground him and with whom he had shared so much—his audience had become irrevocably fewer.

———

Milton's epitaph for Diodati was not his first poem about loss. As a boy, perhaps as part of his schoolwork, Milton had written his share of youthful poems—about birds, flowers, the coming of spring, and the difficulty of waking up early. But later, probably while he was still in college, he composed a pair of longer poems, "L'Allegro" ("The Mirthful Person") and "Il Penseroso" ("The Melancholy, Pensive Person"). These English verses with Italian titles pit the two dispositions against each other, as if Milton were weighing them as moral or vocational alternatives, but he does so playfully, even joyfully—writing both poems in jaunty, shortened couplets. In "L'Allegro" he depicts Mirth as a goddess—"buxom, blithe, and debonair"—tripping "the light fantastic toe" and holding hands with the beautiful nymph Liberty (lines 24, 34). He describes himself indulging in all sorts of pleasurable activities—listening to loud music, going to the theater to see the latest comedies, and generally enjoying "pomp, and feast, and revelry" (line 127).

But serious times call for serious writers. Milton already wanted to be right, not merely entertaining or popular. Although "L'Allegro" and "Il Penseroso" are so intertwined that mirth and pensiveness seem more complementary than contradictory—the poems repeat images, allusions, and phrasings—Milton's own inclination is probably clear from the greater length of "Il Penseroso" and its definitive-sounding ending: "These pleasures Melancholy give, / And I with thee will choose to live" (lines 175–76). The pleasures of melancholy, as Milton enumerates them, include going to the theater to see Greek tragedies, walking alone at night, and finding out a high lonely tower to read philosophy. He also takes inspiration from music—but not the loud "notes, with many a winding bout" in "L'Allegro" (line 139). He now seeks out a church with "storied windows richly dight, / Casting a dim religious light" (lines 159–60) so that he can listen to

> the pealing organ blow,
> To the full-voiced choir below,
> In service high, and anthems clear,
> As may with sweetness, through mine ear,
> Dissolve me into ecstasies,
> And bring all Heav'n before mine eyes. (lines 161–66)

If these "storied windows" refer to images created in stained glass, most often found in Catholic churches, it would explain why the "religious light" is merely "dim": given Milton's upbringing in the Church of England and his opposition to Catholicism, he might find the light there not just subdued but lacking clarity or distinction. Still, the overall effect of the passage is to convey a sense of reverence, inspiration, and solemnity. As a young man setting out on his own, Milton found in church music— regardless of the denomination—a model of what he hoped to accomplish in verse. He was determined to take poetry seriously, not just to amuse or divert readers. He wanted to bring forth "all Heav'n" before readers, to write the truth, and to help his nation through its difficulties.

One of the serious occasions that Milton regularly encountered and chose to write about—even before Diodati's passing—was the death of loved ones and people whom he admired. Death was so much a part of everyday experience in the seventeenth century that parents were encouraged not to form too strong of a bond to their young children. Men and women who survived into their late twenties could live for many years afterward, sometimes well into their seventies, but even a minor sickness could still prove life-threatening. Patients eagerly consulted various types of healers and ingested large doses of medicine, yet few did so with the expectation of complete recovery.[22] Married women in their childbearing years had an especially high risk of death, as did city dwellers; urban water supplies were frequently contaminated, and residents of cities interacted with a great many people and thus tended to contract a great many illnesses.[23] Londoners grew accustomed to the telltale bell of the death cart echoing along cobblestone streets as it clattered past, picking up recently deceased bodies.

Milton would ultimately write about the deaths of acquaintances, one of his wives, two bishops, a postman, a marchioness, a book collector's wife, Shakespeare, Jesus, Samson, an unorthodox Christian sect, and (in *Paradise Lost*) all of humanity. Death is also the subject of his earliest English poem, composed about a dozen years before Diodati's death, probably when Milton was seventeen. "On the Death of a Fair Infant Dying of a Cough" reads like the work of a gifted but still immature poet. Milton begins by concocting a fanciful allegory about Winter, an amorous and desperate deity, who wishes to kiss an infant and accidentally kills her in his cold embrace. Milton may have been addressing his own sister, Anne, who had lost a two-year-old daughter around this time. But the sudden, new sentiment as he tries to console the grieving mother in the final stanza—he tells her the child is now with God in heaven—sounds more studied than felt. He did not yet have the experience or insight that the tragedy demanded.

In another early, funeral poem, "On the Death of the University Carrier," Milton also sounds young. He wrote it while already at Cambridge, seven years before Charles died, to commemorate the town's beloved "carrier" or postman. Thomas Hobson's business was to convey letters, people, and parcels back and forth each week from Cambridge to London, to the Bull Inn in Bishopsgate Street. A surviving portrait shows a distinguished, stocky man, his face framed in a neatly trimmed silver beard; he

FIGURE 7. Engraving of Thomas Hobson by John Payne (1631)

Source: Library of Congress.

wears a ruffled collar, a blue silk doublet, and a wide-brimmed hat with a black velvet cape. Hobson was known, above all, for his strict business sense. When hiring out horses, he regularly chastised students not to tire their mounts. He also inspired the expression "Hobson's choice": when asked if he had a horse to rent, he would insist that mounts be hired in their proper order; customers could have the horse in the stall nearest the stable door, or they could go without. "Hobson's choice" means "no choice at all," and Milton evokes this saying at the start of his poem:

> Here lies old Hobson, Death hath broke his girt,
> And here alas, hath laid him in the dirt;
> Or else the ways being foul, twenty to one,
> He's here stuck in a slough, and overthrown.
> 'Twas such a shifter, that if truth were known,
> Death was half glad when he had got him down;
> For he had any time this ten years full,
> Dodged with him, betwixt Cambridge and the Bull.
>   (lines 1–8)

Milton begins these lines by irreverently offering a choice of two possible scenarios—of Hobson's falling off a horse or lying in a grave—but both of them describe the same thing: the carrier is dead. The impertinent tone is clear from the start as he takes odds on the cause of Hobson's death and calls Death a "shifter" or trickster, cutting the "girt" or belt that secures a saddle to a horse. In the poem's final lines, Milton again personifies death, but instead of a shifter or even the misguided wintery lover from "Fair Infant," Milton now pictures a caring attendant at an inn who showed the octogenarian Hobson

> his room where he must lodge that night,
> Pulled off his boots, and took away the light:
> If any ask for him, it shall be said,
> "Hobson has supped, and 's newly gone to bed."
>   (lines 15–18)

This gentle image anticipates Emily Dickinson's better-known description of a stately Death riding in a carriage and kindly stopping to pick up the poet. Only the insistence of "must" in Milton's lines disrupts an otherwise peaceful scene of almost affectionate attentiveness.[24]

Milton's epitaph poem for Charles Diodati is jarring in its difference. Here Milton took his subject much more seriously and much more personally. Death was no longer a poetic abstraction, and it was no longer kind. But if Milton in his epitaph to Diodati more fully recognizes the seriousness of death, he also demonstrates a more developed understanding of how to cope with it. He continues to subscribe to the standard Christian notion of redemption—he imagines Diodati in heaven, high above, kicking at a rainbow (lines 204–207)—but he also embraces the therapeutic benefits of writing about his friend's passing. The poem allows him to preserve Charles and, in doing so, to persevere and move onward. Finding reassurance in poetic tradition—finding continuity, ongoingness—helps him to keep his friend alive and to outlive the tragedy of Diodati's passing.

––––––

The poem that illustrates this transformation in Milton's thinking is one he wrote the year before Charles Diodati died called "Lycidas." Part of what would make the loss of Charles so difficult for Milton to bear was that exactly twelve months earlier he had lost another friend, who had also died tragically young. And he had lost his mother.

Sara Milton was probably close to sixty-five when she died.[25] Milton wrote a long Latin poem to express his gratitude to his father, but he makes little mention of his mother in any of his works. When he does refer to her, he uses glowing terms—"a woman of purest reputation, celebrated throughout the neighborhood for her acts of charity" (YP IV: 612). An alleged portrait (currently in the possession of the University of South Carolina) reveals a strong resemblance between mother and son: the same full lips, dark eyes, and long nose.[26] Also, she had weak eyes, like her middle child.[27] Sara Milton was buried on 2 April 1637, beneath a plain blue stone, laid flat, in the floor of the chancel of Horton Church. The cause of her death is unknown. Five years earlier, Milton's parents had moved to escape the noise of London, first to the nearby town of Hammersmith, then further north to Horton, a village of mostly pastures and fields and a scattering of homes built around the ancient church.

When, four months after losing his mother, one of Milton's acquaintances from college died suddenly, the young poet must have taken the news especially hard. On 10 August 1637, Edward King died in a shipwreck.[28] The Easter term at Cambridge University had ended, and the twenty-five-year-old King was sailing on the Irish Sea, traveling from Chester Bay to visit his family in Ireland.

Sudden storms made travel to and from Ireland perilous in the summer months, and the Irish Sea was known to be infested with pirates from Ire-

FIGURE 8. Koblenzer Portrait of Sara Milton, the Author's Mother

Source: Robert J. Wickenheiser Collection of John Milton, Irvin Department of Rare Books and Special Collections, University of South Carolina Libraries, Columbia, S.C.

land, the Isle of Man, and as far away as North Africa. Most often, they pursued their prey in small teams, carrying off stolen cargo to friendly harbors near Munster or the beautiful green islands of Roaringwater Bay.[29] King was wise to have made a will shortly before he set sail.

But that Monday there were no signs of treachery, the weather was good, and the waters calm. For hours, the ship carrying King sailed smoothly along the northern shores of Wales, but then, as it headed out of the bay, the hull struck a rock and began to take water rapidly. A few quick-thinking passengers were evidently able to release a lifeboat and escape. Everyone else on board would perish that day. King reportedly remained composed as some of his fellow travelers, fearing the inevitable, scuttled from bow to stern, searching in vain for a way off the sinking ship. He died on his knees—according to one account, holding a Bible[30]—praying to the last as the vessel vanished beneath the waves.

That autumn Cambridge was consumed with the tragedy of King's untimely death. Although only fifty miles north of London, Cambridge with its sheep-filled fens and low-lying meadows was a world unto itself and worlds away from the capital's narrow, crowded streets. The university consisted of 3,000 men and boys, an almost monastic community separate from the life of the town, and Milton and King's college, Christ's—at that time, Cambridge comprised sixteen self-governing colleges—had only 265 members.

King was widely regarded as a rising star at the university, one of the most impressive and promising lecturers—a well-liked, pious, gentle, and cheerful young man. He earned his BA in 1630, the year after Milton; he obtained his MA in 1633, again the year after Milton, who had the distinction of graduating cum laude. It was the younger King, though, whom Charles I subsequently appointed as a fellow of the college because King's family was of a higher social standing and was unwavering in its loyalty to the monarch.

Milton, like King, flourished at Christ's—but his success came more gradually. Milton's nephew recalled that his uncle came to be respected, especially by his college's most esteemed fellows, meaning the thirteen teachers on fellowship who—like, ultimately, King—formed the school's governing body.[31] A few years after Milton enrolled, one of the fellows from his college (we don't know whom) invited him to participate in a university event and recite one of his Latin poems (we're not sure which); Milton then had it printed, probably so that he could give copies as gifts to acquaintances and friends. It was his first printed poem.[32] Again, at age nineteen, he was asked to perform before the school, this time during the summer vacation, serving in the role of stage director at another annual university event.[33]

Milton at this later event gave a raucous oration. He joked confidently and at length in allusive Latin prose, regaling his peers with a mixture of the bawdy and erudite; one notable pun involved the sphinx, a sphincter, and "anal-ytics." Then, in the middle of his performance, he temporarily—surprisingly—adopted an earnest tone. Switching to English pentameter, he announced his devotion to his mother tongue and his aspiration to write one day something serious and heroic. He addressed the English language directly and used a metaphor of clothing to describe his lofty ambition:

FIGURE 9. Frontispiece portrait of Milton (at age twenty-one),
engraved by W. C. Edwards after Cornelius Jansen from *The Poetical
Works of John Milton*, 2 vols. (New York: D. Appleton, 1856).

Source: Robert J. Wickenheiser Collection of John Milton, Irvin Department of Rare Books
and Special Collections, University of South Carolina Libraries, Columbia, S.C.

Yet I had rather, if I were to choose,
Thy service in some graver subject use,
Such as may make thee search thy coffers round,
Before thou clothe my fancy in fit sound:
Such where the deep transported mind may soar
Above the wheeling poles, and at Heav'n's door
Look in. (lines 29–35)

Then, just as abruptly, after his digression, Milton returned to the satiric
task at hand and introduced an arcane academic joke about ten categories
of Aristotelian logic. King, on hand for the entertainment, probably entered here, impersonating one of the scholastic categories.[34]

It is not surprising that, when King died tragically in 1637, several of his friends were moved to verse, and that the next year they published a collection of poems for their dearly departed fellow. The commemorative collection was a common way to honor and remember deceased poets or aristocrats in the seventeenth century.[35] *Justa Edovardo King (Obsequies to Edward King)* contains twenty-three poems in Latin or Greek, followed by thirteen English poems. Here the college's students and tutors primarily praise their friend's faith, learning, and eloquence.

Milton's poem stands out as the final piece in the book and, like his epitaph for Diodati, the single pastoral elegy.[36] It is also one of the greatest poems ever written in English. In stirring lines of varying feet, Milton searchingly probes the meaning of a world where life can be cut so tragically short. He titled his ode simply "Lycidas" after a goatherd in classical poems by Virgil and Theocritus, an allusion that his Cambridge readers would have easily recognized, and he signed it with only his initials, counting again on his peers to know at once the identity of "J. M."

At the start, Milton feels compelled but ill-prepared to write. "Yet once more," he angrily begins (line 1), alluding to a passage on the impermanence of earthly life from Hebrews but also expressing his frustration that he must now write yet another poem of mourning.[37] He furiously plucks at a cluster of evergreen shrubs—laurel, myrtle, and ivy—and "shatters" their leaves to the ground in his rage (line 5). These specific bushes are classical symbols of poetic achievement, but they are also a galling reminder of nature's indifference to his personal feelings. Milton even thinks about giving up, about giving in to pleasure and no longer working so hard to create something great:

> Alas! What boots it with uncessant care
> To tend the homely slighted shepherd's trade,
> And strictly meditate the thankless muse?
> Were it not better done as others use,
> To sport with Amaryllis in the shade,
> Or with the tangels of Neaera's hair? (lines 64–69).

Maybe all the effort and sacrifice—scorning delights and living laborious days (lines 72)—are not worth it, even if a person were to achieve fame, what Milton contemptuously calls "that last infirmity of noble mind" (line 71). No, he abruptly reasons—and part of Milton's accomplishment in "Lycidas" is that he dramatizes his own evolving reaction to his friend's death—sensual pleasure is not better than fame, and true fame should not be measured in worldly terms, but earned and judged on a divine scale.

Little is known about Milton's acquaintance with King—no letters survive like those Milton exchanged with Charles Diodati, and "Lycidas" is the only poem that Milton wrote for the university fellow whom he called his "learned friend."[38] But within the ode, Milton uses the terms of a pastoral kinship to describe an intimate connection with King:

> Together both, ere the high lawns appeared
> Under the opening eyelids of the morn,
> We drove afield, and both together heard
> What time the grayfly winds her sultry horn,
> Batt'ning our flocks with the fresh dews of night,
> Oft till the star that rose, at evening, bright
> Toward heav'n's descent had sloped his westering wheel.
>   (lines 25–31)

Milton may be referring to the life of shepherds, but he seems to be recollecting—and idealizing—the hard work and long days that he and King shared at Christ's College: up before the sun, before they could even see the high lawn, and studying together until the evening star appeared in the night sky.

The opening verses of "Lycidas" contain mostly natural and classical images—sheep, fields, nymphs, and druids—an apparent attempt by Milton to deal with his grief by keeping his friend's death at arm's length. But near the end of the poem, some 165 lines later, Milton begins to embrace his faith and concludes that he need no longer mourn because his friend will be saved by divine grace: "So Lycidas sunk low, but mounted high, / Through the dear might of him that walked the waves" (lines 172–73). He recasts his friend's drowning as a baptism and imagines Lycidas laving his "oozy locks" in the clear waters of the Irish Sea (line 175).

Yet, even as the poem's speaker espouses the standard Christian doctrine of grace and eternal life—near the end he also envisions his late friend at a feast in heaven—he finds solace in continuity and community, as he had in his epitaph to Charles Diodati. He takes comfort in knowing that other poets have for centuries struggled with the same feelings and questions. Reusing the classical name Lycidas is just one connection that Milton traces, as repetition, echoes, and natural cycles provide him emotional reassurance. He comes to accept the notion of Christian redemption not by quoting scripture but by watching the sun's daily course: the "day-star" has, like his drowned friend, sunk below the watery horizon and, also like Lycidas, will rise again (lines 168–72).

As part of this consolation, Milton suggests that the memory he records in his own poem can help to preserve his friend—that is, Lycidas/King has been "mounted high" in Milton's laudatory ode, and so readers should now "weep no more" because, figuratively, Lycidas will never die (lines 165, 172). Like the fame Milton would offer the captain or colonel in the sonnet that he tacked on his door near the start of the civil wars, he presents his ode as a gift to his late friend. But in "Lycidas" the memory of King and the act of creating are a salve for the author's grief, not a means of averting violence nor a bid for personal renown. The poem and the commemorative collection in which it was printed stand in for the body of King that was lost at sea. Taking comfort in the act of writing about—of working through—his feelings, he can now move forward. He envisions himself as a shepherd in the final lines, shrugging on his coat against the chill of evening and heading off tomorrow to new pastures.

With "Lycidas," Milton was well on his way to making his own enduring name for himself. Even if he had never composed *Paradise Lost*, this poem would still be read for its sonorous beauty. Consider these lines before the final consolation, as the poet imagines an elaborate floral arrangement to decorate his friend's hearse:

> Bring the rathe primrose that forsaken dies,
> The tufted crow-toe, and pale jessamine,
> The white pink, and the pansy freaked with jet,
> The glowing violet,

> The musk-rose, and the well-attired woodbine,
> With cowslips wan that hang the pensive head,
> And every flower that sad embroidery wears:
> Bid amaranthus all his beauty shed,
> And daffidilies fill their cups with tears,
> To strew the laureate hearse where Lycid lies.
> For so to interpose a little ease,
> Let our frail thoughts dally with false surmise.
> Ay me! Whilst thee the shores and sounding seas
> Wash far away, wher'er thy bones are hurled.
>   (lines 142–55)

Nature here responds sympathetically to King's death, and as the poem's lines begin to knit themselves into a rhyming pattern, Milton seems on the cusp of peace and understanding. But any "ease" that he momentarily achieves is, he realizes, "frail" and "false." King died at sea, and so a conventional funeral is impossible. Milton comes up short as he remembers that he cannot literally "strew the laureate hearse." His friend's bones will forever be hurled and washed in the sounding waves.

The failure of this floral catalogue also may suggest the limitations of the pastoral mode, as Milton by poem's end is recovering from his initial shock and already looking ahead to his plans to write something more ambitious. But even while he depicts himself moving on in the final verse, he surely would have been pleased to learn that he would ultimately be proven right: for almost four centuries, his ode to King has single-handedly kept alive his learned friend.

———

Milton in his later years may have still found solace in the idea of continuity and poetic achievement, but by the time of *Paradise Lost* he treats death as fearsome. Writing the epic in his forties and fifties, having witnessed the destruction of war and the deaths of two wives, two infants, and his mother and father, he returned to the type of allegorical depiction that he had used in his early poems. But now death is a monster, the incestuous son of Satan and Sin, who tears through his mother's entrails at his birth. Then, overcome with lust, he rapes her, producing a pack of hellhounds that emerges around her waist. The dogs hourly burst forth from her womb, then retreat to chew her insides. She describes them in vivid detail:

> These yelling monsters that with ceaseless cry
> Surround me, as thou saw'st, hourly conceived
> And hourly born, with sorrow infinite
> To me, for when they list into the womb
> That bred them they return, and howl and gnaw
> My bowels, their repast; then bursting forth
> Afresh with conscious terrors vex me round. (Book 2,
>   lines 795–801)

This horrific image of reiterated pain captures Milton's theory of evil—it recoils, only bringing more ruin on itself—but its frightening violence also reflects his mature view of death.

Death in *Paradise Lost* wears a crown, a symbol of his authority; and he shakes a dreadful spear, a symbol of his sometimes violent power. And, when Death almost fights Satan, he threatens his father with a whip of scorpion tails; later, as he travels to Earth with his mother, he smites the ground with a mace. That's all. Milton does not envision Death as a skeleton, according to a long-standing visual tradition, and he provides no more detail about its appearance. On the contrary, he describes Death in one of the poem's memorable passages as a "shape, / If shape it might be called that shape had none" (Book 2, lines 666–67). Death can come in many forms, including sudden illness, old age, or a shipwreck on the Irish Sea.

When God in *Paradise Lost* tells Adam and Eve that He will punish them with death if they disobey and eat from the Tree of Knowledge, the couple has no idea what death entails. "Whate'er death is," Adam says to Eve, "Some dreadful thing no doubt" (Book 4, lines 425–26). Like Milton in his early poems, they do not yet fully comprehend the finality and sadness of dying, but they know it must be bad because God has set it up as the punishment for disobeying his one edict.

FIGURE 10. James Barry, *Satan, Sin and Death*

Source: National Gallery of Victoria, Melbourne.

Adam and Eve also do not understand that they could defeat death. If they had never tasted the Forbidden Fruit and had instead continued to obey God, they would have become like angels and risen to heaven—or so the angel Raphael speculates when he dines with them.[39]

Adam and Eve have yet another option. Even after the Fall, they can overcome death through their descendants. When, just after Eve's creation, she first sees herself reflected in a lake and becomes enamored by her own appearance, God's voice calls her away, promising her instead many images—"multitudes like thyself" (Book 4, line 474)—to replace her single watery shape. Eve's staring at herself in the lake is entirely innocent: she does not understand that the "shape within the wat'ry gleam" is herself (Book 4, line 461). Milton captures her blameless pleasure in verses that beautifully enact the experience of reflection: "I started back, / It started back, but pleased I soon returned, / Pleased it returned as soon with answering looks" (Book 4, lines 462–64). The divine voice that abruptly interrupts this idyll and introduces the idea of fruitless vanity also allows Milton to suggest another cure for mortality: Eve and Adam can have children. The continuity and creativity that Milton found so reassuring are more than poetic.

Milton's own lineage, though, ended with his three adult daughters. Mary never married, Anne died in labor, and Deborah had no children. In the years immediately following Milton's death, no commemorative collection was printed for him; none of his friends published a book of elegies to honor his poetic achievement. The poet who had devoted such care and craft to remembering many of those he knew and loved was not remembered by anyone in the same way.

Instead, Milton's reputation was attacked. In 1689, the literary historian William Winstanley deigned to include Milton in a survey of English poetry, but denounced him as a "notorious Traytor" who "most impiously and villanously bely'd that blessed Martyr *King Charles* the First." Winstanley tartly concludes that Milton's fame had already "gone out like a Candle in a Snuff, and his Memory will always stink."[40] And when, five years later, Milton's nephew published some of his uncle's letters and four of his sonnets, he felt compelled to insert a defensive preface, promising that the book would not give the least offense.[41] Ultimately, Milton would receive his literary due, and his faith in continuity and creation would prove true. But, for decades after Milton's death, his poetry became ensnared by his controversial prose and radical politics. Even though he was not executed after the Restoration, the ongoing life that he imagined for his poems was almost smothered. As the nation recovered from civil war, as Britain was restored to monarchy, the choices that Milton made and the polemical, sometimes angry works he published in those years threatened to undo everything that he worked so hard—and sacrificed so much—to accomplish.

THREE

Combating Injustice

"Need not kings to make them happy"

THE DEATH THAT, MORE THAN any others, came to define the second half of the seventeenth century was not one that Milton wrote about sympathetically. King Charles I's execution—coming seven years after the start of the civil war, just after Milton turned forty—would prove pivotal, both in Milton's life and career and in the nation's political history. But opinion in the months and years afterward varied greatly. The king's supporters called his death murder; Milton saw it as an important step toward England achieving political and religious liberty, not something to mourn but to celebrate.

Details of Charles's death soon circulated widely. On Tuesday, 30 January 1649, he had donned an extra shirt before being led through the new Banqueting House at Whitehall, out a first-story window that had been dismantled for the occasion, and onto the wooden platform that had been hastily erected. It was a fiercely cold day, and the king did not want his shivering to be mistaken for trembling. He also agreed to drink a glass of red wine and eat a piece of bread. He did not want to faint during the long walk to the scaffold.

Stepping onto the wooden platform, the king immediately noticed that it was draped and carpeted with black fabric. It extended into the street, and in the middle, the block and axe sat uncovered. The block was so low that he would not be able to kneel. He would have to lie face down to die. On the scaffold already stood the executioner and his assistant, both of them in black masks to conceal their identities, and in the street around the platform were companies of soldiers—some standing, others on horses. Beyond these groups a crowd of spectators had gathered, extending as far as the eye could see.

The king took out a small piece of paper from which he began to read. His speech lasted about ten minutes and was not entirely coherent; he had been found guilty three days earlier and had not taken much time to prepare. Charles had even thought about saying nothing, about refusing to dignify the charges against him—but he worried that silence would be construed as an admission of guilt. He explained that people can gain liberty by having a government, not by having a *share* in the government because, he emphasized, "A subject and a sovereign are clean different things."[1] When he had finished—"I have delivered my Conscience"[2]—his confessor and friend, the sixty-seven-year-old William Juxon, Bishop of London, had to remind him to add a few words about religion, which he did.

Juxon then handed Charles a white satin cap. The king was not wearing his crown that day, and Juxon and the executioner helped him to tuck in his long hair. Charles removed his cloak, said one last word to the Bishop—"Remember"—and, lying prone on the scaffold, put his neck on the block. The axe fell a second or two later, after the king gave the signal: he stretched out his arms and unclenched his fists.

———

John Milton's impossible task was to write the government's official response to Charles I's execution. Recently appointed Secretary for Foreign Tongues for the newly formed Council of State, Milton had first been required to write a treatise discrediting the Irish for supporting the royalist cause; he chose to focus much of his anger on Charles I and his royalist lieutenant, James Butler, Earl of Ormond. Now, five months later, Milton was being asked to take on the king directly—to confute the suddenly beloved monarch and to challenge the royalists' account of the ruler's final days.

But how could Milton hope to rally the English people against such a popular, tragic king? Dying was Charles I's most successful political act. Coming on the heels of his terrible financial decisions and the civil war—a prolonged military conflict that he had initiated—the king's public humiliation and gruesome death gave people a reason at last to sympathize with the failed monarch. According to one witness, "such a Grone" came from the crowd at the moment of the king's death "as I never heard before & desire I may never hear again."[3] Some accounts have the executioner brandishing Charles's severed head afterward by its hair; other reports would later circulate of shocked reactions, of faintings, miscarriages, and heart attacks. But most accounts suggest the large crowd broke up quickly and quietly, without violence or protest, struggling to fathom what they had just seen.

It was Charles I's mismanagement of the Church of England that escalated into a military conflict and that led ultimately to his trial and death. Members of Parliament in 1640 were dissatisfied with the king's monetary practices—the imposition of new taxes, the creation of monopolies, and the sale of influence, appointments, and knighthoods. Some members were also upset that the king had for the previous eleven years attempted to rule without calling Parliament—the period of Charles I's so-called Personal Rule (1629–1640). But it was the king's religious policy that most rankled the legislature. Just a few generations earlier, Queen Elizabeth I had negotiated a savvy and successful middle way in the nation's religious matters; as opinions about the correct form of worship grew more diverse, she permitted greater latitude in the practices of individual congregations. The succeeding Stuart monarchs, however, struggled to lead the English church with the same restraint. Charles's father, James, forcefully insisted that the national religion was episcopacy, a hierarchical form of church government controlled by a polity of ecclesiastical dignitaries called bishops. James famously said about anyone who sought to reform this power structure, "I will make them conform themselves, or else will *harry* them out of the land, or else do worse, *only hang them*."[4] Charles along with his chief adviser, Archbishop William Laud, even more wholeheartedly pursued a single national church that emphasized ornament and ritual. To enforce this ideal, Charles relied on the church's hierarchy of twenty-six bishops. Each bishop had sacramental and political authority over a group of parishes, and the king expected absolute submission.

To Parliament—and to Milton—this was religious tyranny. When in July 1639 Milton cut short his Grand Tour and returned to England, he was not just upset about the death of Charles Diodati; he wanted to get home before war broke out over Charles I's mishandling of the nation's religion.

But even before Milton had left for the Continent, he had foreseen the controversy that would lead to the civil wars. Twelve years earlier, in the middle of "Lycidas," Milton had devoted an entire verse to criticizing England's unjust bishops. His late friend, Edward King, had been planning to become a priest. If he had lived, Milton suggests, he would have been one of the nation's few good churchmen.

Milton's larger disappointment in "Lycidas" is that he cannot depend on the church in his time of need and must rely on his own spiritual insight to find peace. In the poem, he hammers away at English bishops for their avarice, poor training, and selfishness; they offer no comfort, provide no guidance, and leave their congregations hungry and sick. Milton describes England's clergy as bad shepherds who "scramble at the shearers' feast / And shove away the worthy bidden guest" (lines 117–18). Meanwhile, the citizens suffer:

> The hungry sheep look up, and are not fed,
> But swoll'n with wind, and the rank mist they draw,
> Rot inwardly, and foul contagion spread:
> Besides what the grim wolf with privy paw
> Daily devours apace, and nothing said. (lines 125–29)

This is a disturbing image of the nation's spiritual malaise in the years leading up to the civil wars; people were so desperate for relief, Milton writes, that some were secretly converting to Catholicism, presumably represented here by the "grim wolf with privy paw" because of the two gray wolves in the Jesuits' coat of arms. Milton sums up England's shameful clergy as "blind mouths!" (line 119), an image of sightless monsters, their faces almost entirely taken up by their gaping maws. The root meaning of *bishop* is "one who sees" and of *pastor* is "one who feeds." The nineteenth-century critic John Ruskin was the first to observe that Milton was brilliantly describing the most un-bishoply and un-pastoral churchman, someone who is blind and ravenous.[5]

Milton continued to rail against the English clergy in the prose tracts he published within months of his returning from Italy and France. Living in Aldersgate Street where he taught his nephews and where, at the start of the war, he hung the sonnet on his door, he followed up his attack on the clergy in "Lycidas" with five impassioned tracts criticizing the church's corrupt episcopacy. He was especially incensed that bishops did so little preaching yet accepted sizable benefices, church appointments that came with both property and income. He was furious about the wastefulness and the inequity. The typical bishop, he complained, cared only about satisfying "his canary-sucking, and swan-eating palate" (YP I: 549). Canary is a sweet, imported wine from the Spanish archipelago, and the reference may have been a swipe at the bishops' misplaced refinement and Spanish (Catholic) sympathies. But Milton was also conjuring the image of the clergy as avaricious monsters, consuming birds whole like Polyphemus dining on Odysseus's men.

The five pamphlets that Milton wrote in a burst of activity between May 1641 and April 1642 no doubt paved the way for his later tracts challenging Charles I. How to resist injustice and defeat tyranny? Milton learned early on that he must be bold, tell the truth, and not worry about the status of his adversaries. Of course, the distinction between audacity and arrogance may be in the eye of the beholder, and the opinions of readers in Milton's time probably depended on their religious sympathies; many readers today find his sometimes combative tone difficult to admire. In the 1640s, though, Milton was going up against several highly esteemed public figures, not just ordained clerics but respected scholars and astute

politicians who had the king's ear. Both Bishop James Ussher and Bishop
Joseph Hall—with their distinguished gray beards, towering miters, and
double-breasted black cassocks—must have been intimidating. They were
roughly twice Milton's age (he was then in his thirties) and much more
experienced in ecclesiastical debates than the recent Cambridge graduate.
Milton's other primary opponent in these early tracts was the late Bishop
Lancelot Andrewes, another esteemed academic, perhaps the most highly
respected preacher of his day. His death almost two decades earlier had
only enhanced his reputation, encasing him in a carapace of sentimental
reverence, as his writings were posthumously used to prop up Charles I's
ideas about religion.

FIGURE 11. Lancelot Andrewes. Oil on canvas.

Source: Sotheby's.

Milton was undismayed. He claimed to be chosen by God, and he directly challenged the king's bishops in his five tracts, accusing them of, among other things, hindering the Reformation in England. The English church, Milton felt, had not yet gone far enough in emphasizing its reliance on scripture and personal faith over tradition; the bishops were dragging the nation back to the elaborate decoration and ritual that characterized worship under the Catholic Church before Martin Luther. Such a regressive policy, he argued, was idolatrous.

Milton was by no means alone in his opposition to all things papal. Bloody Mary's five-year reign may have occurred almost 100 years earlier, but the atrocities that she sanctioned continued to fuel a fierce and broad-based anti-Catholicism. It was kept alive in part by publications such as John Foxe's *Acts and Monuments*, a more than 1,000-page illustrated compendium. Foxe's enormously popular book told the stories of the almost 300 Protestants who, under Queen Mary, had been put to death, mostly by burning. Between 1553 and 1558, while Mary was on the throne, a Protestant martyr had been executed, on average, every five days.[6]

Charles I's marriage to a Roman Catholic, Henrietta Maria of France, further stoked anxiety about an attempt by Rome to sponsor a coup and retake the country. In 1626, reports circulated that Charles's queen, accompanied by her retinue, had visited the village of Tyburn, the primary place of the execution of Catholics. She allegedly had descended from her royal carriage and gone forth barefoot, holding a rosary and praying for Catholic martyrs beneath the gallows.

But even with the bishops' unpopularity and widespread fears of Catholicism, Milton was taking a risk in attacking the bishops in the 1640s. He was speaking out against powerful and highly respected officials before he had achieved much of anything—"now while green years are upon my head," as he put it (YP I: 806). In his fourth prose tract opposing episcopacy, *The Reason of Church-Government*, Milton pauses halfway through to introduce and explain himself. His first three tracts had been published anonymously, probably because his name would have added nothing to the force of his arguments. But now, in a long autobiographical digression, he launched into a defense of his conduct and an account of his early years, emphasizing his virtue and insisting that—even as an unknown writer with no priestly power—he is qualified to address such an important topic because he is a pious, concerned, and informed citizen. Also, he adds, boldly projecting his authority into the future, he planned one day to become a great poet.

———

King Charles, of course, did not have to work so hard to prove himself in any of his publications, real or ghostwritten. His authority came simply from his birthright and from the nation's long history of hereditary monarchy. Milton may have had no trouble seeing the king as a mere man, but many of his fellow citizens still believed that the monarch was semidivine, chosen by God to lead the people.

Charles I, though, had never been a very good leader. He was easily irritated and overly sensitive, lacking the confidence that might be expected of the nation's most powerful official. Biographers often trace this deficiency to difficulties that the king experienced in his childhood: he had weak ankles (perhaps caused by rickets) and began walking fairly late. He also developed a stammer as a boy that he never outgrew. Charles may have become a hands-on administrator after he ascended to the throne at age twenty-five, but he struggled to judge and inspire the men who surrounded him at court, and, while he was by no means remote, he also seems to have lacked the imagination and insight to understand his people.

Charles enjoyed spectacle—especially masques, like the one Milton wrote for the Earl of Bridgewater—and years before the civil wars, he was already trying to exploit public displays and performances to project a strong regal image. He also invited the artist Anthony van Dyck to paint him in various poses that compensated for his short stature and youthful appearance. Van Dyck portrayed the king alternately as a Roman emperor, a confident huntsman, and the ultimate patriarch, accompanied by his wife, dog, and two of his children. In the latter painting, the seated Charles looks contemplative and poised; his features are gracefully aged so as to add authority, and he sits in a relaxed pose with his hand almost on the head of the son who would, after the Restoration, be crowned Charles II.

Still, none of these paintings or the successful court spectacles that Charles sponsored could fully compensate for his significant shortcomings as monarch—in particular, his refusal to make concessions and his unwillingness to entertain a reciprocal relation with the leaders of the legislature. With Charles, there was taking but little give.

In 1646, when the First Civil War—Britain's civil war comprised three different conflicts—concluded without a clear-cut victory for either the king or Parliament, Charles realized that he had little hope of ever winning a military fight; the opposition was more passionate, better disciplined, and better organized.[7] Parliament's New Model Army was so named because its leaders emphasized for the first time soldiers' national obligations over their regional ties. The Army's early success was also attributable to its regular pay and the royalists' many tactical blunders.

But, the king understood, the political coalition that Parliament had assembled was fragile. Maybe he could exploit divisions among the Scots, the Presbyterians (in the House of Commons), and the Independents (who dominated the Army). The Scots wanted a strong national church, the Presbyterians came to favor a negotiated settlement with the king, and the Independents insisted on trying the king formally and later pushed for a republican form of government. Maybe, Charles thought, he could hold out until this alliance began to fray. He decided to try to win the peace.

———

Milton was an ardent Independent. Near the start of the war he had provisionally supported the Presbyterians as the best alternative to the corrupt bishops. He had reasoned that, if the English church must have some kind of administration, then elected elders—that is, *presbyters*—were preferable to the lazy, dissolute bishops who were appointed by the king's two archbishops (of York and Canterbury). But already in his tracts objecting to episcopacy Milton had emphasized the authority of the individual con-

FIGURE 12. *Charles I, King of England, from Three Angles* by Anthony Van Dyck, 1636. Oil on canvas. Royal Collection, Windsor Castle, Berkshire.

Source: Photo by David Short. Reproduced with photographer's
permission and under the GNU Free Documentation License.

science and favored obedience to God's spirit over organized religion, over the "fair seeming pretenses of men" (YP I: 937).

Milton's ideal of spiritual liberty—as well as his arguments against the injustice of kingship—grew out of this religious philosophy. He rejected not just the English church's hierarchy but also its orthodox doctrine of predestination, the belief that God from eternity divides humankind into the good and the bad, the elect and the reprobate. Instead, Milton could be described as Arminian, a heretical position named after the theologian Jacob Arminius (1560–1609). Arminians believe that the human will contributes decisively to whether a person is saved or damned.

This was the principle behind Milton's opposition to censorship, which I discuss in chapter 5. Milton believed in the right and responsibility of individual readers to think for themselves. If God gave each person

the gift of reason and the freedom to choose, then everyone can demonstrate their own merit, and no one needs the state to decide which books
have value: "If every action which is good, or evil in man . . . were to be
under . . . prescription, and compulsion, what were virtue but a name,
what praise could be then due to well-doing?" (YP II: 527).

This idea is also at the heart of *Paradise Lost.* After losing the war in
heaven and being cast to hell, Satan tries to blame God for his own failed
rebellion. He says that God had been hiding his power, which tempted
him to revolt: "Till then who knew / The force of those dire arms?"
(Book 1, lines 93–94). Milton's God is surely omnipotent, and Satan's lies
sound plausible, but God is not responsible for the devil's bad decisions.
He gives Satan and all of the angels the choice to rebel or remain loyal,
just as he will give Adam and Eve the choice to eat or refuse the Forbidden Fruit. God says as much to the Son as they gaze down on Earth from
their high prospect and simultaneously take in Adam and Eve working in
the Garden of Eden and Satan coasting through the realm of chaos and
lighting on the outside of the newly created cosmos. God knows that the
devil is on his way to Paradise to see whether he can destroy Adam and
Eve—either by force "or worse, / By some false guile pervert"—and God
knows that Satan will succeed:

> and shall pervert;
> For man will hearken to his glozing lies,
> And easily transgress the sole command,
> Sole pledge of his obedience: so will fall
> He and his faithless progeny: whose fault?
> Whose but his own? Ingrate, he had of me,
> All he could have. (Book 3, lines 91–92, 92–98)

Milton's God is clearly angry here. The repetition of "sole" emphasizes
how little he asks of humanity—a single test, and still Adam and Eve will
fail—while the successive, overlapping questions—"whose fault? / Whose
but his own?"—underscore his frustration. The second sentence should be
the answer to the first: Whose fault? Whose but his own. But by ending
both phrases with the slight uplift of a question, God sounds contemptu-

ous. The unflinching judgment of "ingrate," disrupting the regular iambic rhythm and set off with a strong pause mid-line, drives home divine vexation and human guilt. The gift of free will means that if a person sins, there is no one else to blame. Whose fault? Absolutely not God's.

As God and the Son continue to discuss Satan's bad intention and humanity's impending failure, God explains that he made Adam and Eve

> just and right,
> Sufficient to have stood, though free to fall.
> Such I created all th' ethereal Powers
> And spirits, both them who stood and them who failed;
> Freely they stood who stood, and fell who fell.
> Not free, what proof could they have giv'n sincere
> Of true allegiance, constant faith or love,
> Where only what they needs must do, appeared,
> Not what they would? What praise could they receive?
> What pleasure I from such obedience paid,
> When will and reason (reason also is choice)
> Useless and vain, of freedom both despoiled,
> Made passive both, had served necessity,
> Not me. (Book 3, lines 98–111)

This speech articulates the epic's core principle: without choice, no one can demonstrate true virtue. God does not want preprogrammed figurines who must obey his commands and sing his praises like pieces he moves around a game board. Instead, he wants people (and angels) who must work hard and work up the courage to redress the wrongs they witness. Sometimes the consequence of free will is that angels and people sin and err. But God wants creatures who on their own choose to obey and praise him and, when they falter, who choose to make amends.

The same concept of free will informed Milton's decision to stand up to tyranny, as in "Lycidas," his five tracts against the bishops, and all of his writings against the king. He rejected authoritarianism in all things—in his concept of divinity as well as in church and state, and when he began to write about marriage, he would attempt to frame his defense of divorce as for "the good of both sexes" (YP II: 234). Each person, he believed, has equal access to the truth and equal opportunity to do the right thing. Why should he have been intimidated by powerful opponents like Bishop Ussher and Bishop Hall—or, years later, cower when asked to take on a martyr king? They were all just human beings, like himself.

Still, the emphasis that Milton put on the individual—and thus on himself—can sometimes sound more conceited than courageous. In *Paradise Lost*, his commitment to personal responsibility both vindicates God and pushes against the hierarchy of the sexes: Adam and Eve equally have free will, and each must decide on their own whether to disobey God. But, especially in Milton's prose works, this same ideal can quickly turn self-aggrandizing as he stresses his own heroic righteousness and casts himself as a divinely inspired defender of virtue. "Singular indeed is the favor of God toward me, that He has called me above all others to the defence of liberty," he writes in one tract (YP IV: 735). And in his earlier prose works he implicitly counts himself among those "men of rare abilities, and more than common industry" who are called "not only to look back and revise what hath been taught heretofore, but to gain further and go on, some new enlightn'd steps in the discovery of truth" (YP II: 566). Milton's confident belief in free will and the power of the individual, which prompted and empowered many of his greatest works, also left him susceptible to sounding like the autocrats whom he fought to depose.

———

Despite Milton's confidence, as the civil war progressed, it looked for a while as if Charles's tyrannical rule might prevail, as if the king's tactic of waiting out the tenuous coalition that had formed against him might prove successful. Charles continued to wheedle, negotiate, and strive. When, in late April of 1646, the New Model Army was about to besiege the royalist stronghold of Oxford—the city would fall within two months—he slipped out quietly, disguised as a servant after clipping his hair and beard and donning a rounded hunter's cap. He traveled more than a hundred miles north to Southwell, near Newark, on the River Greet. There, eight days later, on 5 May, he surrendered himself to Scottish commissioners, most likely at an inn called the King's Arms. He had begun secret negotiations with the Scots about a month earlier; now he sent word of his desire to surrender to their commissioners, who had set up headquarters in the archbishop's grand, gothic palace. It was in the palace's splendid, wainscoted State Room with its vaulted ceiling and exposed wooden beams that Cardinal Wolsey in 1530 had retreated in fear when he had failed to obtain a divorce for Henry VIII from Katherine of Aragon. Here the terms of Charles's surrender were now formalized; he reportedly first invited the commissioners to dine with him and turned himself in after the meal.

Negotiations for peace opened between the two sides in the next two months, as Charles was moved to nearby Newcastle, a picturesque medieval town. He remained there in semi-captivity while reviewing Parliament's list of propositions. His basic plan was to delay the process as much as possible: the more time that passed, he figured, the more likely that the delicate alliance between the Scots, Presbyterians, and Independents would deteriorate and fracture. He wanted to be the voice of stability and reason in the midst of the inevitable infighting.

But by early February 1647, the Scots had caught on to Charles's egregious delay tactics. He was never going to meet their demand of a national Presbyterian church to replace the bishops. So they withdrew from the war and handed the king over to Parliament. Charles was next moved to Holmby House, a beautiful country mansion in Northamptonshire, built around two courtyards, with huge, mullioned windows and rows of slender chimneys that enhanced its grand symmetrical facade. The king was glad for the change: he was again able to go hunting.

Charles was also heartened by the cheering crowds who met him at Holmby House. With the war now in its seventh year, with his imprisonment stretching into nine months, he gladly greeted his loyal subjects. That most of these citizens were more committed to the idea of kingship than to his specific administration might have been too nice of a distinction for the still proud monarch. Many of the people who showed up at Holmby House came seeking the royal touch. The custom was for patients with terrible illnesses—most often scrofula but also other diseases

FIGURE 13. Engraving of Charles II touching the scrofulous by R. White (1684)

that caused blisters, sores, and ulcers—to queue up at a special religious ceremony and kneel, one by one, before the king. He then presumed to cure them by gently laying hands on their faces while a clergyman read from scripture (usually Mark 16:18). The practice had allegedly been a long-held tradition in England and France, but Charles and later his son, Charles II, seem to have especially relished the ceremony. According to the long lists of names written in the "Registers of Healing," more than 4,500 people were touched each year by Charles II during his reign.[8] This was the image of monarchy that Charles wanted to promulgate as the war continued to rage. How could a person with such power—who enjoyed such adulation from his people—be reasonably asked to abdicate and submit to the terms of a mere Parliament?

Charles began to plot for his return to power. By May 1647, he offered the legislature a new proposal: he would, at last, agree to a version of the Scots' earlier terms and would allow a Presbyterian national church—but only for three years. In return, he expected the Scots' army to help him regain the throne.

At the same time, the king was exploring his other options. He still held out hope that he would receive aid from France or Ireland, and—even with his comfortable accommodations—he repeatedly tried to escape. On 11 November 1647—probably with the help of the Scottish Covenanters, who worried that the Army and Parliament would not accept Presbyterianism as the national religion—Charles rode off in the night from Hampton Court, another magnificent palace where he had been moved after Holmby House.[9] He made it as far as the Isle of Wight, a mostly rural island in the English Channel distinguished by its rocky coastlines, open chalk hills, and dramatic white sea cliffs. Charles must have felt some optimism as he breathed in the salt air and gazed at the stunning scenery, looking out at the channel and waiting daily for the ship he had ordered from Southampton to take him to France. He would finally be reunited with his queen.

But no vessel ever came—an embargo had been placed on all shipping after the king's escape was known in Westminster[10]—and he was made prisoner once more, this time in Carisbrooke Castle, a twelfth-century fortification built on a raised earthwork surrounded by a ditch and formidable bastion.

In late December 1647, Charles tried again, smuggling secret messages through his chambermaid. This time he made it to a boat off the shore but was left stranded when the direction of the wind changed abruptly. The castle guard was doubled. In March of the next year, the king had a new plan: the forty-eight-year-old monarch was to climb out of his castle window, jump to the lawn below, and meet up with an accomplice who would secrete him away in a nearby fishing trawler. Maybe he could make it across the channel and join his queen in Paris. But Charles never removed the bars from his window and underestimated his girth. He had tested the bars only with his head, assuming his body would fit, but when he tried to climb out, he got stuck.

Stories of such indignities and exploits—of the king's incarceration, persecution, and failed attempts to free himself—helped to cast Charles I

FIGURE 14. Carisbrooke Castle

Source: *Cassell's Illustrated History of England* (London: Cassell, Petter, and Galpin, 1865), volume 3. Photograph by Lori Howard, Georgia State University.

as a sympathetic figure in popular broadsides and pamphlets, and almost certainly prepared readers for his later becoming a religious hero. In November 1648, a newsbook reported that Charles remained resolute in captivity and had bravely pledged that, "for a good peace," he can "with Christ suffer any thing than can befall him."[11] In the same month, another newsbook scorned parliamentarians for tormenting the king; the writer lamented that the monarch's enemies had been so successful in the war that Charles already seemed to have been "crucifi'd."[12]

But if the king was ultimately willing to embrace the role of martyr, he also remained hopeful. Charles had been buoyed by his reception at Holmby House, by the long lines of enthusiastic citizens who patiently waited to receive his royal touch, and by the successful delays that he managed in his negotiations with a divided Parliament. Even as his incarceration dragged on and a royalist defeat on the battlefield seemed imminent, he continued through the winter of 1647 to work on plans for building a sumptuous new royal palace at Whitehall. The opulent edifice was to front the Thames for about 800 to 900 feet and would have been, when complete, twice as large as the seat of the Spanish monarch. The new palace would also subsume the grand, neoclassical Banqueting House that had been recently completed in 1622. In the new design, the house would face a large interior courtyard.

Of course, Charles's ambitious plans were never fulfilled. His trial began on 20 January 1649, and it ended, after seven days of testimony, when he was sentenced to death by beheading. It was outside the new Banqueting House that Charles's performance as martyr would culminate later that month. Ironically, Charles I's death was the event that would galvanize and inspire royalists, and eventually lead to the even more absolutist reign of Charles II. It was also the event that, for Milton, would lead to both his greatest political failure and greatest political success.

———

Milton first made the case for deposing bad leaders in early 1649 in *The Tenure of Kings and Magistrates*. Written while Charles was still on trial, *Tenure* contains a broad critique of negligent or corrupt officials. It is a

COMBATING INJUSTICE   79

landmark argument in the history of modern representative government. Supreme power, Milton argues, always resides with the people, not with a single leader or group:

> No man who knows ought, can be so stupid to deny that all men naturally were born free, being the image and resemblance of God himself, and were by privilege above all the creatures, born to command and not to obey: and that they liv'd so. (YP III: 198–99)

Here was the theoretical justification for deposing a tyrant, for prosecuting Charles I because he had rammed through his unpopular policies, resorting in the end to violence.

Milton never mentions the king by name in *Tenure*, but he vigorously disputes the premise of divine right, the idea that God sanctioned the monarch. Instead, he argues, a people and their ruler have a reciprocal relationship. If a ruler were to break that contract and fail to support the public good—for example, by taking up arms against his people, as Charles I had done in the civil wars—then the ruler can be deposed, even if he were not a tyrant. This was a stunning advance in early modern political theory: Milton was insisting on the rights of the people—"the liberty and right of free born Men, to be govern'd as seems to them best" (YP III: 206). It is an impassioned argument for removing any leader—"be he King, or Tyrant, or Emperor"—who was unjust, who failed to support the public good (YP III: 197). People entrust their government to serve their needs, Milton reasons, not to be their lords and masters. If a king or magistrate proves unfaithful, as had Charles, then he forfeits the people's allegiance and must be replaced. Milton argues that each person should not kowtow to custom or take orders unthinkingly—whether from a king, queen, bishop, or anyone else. The sword of justice, he writes, is superior to all leaders, and the people always wield the sword.

Milton's argument in *Tenure*—first published on 13 February 1649, just weeks after Charles I's execution—resulted in his appointment as Secretary for Foreign Tongues. In the month following its publication, the newly formed Council of State asked one of Milton's acquaintances (we don't know whom) to call on the author at his home in High Holborn

Street in London's inner city. Milton had moved there two years earlier in September or October with the plan of giving up his polemical prose, retiring to his private studies, and concentrating on his poetry. Yet he must have listened with interest as the emissary explained that the council's forty-one members were so impressed by his defense of judicial regicide in *Tenure* that they wanted him firmly ensconced on their side as Secretary for Foreign Tongues.[13] He would earn almost £290 annually, a sizeable salary in the mid-1600s (a skilled tradesman, by comparison, would have earned about £25–40 a year[14]), and mostly he would be expected to work as a translator, producing Latin and English versions of letters and documents, alternatively for and by England's Continental allies, and occasionally writing correspondence and whole treatises on behalf of the new government. He, his wife, and their growing family could move into ample lodgings in the east end of Whitehall Palace: his first daughter, Anne, had been born on 29 July 1646, and Mary followed two years later on 25 October. With more than 1,500 rooms, Whitehall was the largest palace in Europe, boasting tennis courts, a bowling alley, and ornamental gardens; the private rooms were decorated with jasper and enamel. It was an offer Milton could not refuse.

———

One of the first tasks that Milton faced in January 1649 after the death of Charles I was not just presenting the new government's justification for the monarch's trial and execution. He also had to argue against a ghost. Before the king died, he and his advisers anticipated that Parliament would need to legitimize its actions, and they arranged for Charles to have the last word. *Eikon Basilike: The Portraiture of His Sacred Majesty in His Solitudes and Sufferings* claimed to contain the king's prayers and private reflections while he awaited his trial and sentencing. The book was published on the day of his execution, and almost immediately it became a bestseller. The King's Book (as *Eikon Basilike* came to be known; the title literally means, "the king's image") reached more than thirty-five editions in London in just its first year, and twenty-five more editions in Ireland and abroad during the same span.[15] Royalists put a copy on display in their front parlors, next to the family Bible; it was soon translated into Latin, Dutch, German, and French.[16] More than a decade later, in 1662, the Bishop of Exeter, John Gauden, would reveal that the book was largely or wholly a forgery: he claimed that he had in fact written *Eikon Basilike* on Charles's behalf. But by then the book's influence and Charles's status as a martyr were firmly settled. The question of who had actually written the text was no longer so important.

Eikon Basilike began with an elaborate frontispiece portrait that folded out, like a map. It depicted Charles as a Christ-figure, on his knees, penitent, gazing heavenward, and grasping a crown of thorns. Even people who could not read—and about 70 percent of the population could not[17]—immediately got the message: Charles was more sinned against than sinning; he was patient, selfless, and humble, committed to acting in accordance with the will of God and anxious to sacrifice himself for the good of his people.

Milton's primary mistake in writing the government's response was trying to formulate a logical, thorough rebuttal. The king was peddling in raw emotion that could not be gainsaid by a mere citizen. Milton titled his book *Eikonoklastes*—meaning, the *Iconoclast*—as his goal was to smash the image of Charles I that had been constructed in *Eikon Basilike*. Milton proceeded by breaking the text of the King's Book into pieces, following each excerpted passage with a painstaking refutation that showed the disparity between Charles's words and deeds; most of *Eikonoklastes* is a point-by-point and chapter-by-chapter response to the king. The result is a book more than 10,000 words longer than *Eikon Basilike*.

Milton tried to follow the success of *Tenure* by once again adopting an appropriately restrained tone in *Eikonoklastes*, girding his version of events with a stockpile of facts, citations, and quotes. But his basic argument was blunt. Charles was a tyrant, and people must not tolerate a tyrant. Instead, they should be kings of themselves:

> The happiness of a Nation consists in true Religion, Piety, Justice, Prudence, Temperance, Fortitude, and the contempt of Avarice and Ambition. They in whomsoever these virtues dwell eminently,

FIGURE 15. Frontispiece portrait of Charles I from
Eikon Basilike (London, 1649)

Source: Robert J. Wickenheiser Collection of John Milton, Irvin Department of Rare Books
and Special Collections, University of South Carolina Libraries, Columbia, S.C.

need not Kings to make them happy, but are the architects of their own happiness; and whether to themselves or others are not less than Kings. (YP III: 542)

Milton in *Eikonoklastes* not only pits his republican version of events against Charles I's self-serving account but condemns idolatry writ large—including set prayers, church hierarchy, monarchy, and Catholicism. He also cannot conceal his contempt for the "mad multitude" and "image-doting rabble," those fellow citizens who lacked "English fortitude" and, under the influence of corrupt clergy, had fallen for the king's false image (YP III: 345, 601, 344). Even one of Charles's allegedly heartfelt prayers, Milton showed, had been plagiarized: it was cribbed wholesale from a work of fiction, *The Countess of Pembroke's Arcadia* by Philip Sidney.

But Milton's rigor and rhetoric could not trump the populism that Charles fostered. *Eikon Basilike* continued in print throughout the seventeenth century; Milton's *Eikonoklastes* appeared in only one other edition in his lifetime. Milton was learning gradually how best to combat injustice. He would have to wait for his next treatise to try again, to show that the king had deserved to be punished and the new government was just and justified. And this next time Milton would step onto an even larger stage: he would address not just England but all of Europe.

———

In late 1650, the Council of State needed Milton to write another pamphlet. Once again, he was asked to defend England's new government and its decision to depose a tyrant. The year before, the king's eldest son—the future Charles II—had hired the celebrated French linguist Claude de Saumaise to write a treatise defending the prince's father and excoriating the men who had tried and executed him. England's Continental neighbors were monarchies; they did not want their citizens to get any ideas from the English revolution. In *Defensio Regia pro Carolo I* (*Defense of the Reign of Charles I*), Saumaise—more commonly known by his Latinate penname, Salmasius—registers European outrage at Charles's death.

Salmasius devoted most of his tract to the fact that the king's trial had no legal precedent. He argues for the divine rights of kings by appealing to the Old Testament, the New Testament, ancient history, recent history, and the English Constitution. He alleges that defenders of regicide—a "faction of fanatics," as he calls them[18]—had not just subverted their kingdom but also threatened to uproot all of the nation's basic laws.

Salmasius in his tract sounds morally outraged by the king's trial and sentencing. He decries Charles's execution as "savage," "iron-hearted," "bereft of all sense of humanity," and a "miserable and marvelous murder."[19] For mere men to question a semidivine figure—a monarch ordained by God—and then to condemn and sentence him was, in Salmasius's view, an "atrocity," an act of "wickedness," and something to be "mentioned among the disgraces of the century."[20] If Charles I had been a bad king, Salmasius argues, then the blame lies with the English people. God gives people good kings as a reward; bad kings are a form of divine punishment.

This time Milton had learned his lesson and would not hold back. He would bring the same force and emotion that his opponent had shown—and he would out-Latin, out-history, and out-outrage Salmasius. Milton must have realized the intense sympathy that accounts of the king's death had prompted; stories of Charles's moving last visit with two of his children had already begun to circulate, and the king's final prayers and meditations in *Eikon Basilike* were avidly being read both in England and on the Continent. Milton could take some comfort in knowing that he was no longer directly taking on the beloved, late monarch. Instead, he was going up against a public intellectual and, what is more, a Frenchman.

Milton was not challenging a mere academic, however. Once again, he was punching above his weight class. The sixty-year-old Salmasius was the most famous intellectual in Europe, a welcome guest at the most prestigious universities and a trusted adviser at various European courts. One Italian scholar described Salmasius as the "most learned of all who are now living,"[21] and a Danish theologian heaped even more praise on him, calling Salmasius "the miracle of the world, the most learned of all mortals."[22]

Milton, in contrast, was virtually a nobody. While Charles I had been looking for ways to escape and playing Parliament's various factions against each other, Milton was teaching his two nephews, first in Aldersgate Street, then at number 17 Barbican where in fall 1645 he had moved with his wife. He was busy with his growing school, his first collection of poetry, and his new family. Milton was virtually unknown even in his native London. His agreeing to respond to Salmasius might be compared to an undergraduate student in physics suddenly and publicly challenging Stephen Hawking. Or, as Milton's nephew explained, Milton in the conflict was "our little *English David*," while Salmasius represented the "great *French Goliath*."[23] Milton's nephew describes the outcome of the two men's war of words in the same terms. Milton, he crows, gave Salmasius "such a hit in the Forehead, that he presently staggered, and soon after fell."[24]

Salmasius in his tract had asked indignantly about Charles's trial, "By what right or law?" Milton answered that bad leaders must always be deposed, "By that law of Nature and of God which holds that whatever is for the safety of the state is right and just" (YP IV: 317–18). He mostly sidesteps the articles of the English Constitution and the issue of legal precedent. Instead, he insists that the English people, in holding Charles I accountable, had acted morally according to a higher standard, according to "light, truth, reason, and the hopes and teachings of all the great ages of mankind" (YP IV: 307). He then counters that Salmasius was the one behaving immorally. The linguist was doing the bidding of Charles's son and profiting by defending a tyrant.

If Milton in his mid-forties had any lingering doubts about the power of words, his *Defense of the English People* proved to be his single most successful piece of writing during his lifetime. England's new government won much-needed respect on the Continent, Salmasius was irrevocably disgraced (he died before he could publish a reply), and Milton? He became an international celebrity. His book circulated in Germany, Holland, and Sweden—and was publicly burned for its anti-monarchical message in England and on the Continent. Visitors arriving in London began to seek out the home of the previously unknown English author who had defeated the great French linguist.

Milton, though, was not done writing about and opposing tyranny. Three years later, when his response to Salmasius was viciously attacked, he would compose one more treatise on behalf of the Council of State, his *Second Defense of the English People*, again arguing for a people's moral right to hold their political leaders accountable. Around this same time, Milton would turn, at last, to his great poem—"long choosing, and beginning late," as he admitted (Book 9, line 26). In *Paradise Lost*, he would find a new way to think about absolute power and the best ways to oppose it, and now he would approach his subject imaginatively, assuming the perspective of an unjustified, angelic rebel who had the temerity to instigate a civil war not against a mere king but against an omniscient and omnipotent deity.

FOUR

Physical Suffering

"Only stand and wait"

MILTON WENT BLIND WHILE TRYING to complete *A Second Defense of the English People* at the request of the government. He had been suffering from ill health for years and often was able to work for only short intervals, sometimes for only an hour at a time. When doctors warned Milton that his already weak eyes would not bear the strain and that he would go completely blind if he continued to push himself, the forty-three-year-old author ignored their advice.[1] He resolved to sacrifice his sight—as he put it, "while yet I could for the greatest possible benefit to the state" (YP IV: 588). By 1652, he would be completely blind.

Milton had begun losing his sight some ten years earlier, shortly after he hung his sonnet on the door of his house in Aldersgate Street. Even as a boy, he claimed, his eyes had a "natural weakness," which was made worse by his habit of staying up late to read: "This was the first cause of injury to my eyes" (YP IV: 612). But Milton's loss of sight began in his thirties and may have been unrelated to his youthful study habits. He first noticed a mist or clouding in the left part of his left eye. In these years, his vision grew weak only gradually: in a letter from September 1654 to his friend, the Greek-born scholar Leonard Philaras, Milton recollected how he would have difficulty reading in the evenings after dinner, and when he tried to look directly at a lamp a kind of rainbow would obscure it. On bad mornings, if he tried to read, he would immediately feel a stabbing pain and have to stop.[2] Returning to bed on those days, darker colors, he recalled, would "burst forth with violence and a sort of crash from within."[3] Over the next three years, his sight seemed to worsen daily; objects appeared to swim back and forth even when he sat still. Eventually, the white mist would expand and become permanent, and he saw nothing, but if he turned his eyes he might still glimpse the slightest amount of light, like a candle's pulsing glimmer under the crack of a shut door.

Milton had sought consolation in commemorative poems when his friends had died—first Charles Diodati, then Edward King—so it is reasonable to expect that he would turn again to verse to cope with his own pain and illness. And to some extent he did. He once again found some therapeutic benefit in working through his thoughts and feelings in writing, and he was encouraged by the sense of continuity that he found in classical literature. Renowned ancient poets and prophets were also blind: first and foremost Homer, but also Thamyris, Tiresias, and Phineus, all of whom Milton mentions in *Paradise Lost*, as he tries to summon the courage and inspiration to describe heaven and see beyond his own "universal blank" (Book 3, lines 35–36, 48). Surely he, too, could still do great things.

But in practical terms losing his sight made reading and writing much more difficult. How was he going to manage? Could he still fulfill his poetic ambitions? Milton quickly realized that, if he were going to learn to live with his affliction, he would have to get help, to lean on others in a way that he never had.

The new tract that the Council of State asked Milton to write, a sequel to his first *Defense of the English People*, was specifically in reply to an anonymous Latin treatise published in the Netherlands entitled *Regii Sanguinis Clamor* (*The Cry of the Royal Blood*). The unnamed author attacked both Parliament and the Army for breaking the law and killing

King Charles. The author was horrified that England had been turned into a "Popular State"; worse, the perpetrators—those "secret rogues and open robbers"—had committed their crime under the guise of religious devotion. "Compared with this," the unnamed writer sneered, "the crime of the Jews in crucifying Christ was nothing."[4]

Milton was an apt choice to compose the government's official response to *Clamor*, not just because of the success of his *Defense*, but because the anonymous writer had taken pains to call him out personally for writing against Salmasius. The writer devoted part of his tract to lambasting Milton, that "Bestial Blackguard," for having bested and belittled the great French linguist.[5] Such anonymous slander was not surprising. The advent of printed books created more opportunities for ad hominem attacks in the sixteenth and seventeenth centuries. In contrast to the immediacy of sharing works orally or in manuscript, the distance that print interposed between author and audience provided greater opportunity for readers to talk back, to disguise or hide their own identities and say something controversial, mean, or even scurrilous. The still uncharted world of print at that time was like online social media now—a new, barely regulated forum for opining, complaining, accusing, replying, and flaming. There were bound to be trolls.

Milton had framed some of his early prose works as responses. In 1645 in *Colasterion*, he refuted an anonymous critic of his defense of divorce. The title of Milton's tract literally means "instrument of punishment," a phrase that accurately captures the pamphlet's quarrelsome tone: Milton emphasizes that a "conversing solace, & peaceful society" are "the prime end of marriage," but he also attacks his attacker, calling him, among other names, a "brain-worm" and "phlegmy clod" (YP II: 739–43). Four years earlier in *Animadversions*, Milton had written another contemptuous reply, this time coming to the aid of a group of anti-episcopal clergymen who published their tracts under the pseudonym "Smectymnuus" (the five authors disguised their identities by combining their initials).[6] Milton systematically answered one of the group's detractors, Bishop Joseph Hall, and again wrote with equal parts logic and vitriol. Anticipating the style of *Eikonoklastes*, where he tried to reply to Charles I's book section by section and point by point, Milton here alternated short quotations from Hall's tract with his own heated replies. In some places, Milton argues passionately and persuasively against church hierarchy; in other places, his response is harsh and blunt. To Hall's praise of England's bishops, Milton responds simply, "Ha, ha, ha" (YP II: 726).

A decade later, when Milton accepted the Council of State's charge to write a sequel to his *Defense of the English People*, he no doubt drew on all of this previous experience. He had three goals: to justify the new government, to argue again for the right of the citizenry to hold their leaders accountable, and to answer, point by point, the new unnamed author for all of the insults he had lobbed at him. The author of *Clamor* had incorporated a series of cruel remarks throughout the eight chapters and also ridiculed Milton in a separate set of Latin verses at the end of his tract—a total of some 245 lines. He called Milton a "monster of a man," a "loathsome executioner," and an "insignificant piece of mud."[7] Mothers, he said, would use the Englishman's execrable name to frighten their children. And that Milton was losing his sight? Well, God must be blinding him as punishment for supporting the king's murder.

Milton was up against probably his most capable adversary. He knew he had to respond with both his head and heart, and he deployed a nimble blend of widely divergent styles in exquisite modern Latin. His *Second Defense of the English People* (*Pro Populo Anglicano Defensio Secunda*) sounds by turns aphoristic, insulting, learned, laudatory, and lofty. At one moment, he goes on the offensive, unleashing a torrent of invective on the anonymous author like the one he had used to assault Salmasius in the *Defense*. In the next, he is praising his countrymen and singling out Oliver Cromwell, the brilliant and ruthless lieutenant-general who led the Parliamentary forces during the civil war. Then, Milton changes again and takes a teacherly tone, warning Cromwell, who had recently accepted the lifetime appointment of Lord Protector, which Milton and many other members of Parliament worried was a betrayal of the war's republican ideals. Milton urges Cromwell and his fellow citizens to build on the liberty that they had achieved—and to avoid the pitfalls that had vexed Charles I's government: "If you begin to slip into the same vices, to

FIGURE 16. Oliver Cromwell by H. Robinson, based on
the painting by Robert Walker. Oil on canvas.

Source: New York Public Library.

imitate those men, to seek the same goals, to clutch at the same vanities,
you actually are royalists yourselves" (YP IV: 681).

———

While Milton was coping with his rapidly diminishing sight, he was
plagued with a series of other painful, personal losses that would lead to
his reaching out and seeking help. Just as copies of the blistering attack
he suffered in *Clamor* began to reach his friends and acquaintances, he
lost his wife of nine years. Mary (Powell) Milton died in May 1652, at age
twenty-seven, probably of complications from the birth of the couple's
third daughter, Deborah. Six weeks later, Milton buried his only son,
John, at fifteen months. Milton's nephew Edward Phillips attributed the
second tragedy to poor nutrition—"the ill usage, or bad Constitution of

an ill chosen Nurse"[8]—a cause that must have filled the still new father with sorrow and regret, and maybe guilt. At age forty-three, he suddenly found himself a single parent, struggling to raise three very young girls on his own: Anne was six, Mary was four, and Deborah was almost one month. In December of the previous year, the family had moved out of their opulent government rooms into a nearby residence on a short street called Petty France in the same district of Westminster. With the sudden deaths of his wife and son, the new house—even as it was filled with the noise of three young girls—must have seemed strangely empty.

Milton refused to be bowed, and he once again channeled his grief and confusion into his writing, presumably depending on nurses and family to take care of his three daughters, although no specific evidence survives. This time he tried to force himself to concentrate on larger, national concerns, perhaps to keep his own losses at bay and in perspective. It almost worked. In addition to drafting his *Second Defense* for the Council of State, it was during these months that he composed cautionary political sonnets to two leaders from the revolution, Henry Vane and Oliver Cromwell, urging them to keep church and state separate.

Sonnet 17 "To Sir Henry Vane the Younger" begins by complimenting the statesman for his intelligence—"young in years, but in sage counsel old" (line 1)—before Milton gets down to business and encourages Vane to preserve religious liberty: "Both spiritual power and civil, what each means, / What severs each, thou hast learnt, which few have done" (lines 10–11). During the wars, Vane had worked closely with Cromwell to negotiate a settlement with Charles I and helped to establish a new government after the king's trial and execution. But, the year after Milton wrote this poem, the two politicians had an irreparable falling out: Vane was outraged when Cromwell in 1653 agreed to become Lord Protector, which looked to Vane like a power grab.

Milton's Sonnet 16 to the more powerful Cromwell is a mix of praise and warning:

> Cromwell, our chief of men, who through a cloud
> Not of war only, but detractions rude,

Guided by faith and matchless fortitude
To peace and truth thy glorious way hast ploughed,
And on the neck of crownèd Fortune proud
Hast reared God's trophies and his work pursued,
While Darwen stream with blood of Scots imbrued,
And Dunbar field resounds thy praises loud,
And Worcester's laureate wreath; yet much remains
To conquer still; peace hath her victories
No less renowned than war, new foes arise
Threat'ning to blind our souls with secular chains:
Help us to save free conscience from the paw
Of hireling wolves whose Gospel is their maw.

Again, Milton was using the sonnet form to make an explicitly political point. The long, winding, opening sentence—its fills the first eight and a half lines—sums up Cromwell's decisive military victories almost hurriedly. The list of battles—near Darwen stream, in Dunbar, at Worcester—then comes up short, interrupted mid-line, as Milton abruptly shifts to a admonitory tone: "Yet much remains / To conquer still." The change is all the more jolting because the thought breaks over two lines: Milton is emphasizing a greater, more difficult task that lies ahead for the Lord Protector—to govern well—and implores him to keep separate church and state. The final image of wolfish ministers suggests the corruption that will occur if Cromwell ignores the poet's appeal and the clergy are paid by the government.

But even as Milton in his mid-forties looked to politics as a solution or distraction, he could not stop thinking about his late wife. In this same period, he probably wrote one of his most moving poems, an apparently personal sonnet on Mary's tragic death.[9]

Methought I saw my late espousèd saint
Brought to me like Alcestis from the grave,
Whom Jove's great son to her glad husband gave,
Rescued from death by force though pale and faint.

Mine as whom washed from spot of child-bed taint
Purification in the Old Law did save,
And such, as yet once more I trust to have
Full sight of her in Heaven without restraint,
Came vested all in white, pure as her mind:
Her face was veiled, yet to my fancied sight,
Love, sweetness, goodness in her person shined
So clear, as in no face with more delight.
But O as to embrace me she inclined,
I waked, she fled, and day brought back my night.

Milton, as he had in "Lycidas" and his epitaph to Charles Diodati, again begins by trying to take comfort in continuity. He compares himself with Admetus, a widower from antiquity, who is reunited with his late wife, the beautiful Alcestis, through the supernatural assistance of Hercules, "Jove's great son." Milton was trying to reassure himself that the great son of his own God would ultimately reunite him with his wife, that despite his blindness he could one day enjoy "full sight of her in Heaven without restraint." The poem may begin tentatively—"*Methought* I saw my late espousèd saint"—but the almost redundancy of "full sight" and "without restraint" suggests how desperately he wants to see his wife now. She appears to him in his dream dressed in white with her face veiled—apparent symbols of, respectively, her virtue and irrevocable separation—and for most of the sonnet, he sounds hopeful, almost happy—"Love, sweetness, goodness in her person shined / So clear." But in the end, he cannot hold on to his beloved "saint," like Orpheus with his half-regained Eurydice or Aeneas unable to embrace the shade of his late wife Creusa: "But O as to embrace me she inclined, / I waked, she fled, and day brought back my night." The slowly unfolding syntax in the first of these lines—Milton delays the subject and verb until the very end—suggests the poet's yearning and his wife's straining reach. In contrast, the rush of action in the final line—three subjects, three verbs—drives home the suddenness and finality of his disappointment.

As Milton fantasized about seeing his wife again, his actual sight was worsening daily. If he worked too long or read too much, he was wracked with headaches and had to rest. He also began experiencing intestinal pain; he wrote that around the same time "my spleen and all my viscera [were] burdened and shaken with flatulence."[10] Milton must have genuinely wondered whether God was punishing him, as the anonymous author of *Clamor* had cruelly alleged. During the seventeenth century, Job remained the model of virtuous suffering, but the more common assumption was that physical afflictions indicated a lack of righteousness. In the case of Milton's health, he had to suffer twice—first, going blind; second, having his blindness mocked by his political adversaries. In the middle of his *Second Defense*, he felt it necessary to pause and assess his own behavior:

> For my part, I call upon Thee, my God, who knowest my inmost mind and all my thoughts, to witness that (although I have repeatedly examined myself on this point as earnestly as I could, and have searched all the corners of my life) I am conscious of nothing, or of no deed, either recent or remote, whose wickedness could justly occasion or invite upon me this supreme misfortune. (YP IV: 587)

Perhaps more striking than the connection Milton accepts here between his morality and his misfortune is the fact that he does not sound resentful about his blindness. He does not know why he lost his sight, but he does not blame God, and he does not consider slowing down. He just wishes to establish—for his readers and for himself—that it is not his own fault. His efforts to search "all the corners of my life" indicate a painful commitment to self-examination and honesty.

The closest Milton comes to anger about his blindness is in *Samson Agonistes*, published some seventeen years later in 1671, as he reimagines the story of the Hebrew hero from the Book of Judges. When the poem opens, Samson finds himself in chains, enslaved, humiliated, and betrayed by Dalila. But the hardship that most upsets him is his blindness. Milton's poetry nowhere sounds more gut-wrenching:

O loss of sight, of thee I most complain!
Blind among enemies, O worse than chains,
Dungeon, or beggary, or decrepit age!
Light, the prime work of God, to me is extinct,
And all her various objects of delight
Annulled, which might in part my grief have eased,
Inferior to the vilest now become
Of man or worm; the vilest here excel me,
They creep, yet see; I dark in light exposed
To daily fraud, contempt, abuse and wrong,
Within doors, or without, still as a fool,
In power of others, never in my own;
Scarce half I seem to live, dead more than half.
O dark, dark, dark, amid the blaze of noon,
Irrevocably dark, total eclipse
Without all hope of day! (lines 67–82)

It is easy to understand why many early readers assumed that Milton was writing about himself in *Samson*. He seems to be pouring his own personal suffering directly into the mouth of his protagonist. The four successive stresses—"O dark, dark, dark"—shred the poem's meter and underscore the fallen hero's anguish. He feels more dead than alive, completely out of control, lower than a worm or reptile.

Yet even Samson, each time that he almost lashes out at God, refuses to criticize divine authority for his shame and suffering. "But peace, I must not quarrel with the will / Of highest dispensation," Samson willfully concludes in his opening soliloquy (lines 60–61). Of course, Milton had not, like Samson, divulged a secret that led to his persecution, but he must have had private doubts about divine justice. Like Samson's father in the poem, he must have wondered why God seemed to be in hiding. He had repeatedly tried to do the right thing—to be, like Samson, God's faithful champion. How was he now supposed to write?

The exact cause of Milton's blindness remains unknown. Based on the symptoms he detailed in the letter to his friend Leonard Philaras he probably suffered from a rare condition, a pituitary tumor that put pressure on his optic nerve and caused his sight to deteriorate.[11] Less likely is that Milton experienced what is called a bilateral retinal detachment: the lining in the back of his eyes would have become separated from his optical blood vessels.[12] But while retinal detachment is more common than a pituitary tumor, it typically occurs abruptly and is preceded by severe and progressive myopia, a condition which, so far as is known, Milton did not have.

Part of what would have made the onset of blindness so difficult to bear were the futile, torturous treatments that were commonly administered during the seventeenth century. Among the most frequent cures for afflictions of the eyes were bloodletting, cauterizing below the ears, and powerful laxatives. Milton probably also underwent one of the period's standard operations for inflammation of the eyes.[13] A physician would ask the patient to sit in a chair and to lean his head back. Pincers would then squeeze together, either vertically or horizontally, some of the patient's skin just below the hairline. The pinching may have been meant to reduce the more intense pain that followed. A hot, diamond-pointed cautery was inserted repeatedly through holes in the pincers; the cautery was connected to a thick cotton thread soaked in egg whites or rose oil, which, it was thought, would reduce swelling as the patient's flesh burned and bled.

But beyond the private letter that Milton wrote to his friend Philaras, he does not mention the physical discomfort that came with his worsening sight. Instead, he lingers on his psychological suffering and focuses on the task ahead. This comes through most clearly in one of two sonnets that he seems to have written on his blindness. He wants to know how he will still serve God if he is deprived of "light." Here, in Sonnet 19, he alludes to the Parable of the Talents from Matthew 25:

When I consider how my light is spent,
Ere half my days, in this dark world and wide,
And that one talent which is death to hide,
Lodged with me useless, though my soul more bent
To serve therewith my Maker, and present
My true account, lest he returning chide,
"Doth God exact day labor, light denied?"

> I fondly ask; but patience to prevent
> That murmur soon replies, "God doth not need
> Either man's work or his own gifts; who best
> Bear his mild yoke, they serve him best; his state
> Is kingly. Thousands at his bidding speed
> And post o'er land and ocean without rest:
> They also serve who only stand and wait."

In the first half of the sonnet, the speaker's tone is anxious, almost diffident; in one long seven-and-a-half-line sentence, he delays his central question—"Doth God exact day labor, light denied?"—encumbering it with a cluster of modifying phrases and clauses, as if steeling himself to ask what is now expected of him. He knows the question must sound fond, meaning "foolish," and tries to downplay his uncertainty by calling it a mere "murmur." He is more determined than ever—his soul is "more bent"—but what if his "talent," a monetary unit meted out according to ability in the biblical parable, has become "useless"?

It is in the poem's second half that the poet finds reassurance—and it comes suddenly, mid-line, as if patience wants to "prevent" his imagined question as soon as he utters the thought. God does not need his work; God can be served by persisting, simply by his going on and—according to the sonnet's most widely held reading—accepting that he is now blind. Thousands of angels may race across the world doing God's commands, but a person need only stand fast and "wait," a word in the seventeenth century that meant not just serving or standing in readiness but also placing hope in the divine.

For Milton, such waiting would not have come easy. As he had already announced—in his poem at Cambridge, in his tracts against the bishops, and in his correspondence with Charles Diodati—he had much that he wished to accomplish. The strain comes through in this sonnet as the speaker's thoughts rush onward, tumbling from line to line without pause, especially in the poem's second half, until he suddenly comes up short with the definite, divine disruption "Is kingly." Milton came to oppose monarchy as a form of earthly government, but he was still able to accept God's absolute authority. The sonnet shows Milton in the middle of his life, on the verge of writing his poetic masterpiece: he wants to be one of the speeding thousands, but he is gritting his teeth and trying to accept that his lost light is not a permanent setback.[14] He desperately hopes that he must only wait a little longer and put his faith in God to write the great poem that he had been so long planning.

———

To write this great poem, Milton also had to admit that he needed help. He liked to envision himself as a lone champion. In recalling his defeat of Salmasius, he wrote, "I met him in single combat and plunged into his reviling throat this pen" (YP IV: 556), and in "On the Morning of Christ's Nativity," he imagines getting to the manger first and presenting his ode at Jesus's feet before the arrival of the star-led magi. Later, in *Paradise Lost*, he invents a possible surrogate, the angel Abdiel, a solitary hero who refuses to join Satan's rebellion and—just as Milton was trying to do in his epic theodicy—eloquently defends the ways of God.

> Shalt thou give law to God, shalt thou dispute
> With him the points of liberty, who made
> Thee what thou art, and formed the pow'rs of Heav'n
> Such as he pleased, and circumscribed their being?
> Yet by experience taught we know how good,
> And of our good, and of our dignity
> How provident he is, how far from thought
> To make us less, bent rather to exalt
> Our happy state under one head more near
> United. (Book 5, lines 822–31)

When Abdiel then rushes to the divine throne and tries to alert God about Satan's malicious plotting—God already knows, of course, and Abdiel is met with a vast, dazzling assembly of embattled squadrons—the Deity praises his "dreadless angel" (Book 6, line 1) in terms that could also describe Milton's own polemical achievements:

> Servant of God, well done, well hast thou fought
> The better fight, who single hast maintained
> Against revolted multitudes the cause
> Of truth, in word mightier than they in arms;
> And for the testimony of truth hast borne
> Universal reproach, far worse to bear
> Than violence. (Book 6, lines 29–35)

Here again was Milton's belief in the power of language, given new authority as spoken by God and now sounding almost self-congratulatory as Milton seems to ally himself with a lone, brave angel.

Blindness, though, brought Milton a new humility. This was a time before schools and training for the blind, when a person on the streets of London who could not see was assumed to be a sinner justly punished for some reprehensible crime.[15] Ancient Greek art and literature had offered the auspicious image of the blind seer—the elderly man endowed with supernatural vision in place of his lost sight—but the classical tradition also included figures for whom blindness was an extreme form of suffering, whether a self-inflicted badge of shame and remorse (Oedipus) or a curse from the gods (Tiresias). Since the medieval period, blindness in England was mostly associated with itinerant beggars who congregated on the streets and were given to drinking and debauchery. The Calvinist doctrine of providence was still accepted by most theologians and moralists, and tales circulated widely of God's swift punishments for all manner of impiety. Blindness was thought to be the worst debasement that God could inflict. When in 1679, for example, a woman named Elizabeth Middleton publicly wished God to judge her if rumors of a Catholic conspiracy were true, she was purportedly "strucken stark Blind" within two days.[16] Milton must have had to defend himself repeatedly for his disability even as he was learning to live an entirely new life. And, if he wanted to continue to pursue his studies and to write again, he had to find a group of friends and family on whom he could rely.

Early on, despite emphasizing his ambition and individual achievement, Milton had been a social author. His tracts against the bishops were part of a larger religious and political conversation, and he seems to have collaborated with his first tutor, the devout Presbyterian Thomas Young. Milton probably penned the postscript for one of the treatises criticizing bishops that Young wrote with the four other, like-minded clergymen, collectively known as "Smectymnuus." Given the back-and-forth of pamphlets-writing in this period—authors published arguments, responses, and counterarguments on topics ranging from coffeehouses to church ceremony—it is not surprising that Milton extolled the value of a shared process of writing, one that required "much arguing, much writing, many opinions" (YP II: 554). He also used a metaphor of building a temple to describe the pursuit of truth as a collective endeavor, "some cutting, some squaring the marble, others hewing the cedars" (YP II: 555).

Among Milton's early poems, the courtly entertainment, *A Masque Presented at Ludlow Castle*, stands out as his most obviously collaborative creation, commissioned by the Earl of Bridgewater, dependent on the performances of the Earl's three children, and enhanced by the music of Henry Lawes. But Milton understood the benefit of working with others for even his nondramatic lyrics. He and Charles Diodati shared their poems with each other, and Milton also gave copies of his poetry to Alexander Gill Jr., the son of his headmaster at St. Paul's grammar school. Milton came to enjoy the company of a close circle of friends—boyhood and college classmates, acquaintances he met during his European travels, and a growing coterie of intellectuals, both men and women, as well as his own former students. Even before he went blind, he sought some of these friends' advice and guidance.

In Milton's later years, as he continued to live with his blindness, this social network must have deepened and expanded. Two years before the publication of *Paradise Lost*, for example, he shared a manuscript copy with one of his former students. Thomas Ellwood was a young Quaker who helped Milton find lodgings in the village of Chalfont. Milton and his family temporarily moved there in 1665—to a two-story, timbered cottage—to escape the plague that was then overwhelming London. Ellwood recollected how his friend and former teacher had followed up with him about his epic poem:

He asked me how I liked it, and what I thought of it, which I modestly but freely told him: and after some further Discourse about it, I pleasantly said to him, Thou hast said much here of *Paradise lost*, but what hast thou to say of *Paradise found*? He made me no Answer, but sate some time in a Muse; then brake off that Discourse, and fell upon another Subject.[17]

This anecdote suggests that Milton took his pupil's advice seriously, and Ellwood goes on to report that his influence was even more significant than he expected. A few months later, he visited Milton yet again, and the author handed him a copy of a second long poem, *Paradise Regained*: "In a pleasant Tone [he] said to me, *This is owing to you: for you put it into my Head, by the Question you put to me at* Chalfont; *which before I had not thought of.*"[18]

Milton was also not above taking advice from readers at large. In a reissue of the first edition of *Paradise Lost*, he added a paragraph explaining why the poem did not rhyme (rhyming was then the fashion) along with brief, prose summaries of each of the epic's books. Why? Because the poem's printer and publisher, Samuel Simmons—the son of Milton's longtime friend, the Stationer Matthew Simmons—asked the author to make these revisions. Some early readers, Samuel Simmons reported, had "stumbled" through the poem's first issue and needed further assistance.[19] Milton readily complied.

But for Milton in his blindness suddenly to need help even with his reading, for him to have to wait on amanuenses to take down and help correct all of his writings—this was a new level of reliance, and it was slow and sometimes frustrating. He would never be one of the speeding thousands doing God's bidding. He had gone from freely collaborating to feeling utterly dependent.

Here is the routine that Milton came to follow. He would awaken at 4:00 a.m., have an attendant read to him from the Hebrew Bible for about a half hour, and then spend time in quiet contemplation. At 7:00 a.m., the attendant returned, and Milton liked to sit in his easy chair and lean back obliquely with his leg flung over the armrest. He would then dictate the stock of verses that he had formulated during the previous night. On a good morning, he might recite some forty lines before breakfast, but he would then painstakingly review and revise the verses with his attendant, and reduce them to half.[20]

Milton in his blindness worked with a large group of amanuenses. The various hands in the surviving manuscript of his theological treatise indicate that he learned to lean on many friends and many scribes. In his later years, after the success of his first *Defense*, acquaintances snatched at the opportunity to assist the internationally renowned writer, and hopeful parents eagerly volunteered their young sons to work for—and learn from—the great author. But even casual visitors might be pressed into service to help correct and fine-tune his manuscripts. One of Milton's nephews, Edward Phillips, recalls often being asked to assist his demanding uncle. In particular, Phillips lent a hand with *Paradise Lost*:

> I had the perusal of it from the very beginning; for some years, as I went from time to time, to Visit him, in a Parcel of Ten, Twenty, or Thirty Verses at a Time, which being Written by whatever hand came next, might possibly want Correction as to the Orthography and Pointing.[21]

Phillips's account provides a rare glimpse into the creation of a literary masterpiece. It suggests at once Milton's scrupulous attention to detail, his refusal to be limited by his disability, and his reliance on family and friends to be his eyes.

————

Milton's own children proved to be less than enthusiastic assistants. By 1661, when the family moved from Petty France to a new house in Jewin Street (to a neighborhood in northwest London), Mary (age thirteen) and Deborah (age nine) were routinely expected to read to their father, while only the eldest of his three children, Anne (age fifteen), was excused, most likely because of a speech impediment. Milton's daughters probably did not understand all of the languages that he asked them to read. Gentlewomen in the seventeenth century were typically educated in dancing, drawing, music, needlework, and French. Mary and Deborah would have been expected to read in English and French as well as Latin, Italian, Spanish, Greek, Hebrew, and Syriac. The girls are reported to have had exact pronunciation, but they would have been taught these other languages only phonetically, without instruction in the words' meanings.

This work must have been trying and tedious for Milton's daughters. Day after day, presumably for hours at a time, they would have sat and recited some of the most influential and profound works ever written—classical and contemporary works as well as the Bible—and the girls may have been cut off from the meaning of words that they could only parrot. According to one of his daughters, he even refused to teach them other languages. She said that he believed—and repeated often in their hearing—"one Tongue was enough for a Woman."[22] No doubt Milton intended this attempt at a quip to sound humorous—women talk too much!—but such casual misogyny is disturbing and jarring. Was he lashing out at his daughters because he resented how much he now needed their help? In his prose writings on marriage and divorce, Milton had insisted that both spouses suffer, but (as I discuss in the next chapter) he also let some ugly things creep into his prose, and he sometimes cast the man as the injured party and blamed the woman for not being intellectually and socially companionable.[23] A larger, deep-seated bias against women may have blinded him to his own daughters' gifts and intelligence.

Generally, fathers during the early modern period were expected to foster their children's respect and admiration more than their love. Milton lived during a time when showing fatherly affection, at least among the aristocracy, was scoffed at. As late as 1732 a magazine article entitled "Foolish Fondness" criticized the "common people" for feeling too strongly about their children,[24] and the antiquarian and essayist John Aubrey—who some ten years later would, coincidentally, compose one of the earliest biographies of Milton—observed in 1670 that parents were expected not to indulge their offspring: "The Gentry and the Citizens . . . were as severe to their children as their Schoolmasters; and their Schoolmasters, as masters of the House of correction. The child perfectly loathed the sight of his parents, as the slave his Torturor."[25] Aubrey might be overstating his point here—perhaps such treatment was not so intense and not so widespread—

but other writers, such as Hannah Woolley in *The Gentlewoman's Companion* (1673), reinforce the general sentiment. Woolley tells mothers to inspire their children's submission to their father, and she describes children's paternal attitudes with phrases such as "so much awe," "awful regard," and as "much or more obedience to him than your selfe."[26]

In Milton's case, the surviving evidence is secondhand and scant, and it was recorded decades afterward by scholars who were sometimes willing to pay for news about the infamous defender of regicide.[27] Still, "awful regard" might aptly describe the attitude of Milton's daughters toward him, at least for a time. His nephew's own conflicted feelings about Milton's expectations come through as he describes the girls' reactions with a string of contrastive clauses. Edward Phillips writes that Mary and Deborah found reading to their blind father to be

> a Trial of Patience, almost beyond endurance; yet it was endured
> by both for a long time; yet the irksomeness of this employment
> could not always be concealed, but broke out more and more into
> expressions of uneasiness.[28]

According to a former maidservant, Elizabeth Fisher, the girls grew so frustrated that they sold off some of their father's books without his knowledge; they tried to sell the rest for scrap paper. Milton, of course, an avid reader and bibliophile, depended on his books for his writing. This theft, if true, would have been devastating. The same maidservant went on to report that the girls encouraged her to steal from the household expenses and that Mary, told of her father's plans to marry his third wife, was indifferent. Instead, she wanted to be told only that he died.

Surely some readers will sympathize with the widower Milton, struggling to cope with his newly dark world, to keep up with his secretaryship, to fulfill his lofty poetic goals—and to relate to three teenage daughters as their thoughts were turning to marriage. But we must also sympathize with Deborah, Mary, and Anne if they came to resent their father for requiring them to help with his work without understanding what they were reading. Their busy and distracted father's high standards and high-mindedness must have seemed less noble than impractical and selfish.

Also difficult for the three girls would have been growing up without a mother for most of their adolescence. Four years after Mary died, Milton had married again. Almost nothing is known about this second wife, Katherine Woodcock, but the couple had a daughter about a year later, and they named her after her mother. For a time, Katherine Woodcock seems to have brought peace and order to the author's home; the couple was probably happy.[29] But this second union proved brief and ended tragically: Katherine died four months after giving birth, and her baby died a month after her. Milton was again distraught, and he must have struggled with this new grief as he once again found himself raising three daughters on his own.

For Milton's third wife, the girls had little affection. In 1663, the fifty-four-year-old author again married a much younger woman. Elizabeth Minshull was twenty-four years old, reportedly gentle and agreeable, and skilled as a reader, writer, and singer. From the little surviving evidence, she and Milton had an affectionate and mutually satisfying marriage.[30] Milton's daughters, though, resented young Elizabeth's attempts to control them, and they worried that she would inherit Milton's estate in their place, which ultimately she did.

Still, some scholars have argued that reports of Milton's cruelty to his daughters have been exaggerated.[31] Wouldn't the former schoolteacher have wished for his daughters to understand as many languages as possible, and wouldn't he have taken measures to make sure that his children could write?[32] At least Deborah, it has been established, knew Latin and, because she could write, also likely served as one of her father's amanuenses. After Milton died, she spoke fondly of him and remembered him as convivial and well-liked.[33] The early biographer Aubrey also reports that Milton taught Deborah to read Greek. She would eventually follow in her father's footsteps and go on to keep a school, and in her later years, she had not forgotten all that she had learned from Milton. She allegedly could still recite whole passages from Ovid's *Metamorphoses*, an anecdote which may belie the claim that Milton had restricted his daughters' education.

The idea of Milton as a patriarchal tyrant is in part an invention of the nineteenth century. The image of a detached, older poet dictating to his timid, laboring daughters emerged from lingering contempt for Milton's opposition to monarchy and his attacks of the beloved King Charles. Anne Manning, a Victorian fiction writer, for one, published a popular epistolary novel, *Maiden and Married Life of Mary Powell* (1852). It was told from the perspective of the poet's first wife, and imagined a Milton who was sometimes aloof and self-absorbed—although deep down he was dedicated to his "sweet Moll," his "precious Wife."[34] Even more influential and less flattering was probably George Romney's engraving "Milton and His Daughters," first published in a 1794 edition of Milton's poetry edited by the scholar William Hayley and later adapted by biographers and other artists. It shows a sullen figure sitting apart from two of his young daughters, bent over a table and looking anxious and cowed.

Milton in his writings suggests that he struggled to relate to his own father. In his Latin poem "Ad Patrem" ("To His Father"), he thanks the senior John Milton for not forcing him to study business or law. But Milton also sounds defensive about his poetic ambitions: "Do not, I pray, keep scorning the sacred Muses, and do not think them vain and useless, you who skilled in their gift set a thousand songs to fit rhythm" (lines 56–59). It is unclear how playfully or seriously Milton made such appeals. Did his father genuinely disapprove of his literary aspirations? Although a Scrivener by trade, his father had achieved some fame in his own right as a musician. He was invited to contribute to a collection of madrigals published as a tribute to Queen Elizabeth, and he received a medal for his musical compositions from a Polish prince visiting London. But most striking in "Ad Patrem" is Milton's belief in a generational affinity. He thus asks his father defensively, "Why should it surprise you if it happened I was begotten a poet—if, so closely joined to you by dear blood, we pursued related arts and kindred study?" (lines 61–63).

Milton goes on to thank his father for helping with his education, specifically attributing to him his own knowledge of languages—Latin, Greek, French, and Italian.[35] Perhaps this personal experience made it especially challenging for Milton to accept any difficulties that his daughters had in mastering the languages that he understood as his own paternal

FIGURE 17. *Milton and His Daughters* by George Romney from *The Poetical Works of John Milton*, 3 vols., ed. William Hayley (London, 1794–1797).

Source: Robert J. Wickenheiser Collection of John Milton, Irvin Department of Rare Books and Special Collections, University of South Carolina Libraries, Columbia, S.C.

inheritance. According to Milton's nephew, Mary, Anne, and Deborah simply lacked their father's scholarly interests:

> It had been happy indeed if the Daughters of such a Person had been made in some measure Inheritrixes of their Father's Learning; but since Fate otherwise decreed, the greatest Honour that can be ascribed to this now living (and so would have been to the others, had they lived) is to be Daughter to a man of his extraordinary Character.[36]

Readers of Milton's poetry and prose can no doubt accept this assessment more easily than the children who found themselves, for whatever reason, unable to share their father's passion and drive. Milton might not have been able to see beyond his own poetic aspirations to fathom that his daughters deserved the opportunity, like he had, to follow their own dreams and find their own voices, regardless of what their father wanted.

———

For Milton to pursue his plans, he knew he needed yet another kind of help. In *Paradise Lost*, as he catalogues some of the sights that he can no longer see, he looks for a less practical type of assistance:

> Thus with the year
> Seasons return, but not to me returns
> Day, or the sweet approach of ev'n or morn,
> Or sight of vernal bloom, or summer's rose,
> Or flocks, or herds, or human face divine;
> But cloud instead, and ever-during dark
> Surrounds me, from the cheerful ways of men
> Cut off, and for the book of knowledge fair
> Presented with a universal blank
> Of Nature's works to me expunged and razed,
> And wisdom at one entrance quite shut out.
> So much the rather thou celestial light
> Shine inward, and the mind through all her powers
> Irradiate, there plant eyes, all mist from thence
> Purge and disperse, that I may see and tell
> Of things invisible to mortal sight. (Book 3, lines 40–55)

The stock images of flocks and herds might sound removed from Milton's firsthand experience in seventeenth-century London; perhaps to help him cope with the new affliction he once again was turning to classical literature—to the pastoral tradition of the authors he and Charles Diodati had read as boys in grammar school. But the glimpse of simple, natural things in Milton's epic—sheep, cattle, a summer's rose—also fits with other evidence that he especially enjoyed nature and repeatedly tried to live near and go for walks in the city's many green spaces. The hardship of Milton's condition comes through in the repetition of violent removal—

"expunged," "razed," "cut off," and "shut out"—as well as the finality of "universal blank" and "ever-during dark."

Milton's only hope in this passage is a celestial patroness, a muse, who will compensate him for his blindness by granting him new insight into the workings of the world. At first, this gesture might seem to be mere poetic posturing. Of course, Milton did not really believe in a muse; he was writing according to an ancient tradition, in which poets would call on one of nine classical deities for inspiration. Milton had included a similar gesture of invoking a muse in some of his early, sighted poems such as "On the Morning of Christ's Nativity."

But the use of a muse in Milton's later works is repeatedly connected to his loss of sight. He does not mention one without the other, so that he again looks for divine assistance in another sonnet about his blindness. In Sonnet 22, he interrupts a list of what he can no longer see by insisting, once again like Samson, that he does not blame God: he is now bereft "Of sun or moon or star throughout the year, / Or man or woman. Yet I argue not / Against Heaven's hand or will" (lines 5–7). The brief list of lost sights seems to be in ascending order of importance. It culminates with the pain of isolation: the social writer can no longer see the faces of his family or friends. The strong pause mid-line and the abrupt interruption of the new sentence, "Yet I argue not," painfully betrays the willfulness required for maintaining a sanguine outlook. He takes some comfort in knowing that he sacrificed his sight for the sake of defending liberty in his first *Defense*—"my noble task, / Of which all Europe talks from side to side" (lines 11–12)—but again his primary consolation seems to be through prayer or inspiration. He concludes the sonnet by invoking God or a heavenly muse, someone or something whom he calls only his "better guide" (line 14).

How to cope with physical suffering? Milton's answer seems to be a combination of poetry, prayer, and fellowship. The epithet "heav'nly Muse" in *Paradise Lost* (Book 1, line 6) neatly encapsulates these sources of comfort; it is at once a wellspring of inspiration, divinity, and companionship. His invocation of a muse was in part a humble admission that he needed help to accomplish his greatest poetic task—as he put it, "to soar

/ Above th' Aonian mount, while it pursues / Things unattempted yet in prose or rhyme" (Book 1, lines 14–16). He calls on his muse not just to "instruct" him but to "illumine, . . . raise and support" (Book 1, lines 19, 23), and he describes her visiting his slumbers nightly or appearing at dawn to fill him with verse (Book 7, lines 29–30). She provides Milton with both insight and company.

After the Restoration, fearing for his life, concentrating his waning energy at last on his epic, Milton did not paint a rosy picture of his circumstances. He admits he had "fall'n on evil days, / On evil days though fall'n, and evil tongues; / In darkness, and with dangers compassed round, / And solitude" (Book 7, lines 25–28). But, as his muse visits and inspires him, he immediately finds hope: he is "not alone," after all, and his voice is still strong even in the darkness.

FIVE

Free Speech
"Precious lifeblood"

BEFORE MILTON COULD START WORK in earnest on *Paradise Lost*, he found himself having to answer for something he had done as a government secretary—or, more accurately, something he had not done. He was called to testify before a special parliamentary commission and grilled about allowing the publication of a heretical, Polish book. Given how seriously Milton took language, his opposition to the book's censorship should come as no surprise, which is exactly what he told Parliament.

Today the Palace of Westminster is stately and iconic, a neo-Gothic structure designed by Charles Barry and Augustus Pugin in the early 1800s, but when Milton was questioned there in February 1652 the Palace of Westminster comprised a confused collection of buildings— some with towers, others with pinnacles, still others with turrets. Milton, almost completely blind (he would lose his remaining sight in the next few weeks), would have needed to be led through the ancient stone structure into the House of Commons, maybe on the arm of a former student or holding his wife Mary's hand. He may have also leaned on his walking stick.[1]

Still, he surely recognized the voices of the special committee's members, especially Oliver Cromwell and the other men who also served on the Council of State. Milton had at this point been working for the Council as Secretary for Foreign Tongues for three years, since March 1649; he would ultimately serve for nearly seven more. As part of his secretaryship, he was required to do a great deal of routine administrative work. His eloquent, impassioned writings in defense of regicide and republicanism naturally continued to garner the most attention, but on a day-to-day basis Milton was mostly handling and translating many, many documents to, from, and about other European states.

The council also regularly called on Milton to do some light police work—to oversee (grant an official license for) a periodical that endorsed the new government, and to search through and seize the papers of people whom the council suspected of breaking the law or continuing to support the late monarch.[2] It was acting in this general capacity that led to Milton's being called before Parliament in the winter of 1652. The commission wanted him to explain his role in the publication of *Catechesis Ecclesiarum quae in Regno Poloniae*, a Latin translation of an anonymous heretical manifesto that became known as *The Racovian Catechism* because it had originally been published in Raków, Poland. The book's author advocated the separation of church and state, and much more radically, he was anti-Trinitarian: he denied that Jesus was God. He also rejected the Atonement, dismissed the doctrine of Original Sin, and refused the divinity of the Holy Spirit. This was a time when Christianity influenced and was entangled with all aspects of society, when a person who skipped church on Sunday committed a criminal offense. The English church dominated the regulation of the book trade, the licensing of physicians and schoolmasters, and the administration of universities.[3] For a tract openly to defy church authority and oppose the fundamental tenets of Christianity was tantamount to casting doubt on the underlying assumptions of English identity and culture.

Milton did not mince words. The special committee had already conducted a month-long inquiry into the catechism: How had such an egregiously anti-Trinitarian book come to be published in England?[4] Milton told the commission plainly that, of course, he was the one who had approved the catechism. He did not think such ideas should be suppressed. He also reminded the committee that he had written a whole tract on the subject of regulating the press; in permitting the catechism to go forward he had "done no more than what his opinion was."[5]

Milton's was certainly a minority view—and his tract opposing regulation was a watershed moment in the history of free expression. Practices of censorship may have differed widely during his lifetime, but since 1476, when the merchant and writer William Caxton first introduced printing in England, no sitting monarch had allowed a free press. Anyone who wished to publish a text—a book, pamphlet, or paper—had to do two things. The first step was going to the Stationers' Company, then housed in Ave Maria Lane, near St. Paul's Cathedral, the largest open area in the city and the heart of the English book trade. Dozens of shops lined the perimeter, and each bookseller hung out a unique wooden sign—a harp, a crane, a hand and plough—so as to distinguish his stock from his peers' books. Beginning in 1557, the crown had chartered the Stationers' Company to oversee these shops or "stations" and to supervise the printing and publishing of all texts.[6] For a fee, a member of the company entered by hand the book's title and the owner's name in the Stationers' massive *Register*.

The second step for publishing a text was going to the Star Chamber, a court housed among the many buildings of the Palace of Westminster, so named because the ceiling was decorated with gilt stars.[7] Here a group of government-appointed officials, many of them clerics, were required to examine thoroughly each text before it was printed. They were to approve—to license—only those works that they deemed acceptable.

With the start of the civil wars in 1642—as the king set up an alternative government in Oxford and the Court of Star Chamber was eliminated—this second type of censorship foundered, inaugurating the nation's first period of virtually unrestricted publication. Suddenly, the number of printed texts soared. In 1640, about 867 items had been printed; in the following three years, 1,850, 2,968, and 1,495 texts appeared.[8] Parliament scrambled to stop the deluge. On 16 June 1643, the government revived key protocols from earlier Tudor and Stuart legislation. Parliament stipulated anew that no book, pamphlet, or paper could be printed, unless it were first approved by a government licenser.

Mostly, the government attempted to prosecute Stationers who repeatedly created unlawful texts or who produced works that contained slander, sedition, or heresy. Corporal punishments for these latter crimes, though rare, were dramatic, meant to linger long afterward in the minds of the public. Most notorious was probably the case of the lawyer John Stubbe, who in 1579 published *The Discoverie of a Gaping Gulf.* As Queen Elizabeth entertained the possibility of marrying the French Duke of Alençon, Stubbe used his tract to rail against the proposed alliance as well as all things French. The Queen was incensed. She had Stubbe removed from the bench and imprisoned along with both the tract's printer, Hugh Singleton, and a member of Parliament, William Page, who had attempted to distribute about fifty copies. All three men were also sentenced to have their right hands chopped off, although the octogenarian Singleton was later pardoned, perhaps because of his age.[9] A stage was hastily constructed in the marketplace at Westminster so that the punishment could be carried out in plain view. According to reports, immediately after Stubbe's right hand dropped onto the wooden stage, he doffed his cap with his left, shouted to the crowd, "God save the queen"—then crumpled to the platform as his knees buckled from the pain and loss of blood.[10]

Milton in 1652 probably feared most immediately that he would lose his government position, not his hand, but he knew he could be fined, imprisoned, or worse for seeming to endorse the catechism's heresy. Four years earlier, on 2 May, Parliament had passed an "Ordinance for the Suppression of Blasphemies and Heresies," and its provisions included the death penalty for espousing anti-Trinitarianism. The last man burned at the stake in England had also been anti-Trinitarian.[11] On 11 April 1612, the sheriff of Lichfield ignored Edward Wightman's screams of pain as his body was engulfed in smoke and flames and he tried in vain to recant his heresies.

Sometimes it was heretical or seditious publications that were set ablaze—not with the aspiration of destroying every copy but with the aim of demonstrating that such works would not be tolerated. Eventually, it became tradition that the common hangman would be the one to toss in copies of the offending book, one after the other, his presence meant to suggest the burning of the perpetrators in effigy. Even in the early 1640s, after the outbreak of civil war, as Parliament assumed control of the government, more than a dozen book burnings were staged in the capital, a greater number than during Charles I's previous seventeen-year reign.[12]

But it was under King Charles that these spectacles became especially elaborate. The most memorable case was of the Puritan William Prynne. In 1633—the year before Milton's masque at Ludlow—Prynne published *Histriomastix*, a more than 1,000-page treatise against all manner of stage plays. He believed that the theater distracted people from attending church, corrupted actors who imitated immoral characters, and encouraged audiences to commit the sins that they saw portrayed. Prynne went so far as to suggest that any woman who acted in a dramatic work was a whore, a charge that Charles I did not take lightly. His wife, Queen Henrietta Maria, was widely known to enjoy courtly entertainments and was at the time readying to perform in a royal masque, like the one Milton had written for the Egerton family.

The Court of Star Chamber found Prynne guilty of sedition, and he was imprisoned, fined £5,000, barred from practicing law, and stripped of his university degrees. But even that sentence was not deemed sufficient. He was also forced to stand with his head and hands in the pillory at Westminster, in the same place where Stubbe and Page had their hands amputated. A paper declaring Prynne's crime in black letter type was put on his head—it read, "seditious, libelous railing"[13]—and part of one of his ears was sliced off by a barber surgeon. Prynne was then taken to an open square in the parish of Cheapside, the paper again propped on his head, and part of his other ear removed as he stood in the pillory with his head bowed between his raised arms. When a fire was set in front of him, the hangman began to drop into the flames hundreds of copies of Prynne's thick book, creating so much noxious black smoke that the bleeding prisoner choked and almost passed out.[14]

Four years later, the unrepentant Prynne would find himself again on the scaffold for another treasonous tract along with two other men

FIGURE 18. William Prynne in the pillory

Source: *Cassell's Illustrated History of England* (London: Cassell, Petter, and Galpin, 1865), volume 3. Photograph by Lori Howard, Georgia State University.

accused of sedition—Henry Burton, a priest, and John Bastwick, a physician. As a repeat offender, Prynne had his nose slit and his cheeks branded with the letters "S. L." for "Seditious Libeller."[15] All three men also had their ears cut off, but this time Prynne's ears were sheared even closer to his head—so close, he reported, that the executioner hacked off a piece of his cheek, and the blade then slid into his neck. With the second ear, the executioner—perhaps eager to be done with the whole grisly business— descended the scaffold prematurely and had to be called back by the attending surgeon. He had to finish severing Prynne's dangling lobe.

———

Milton would later have his own complaint against Prynne, but certainly he sympathized with the Puritan's cruel punishment. On 23 November 1644, Milton published a vigorous attack on regulating the press in which he articulated a far-reaching position against censorship. He titled it *Areopagitica* after the Areopagus, a huge rocky hill in Athens across from the Acropolis (named for Ares, the god of war). In ancient times, a highly respected court met there, and Milton was evoking the court's name to imply that England's Parliament should emulate the Areopagus and, in particular, abolish prepublication censorship. When he appeared before the parliamentary commission and reminded the members that he had written on the regulation of printing and "published a tract on that subject, that men should refrain from forbidding books," he was referring to *Areopagitica*.[16]

For Milton, it did not matter that England's system of censorship was never consistently enforced or that in 1644, the year *Areopagitica* was published, only 20 percent of all printed texts were registered with the Stationers' Company.[17] Just the requirement of obtaining a license for a book before it was published affected what authors dared to write. Why bother to compose something that would never be allowed to see print? No records survive to show how many books the licensers refused to publish or whether licensers often redacted books that were then printed. In the case of *Paradise Lost*, one early biographer reports that "among other frivolous Exceptions," the licenser objected to an oblique reference to kingship in a description of Satan in hell:[18]

> his form had yet not lost
> All her original brightness, nor appeared
> Less than Archangel ruined, and th' excess
> Of glory obscured: as when the sun new ris'n
> Looks through the horizontal misty air
> Shorn of his beams, or from behind the moon
> In dim eclipse disastrous twilight sheds
> On half the nations, and with fear of change
> Perplexes monarchs. Darkened so, yet shone
> Above them all th' Archangel. (Book 1, lines 591–600)

Apparently, the licenser thought the passing reference to a fearful, perplexed monarch was treasonous, but Milton or someone arguing on his behalf convinced the licenser otherwise because the lines have been

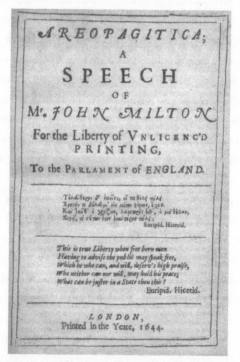

FIGURE 19. Title page of *Areopagitica* by John Milton (London, 1644)

Source: Robert J. Wickenheiser Collection of John Milton, Irvin Department of Rare Books and Special Collections, University of South Carolina Libraries, Columbia, S.C.

printed as quoted here since the poem's first edition. If the licenser's other "Exceptions" resulted in any revisions, no record of them survives.

Milton objected to all such interference. He writes in *Areopagitica* that the discernment of "truth and falsehood" depends on "what should be printed and what suppressed"—a remarkably prescient description of how technology and the wider distribution of texts would affect knowledge and inspire political change in the ensuing centuries (YP IV: 626). He allied the unfettered operation of the printing press "with truth, with learning, and the Commonwealth" (YP II: 488). In other words, a free press, according to Milton, is essential for a nation's religion, education, and government.

Milton did not think Parliament should completely deregulate the still relatively new technology of print, however. He accepted that books could be suppressed *after* publication—in his words, if a book "prov'd a Monster, . . . it was justly burnt, or sunk into the Sea" (YP II: 505). He would not have approved of libel or hate speech, for instance. His position was that all books, good or bad, should be published and read, but authors should answer for impious, libelous, or evil publications. For Milton, the latter included Catholic books because, he reasoned, any religion that opposed toleration could not, in turn, be tolerated; otherwise, the law would "unlaw" itself (YP II: 565).

How should such limitations be imposed? Milton believed that arriving at truth depends on debate—as we have seen, "much arguing, much writing, many opinions"—and, he added, "opinion in good men is but knowledge in the making" (YP II: 554). In contrast, he complained that censorship discouraged people from thinking for themselves and produced a "gross conforming stupidity" (YP II: 564). But instead of offering a specific practical policy for regulating the print trade, Milton trusted that an educated citizenry could peruse and judge books on their own to discover which should be read and which ignored, without the interference of church or state. He celebrates the benefits of free expression in richly metaphorical language. Good readers, he says, are like good refiners, able to sieve gold out of the "drossiest volume" (YP II: 521). They are also like well-practiced apothecaries, tempering and composing effective medicines out of useful drugs and herbs, and they are like the maiden Psyche from mythology, sifting through the heap of "confused seeds" that Venus required her to cull and sort to win back her husband Cupid (YP II: 514). Milton also imagines a battlefield of ideas: Parliament should permit the publication of both truth and falsehood and let them "grapple" because, he predicts, the truth will always win "in a free and open encounter" (YP II: 561). Bad books will perish (he does not explain exactly how), and the best works will survive to inspire and inform future readers.

More than six decades before England's first copyright law in 1709, Milton also stressed the rights of authors. Books were not another ware that Parliament could regulate, like wool or tobacco, but instead uniquely preserved an author's soul. He compares books to the mythical dragon's teeth that Cadmus planted in founding Thebes. According to legend, a ferocious army sprang up and began to fight each other until only five soldiers survived, and these helped Cadmus to build the new city's citadel. Books are similarly magical, sown with the author's ideas and able to generate strong readers, armed with new knowledge and insights. As Milton put it, a "good Book" contains "the precious life-blood of a master spirit, imbalm'd and treasur'd up on purpose to a life beyond life" (YP II: 493). This last quotation is embossed over the entrance in the primary reading

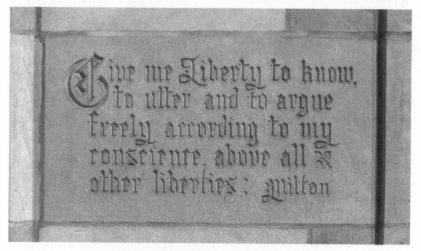

FIGURE 20. Dedication to the Tribune Tower

Source: Photo by David Hallberg.

room of the New York Public Library, and another quotation—"Give me the liberty to know, to utter, and to argue freely according to conscience, above all liberties" (YP II: 560)—is inscribed in a gray brick on the outside of Chicago's Tribune Tower on Michigan Avenue. Milton's broader argument against regulating the press profoundly influenced, among other writers, the philosopher John Stuart Mill, whose *On Liberty* (1859) echoes the First Amendment to the U.S. Constitution, and in cases involving freedom of expression, the U.S. Supreme Court has cited *Areopagitica* by name five times.

———

Milton's opposition to censorship was broad-minded and forward-thinking, but it was also personal. Shortly before he appeared in front of the parliamentary commission, one of his own writings had suffered an incendiary fate. In June 1651, an English translation of his anti-monarchical *Defense of the English People* was publicly burned in Toulouse and Paris, and its further sale was outlawed.[19] On 23 August of the same year, a clergyman named Edward Hyde expressed his disappointment that Milton's *Defense* was available in Germany; he hoped that it would soon be burned and banned.[20] Even one of the Earl of Bridgewater's two sons, John Egerton, who had performed as the Elder Brother in *A Masque Presented at Ludlow Castle*, angrily jotted on his copy of Milton's defense of regicide, "Liber igni, Author furca, dignissimi" ("The book is most deserving of burning, the author [deserving] of the gallows").[21]

But when Milton sat down to compose *Areopagitica* in 1644, he was specifically thinking of the religious controversy surrounding his writings on marriage. Just one year earlier, he had first taken the unconventional position of defending divorce. Henry VIII may have broken with the Catholic Church in 1534 because he wished to dissolve his first marriage (to Katherine of Aragon), but the medieval Catholic doctrine prohibiting divorce remained intact in the Church of England; a marriage that was deemed valid could be dissolved only by the death of the wife or husband. In *The Doctrine and Discipline of Divorce* (1643), Milton instead followed Continental Protestant practices in asserting that divorce should be permitted—and he went further, breaking new ground. The ideas that he advocated were not made legal in England for more than 300 years.

Milton defended the rights of both spouses to remarry (not just the victim of an unfaithful spouse), argued that the right to dissolve a marriage should reside solely with the spouses (not ecclesiastical or civil courts), and expanded the valid reasons for divorce to include emotional incompatibility (not just adultery). If divorce were allowed only in cases of adultery, Milton insisted, the law would wrongly suggest that marriage is mostly about sex. Instead, he described marriage as a cure for loneliness. He compared it to an "apt and cheerful conversation" (YP II: 235), a metaphor that underscores the significance he attached to a couple's reciprocity and feelings of sympathy.

Milton's defense of divorce fit his broader belief in free will and personal responsibility, which were also of course fundamental to his arguments against censorship. He makes this point right at the start of his first divorce tract, derisively personifying Custom as the teacher most influential in matters of faith and culture. People may commend Virtue and Conscience as the best guides, but still Custom is the one most often followed:

> Except it be, because her method is glib and easy, in some manner like to that vision of Ezekiel, rolling up her sudden book of implicit knowledge for him that will to take and swallow down at pleasure, which proving but of bad nourishment in the concoction, as it was heedless in the devouring, puffs up unhealthily a certain big face of pretended learning, mistaken among credulous men for the wholesome habit of soundness and good constitution, but is indeed no other than that swollen visage of counterfeit knowledge and literature, which not only in private mars our education but also in public is the common climber into every chair where either religion is preached or law reported, filling each estate of life and profession with abject and servile principles, depressing the high heaven-born spirit of man far beneath the condition wherein either God created him or sin hath sunk him. (YP II: 222–23)

Compared to today's conventions of writing, this one sentence—151 words—looks cumbersome and formidably drawn out. But, when read aloud, it is actually lucid, even beautiful. Long before Milton went blind, he wrote for the ear, punctuating his prose rhetorically instead of according to a strict set of grammatical rules. In the midst of polemical tracts such as his *Doctrine and Discipline of Divorce* and *Areopagitica*, he also readily drew on the vivid language and figures that he relied on in his verse. Here, in the revised, second edition of his first divorce tract, he sets the stage for his argument that England needs to think in a new way about its marriage laws. He compares Custom to the sweet scroll that God commanded Ezekiel to eat so that he could prophesize (Ezekiel 2:8–3:3), but Custom is instead a type of junk food, pleasurable and easy to swallow but providing little nourishment and with the unpleasant side effect of causing a puffy face, what today would be called a big head. A person who follows custom becomes overconfident and has no real knowledge; the custom follower does things unthinkingly, simply because that is how things were always done. According to Milton, this is what was ruining the nation's education, religion, and law.

Milton then switches metaphors and describes Custom as a mask:

> To pursue the allegory, Custom being but a mere face, as echo is a mere voice, rests not in her unaccomplishment until by secret inclination she accorporate herself with Error, who being a blind and serpentine body without a head, willingly accepts what he wants and supplies what her incompleteness went seeking. Hence it is that Error supports Custom, Custom countenances Error. (YP II: 223)

Clearly this passage anticipates the serpent in the Garden of Eden, the shape that Satan takes to seduce Eve in *Paradise Lost*. Milton is arguing that customs are upheld mistakenly and that appeals to custom merely put a good face on making mistakes; the chiasmus in the final sentence—"Error supports Custom, Custom countenances Error"—dramatizes the complementary relationship between the two things. Instead, Milton wants people to think for themselves and apply what in *Paradise Lost* he calls "right reason," a combination of rationality and conscience for deducing what is good and virtuous (Book 6, line 42). If God created matrimony out of love, Milton reasons, then couples should be allowed to dissolve a bad marriage. God would not want people to suffer in a "drooping and disconsolate household captivity" (YP II: 235), what Milton also describes more painfully as "grind[ing] in the mill of an undelighted and servile copulation" (YP II: 258).

The thinking that Milton was working out in his defense of divorce would prove to be important for his arguments against monarchy during the civil war years. Milton in his tracts on marriage distinguishes between two types of natural law—a primary law of nature that applied only to life in Eden before the Fall, and a secondary law after the Fall that God gave to humanity to cope with and find relief from its sinfulness. The permission to dissolve a bad marriage, Milton argues, is part of this second type; it is necessary because humankind is now "imperfect and degenerate" (YP II: 661). But he also calls this secondary law for dealing with a fallen world the "secondary law of nature *and of nations*," a phrase which anticipates his later political stance (YP II: 661, my emphasis).[22] He would come to believe that people have the natural right to separate from a bad spouse or a bad leader.

Still, if Milton repeatedly tried to stake out a principled position in his divorce tracts and to argue for a blameless incompatibility as the reason for allowing divorce, he more than wavered in his attempt to hold both sexes equally accountable. In places, he clearly accepts Paul's hierarchy by which men are thought to be superior to women (for example, in 1 Corinthians 11:3). Milton writes in *The Doctrine and Discipline of Divorce* that whether to dissolve a marriage should be decided privately, according to "the will and consent of both parties, *or of the husband alone*" (YP II: 344, my emphasis), and his language to describe an incompatible marriage sometimes sounds horrible, as when he bemoans the husband who finds himself "bound fast to an uncomplying discord of nature, or, as it oft happens, to an image of earth and phlegm" (YP II: 254).

Milton sounds even angrier in his later divorce tracts (he ultimately wrote four). Especially in the final one, *Tetrachordon* (1645)—literally meaning "four-stringed" after the four places in scriptures that deal with marriage—he repeatedly assigns the fault for a bad marriage to a wife who is stubborn or ill-natured.[23] He still admits that some women are superior to men and so should have authority over their husbands: "If she exceed her husband in prudence and dexterity, and he contentedly yield, for then a superior and more natural law comes in, that the wiser should govern the less wise, whether male or female" (YP II: 589).[24] But even in such moments he suggests that a less intelligent man must consent— "contentedly yield"—before the more prudent and skilled wife is allowed to govern the marriage.

In all of Milton's writings on divorce, his larger argument thus cuts two ways. His emphasis on spiritual and emotional compatibility as the primary purpose of marriage—and his downplaying of the importance of reproduction—lays the groundwork for ignoring sexual differences altogether. His argument is opening up the possibility of a marriage between anyone, between two men or between two women. But Milton himself absolutely did not recognize this potential implication, and in other places, instead of deemphasizing sexuality, he cannot see beyond it, doubling down on a hierarchy of the sexes that denigrates women. In these moments, he assumes that marriage is meant to cure the loneliness of only men.

———

The controversy over Milton's writings about divorce during his own lifetime, though, had nothing to do with his gender bias. He was instead attacked for his apparent immorality in allowing both spouses to divorce and remarry. Nine years later, as he sat in front of the parliamentary commission, he was still smarting from the public scorn and outrage. First an anonymous critic had published a caustic reply to his *Doctrine and Discipline of Divorce*, complaining of Milton's "intolerable abuse of Scripture" and concluding that his book deserved to be burned by the hangman.[25] Then on Tuesday, 13 August 1644, a small, round-shouldered priest named Herbert Palmer stood up in front of Parliament in his skullcap and white cravat. Palmer demanded in loud, vigorous tones that Milton's "wicked booke" should be publicly burned; the House of Commons conceded that the Committee for Printing, which oversaw the publication and licensing of books, would begin an investigation.[26] One month later, on 16 September, it was Prynne himself who spoke out against Milton.

Having grown out his hair on both sides to cover the gashes where his ears had been, Prynne continued to take up his pen against what he perceived to be instances of immorality; ultimately he would produce more than 200 topical pamphlets. This time he singled out Milton's argument for allowing unhappy spouses to dissolve a bad marriage, what Prynne mischaracterized as an argument for "divorce at pleasure." This book, Prynne argued, should be suppressed.[27]

Milton's response to all of these attacks was not just to write *Areopagitica* but also to redouble his efforts in writing about marriage. Between August 1643 and February 1644, he thoroughly revised his divorce tract, increasing its length more than twofold between the first and second editions. Perhaps, if he just explained himself more clearly and more fully, if he added a new introduction and inserted better signposts, he could win over some of his opponents. He wanted to show that in all things he supported liberty, not license.

——————

If Milton in 1652 was upholding the ideals he articulated in *Areopagitica* and approving *The Racovian Catechism* on principle, he also privately agreed with some of the latter tract's most heretical provisions. Around the time that he testified before Parliament he began working intently on his own theological treatise, *De Doctrina Christiana* (*On Christian Doctrine*).[28] Milton would have depended on a free press if he ever wanted to air these religious views. He openly and at length denies the divinity of both the Son and Holy Spirit. He does not go as far as the anonymous author of the catechism in declaring Jesus a mere man; instead, his mature Christology could be classified as Arian, meaning it resembles the theology of Arius of Alexander (c. 250–336), an early Christian who distinguished between the essences of God and the Son.[29] For Milton, the Son who is "begotten" in the Bible cannot be co-eternal and self-existent and thus cannot be the same essence as the one deity.[30]

The other heterodox views that Milton espouses in his treatise would have also been highly controversial. He opposes infant baptism, rejects creation ex nihilo, denies predestination, and argues for the legality of polygamy; he also avows mortalism, the heresy that when a person dies, the soul dies with the body. He called his treatise "my best and most precious possession,"[31] and the work that it represents is formidable. He must have read through the Bible systematically, again and again, until he had much of it by heart, puzzling out ambiguities and inconsistencies, and compiling some 8,000 citations on related topics.

Blindness, of course, would have hampered Milton's progress, but he persevered, relying on a large group of amanuenses. Milton's nephew Edward Phillips recalled often being asked to assist his demanding uncle. In particular, he remembered that Milton requested him and his brother John to write "from his own dictation, some part, from time to time, of a Tractate which he thought fit to collect from the ablest of Divines"—a description that sounds a bit like Milton's theological treatise. Phillips added that even before Milton went blind he "set out several Treatises" about the clergy, an account that invites readers to imagine the author, lost in thought, pacing around his room, and composing aloud, as his nephews took dictation.[32]

The thrust of Milton's theological treatise also helps to explain why he was apparently so forthcoming about his decision to permit *The Racovian Catechism* when he spoke to Parliament's investigating commission. He thought that true religion had to be pursued individually, not determined by a church or government. His scrupulous method of reading in *Christian Doctrine* indicates a devout belief in the Bible as the inspired word of God. But Milton also believed that a person's internal "Spirit" should supersede even the Bible if the two were ever to come in conflict. The scriptures, he maintained, include errors, especially the New Testament, and all such outward forms of religious authority should not encroach on a person's inner knowledge:

> Anyone . . . who imposes any sanctions and dogmas of his own on the faithful—each one of whom is ruled by God's spirit—against their will, [whether he does it] in the name of the church or in that of a Christian magistrate, is imposing a yoke not only on human beings but also on the holy spirit itself.[33]

Milton concludes that his own theological treatise should serve only as a model, not a general prescription. He expected readers to work out their individual understanding of God and did not want to persuade anyone of his specific religious ideas. On the contrary, he invited readers to arrive at their own informed opinions about the church's doctrines based on their inspired personal beliefs. He writes that readers should have the freedom "not simply to probing every doctrine, and of winnowing it in public, but also of thinking and indeed of writing about it, in accordance with each person's firm belief."[34]

Milton in his treatise goes so far as to suggest that individuals who follow their conscience in the pursuit of truth might, in some cases, need to break the law:

> If I observe the sabbath in compliance with the Ten Commandments though faith meanwhile tells me [to do] something else, that meticulous compliance with the commandments will be reckoned to me . . . as sin and *anomia* [violation of the law]. For indeed it is faith that justifies, not congruency with the Ten Commandments, and only that which justifies can make each individual work be good.[35]

Here are the seeds of Henry David Thoreau's argument for civil disobedience, first published 200 years later in 1848 and then developed independently by Gandhi and American civil rights leaders. What matters is not only *what* a person believes, but *why* a person does so. To do the right thing—out of custom, out of obligation—without first doing the hard work of understanding why is to be a "heretic in the truth" (YP II: 543). Milton is claiming that a person with good cause can break a civil government's laws; he argues that individuals must, above all, follow their conscience.

Who was to say, then, that *The Racovian Catechism* should be suppressed if its author arrived at his theology—including a rejection of the Trinity—through reason and conscience? In *Areopagitica*, despite his own sense of self-importance, Milton describes the search for truth as ultimately a collaborative process. As with the building of a temple, it requires various perspectives and ideas—"many schisms and many dissections . . . in the quarry and in the timber" (YP II: 555). And every piece of the structure should not be exactly the same; the building's strength and symmetry arise out of its many varieties and disagreements.

————

The special commission to which Milton testified in late February 1652 was apparently satisfied with his answers and decided that he should not shoulder any blame for the heretical catechism. He had not, after all, authored or translated the book, nor had he sought to profit from its printing. He wisely chose not to reveal that he agreed with the catechism's anti-Trinitarianism.

Six weeks later, when the committee submitted its official resolutions to Parliament, no mention was made of the secretary-poet. Instead, the commission included the results of its several examinations of Henry Walley, clerk of the Stationers' Company; Francis Gouldman, a clergyman and lexicographer; and William Dugard, the tract's printer. Gouldman and Dugard were found guilty of printing and publishing the catechism, although neither was apparently punished aside from the financial loss of having his work confiscated. Parliament declared the tract to be "Blasphemous, Erronious and Scandalous," and all copies were to be seized and destroyed.[36]

Milton continued to serve as Secretary for Foreign Tongues. But in the following weeks and months as he lost his remaining sight and his health worsened, the council reduced his official duties. The Secretary to the Council of State, John Thurloe, took over many of Milton's responsibilities, and the councilors also came to depend on Philip Meadows, whom Thurloe had tapped to serve as Milton's assistant (initially over Milton's choice, Andrew Marvell).[37] The efficient Thurloe, a skilled Latinist, was quickly promoted to Milton's post, but for the government's most important letters, it continued to call on Milton, a practice which remained unchanged even when Oliver Cromwell was appointed Lord Protector in December 1653 and five years later when he was then briefly succeeded by Richard, his eldest son.

Years after testifying before the parliamentary commission, Milton seems to have been still thinking about the controversy surrounding

The Racovian Catechism. When in September 1658 Richard Cromwell was named Lord Protector, some members of Parliament thought it was a good opportunity for the government to take more drastic measures against Quakers, Jews, and anti-Trinitarians. Milton wanted the new Protectorate to embrace instead an even broader policy of toleration than Richard's father had allowed.[38] In mid-February 1659—seven years after Milton testified about *The Racovian Catechism*—he published *A Treatise of Civil Power in Ecclesiastical Causes,* in which he stressed again the dignity of individual believers: "It is not lawful for any power on earth to compel in matters of Religion" (YP VII: 238). He may have also been laying the groundwork for the publication of his own theological treatise.

Yet, Milton never published his *Christian Doctrine.* As the nation reverted to monarchy over the next few months, he had reason to fear that reprisals for putting forth controversial views would be even harsher under Charles II than during the commonwealth period. In 1660, the House of Commons asked Charles II to call in two of Milton's books defending regicide, and in late August of the same year, copies of Milton's *Defense* were set on fire by the hangman outside the Old Bailey, the nation's central criminal court. Priests and academics as far away as West Yorkshire spent great sums buying up copies of Milton's prose works for the pleasure of setting them on fire and watching them burn. The bookseller John Swale reported that one group of clergymen in Leeds would meet annually, fortifying themselves with strong beer, then building a fire and tossing in copies of both Milton's *Defense* and his most thorough criticism of Charles I, *Eikonoklastes.*[39] Twenty years later, on 21 July 1683, the doctors and masters at Oxford University—the school's principal governing body—condemned all of Milton's books defending regicide. Members of the university were prohibited from reading these works, and the university's convocation had copies burned symbolically at the Schools Quadrangle, a part of the Bodleian Library.[40]

The only surviving copy of Milton's *On Christian Doctrine* was not discovered until more than a century after Milton's death. An archivist named Robert Lemon stumbled upon the 724-page manuscript in London's Old State Paper Office in Whitehall.[41] In the Middle Treasury Gal-

FIGURE 21. First page of the surviving manuscript of Milton's *Christian Doctrine*

Source: The National Archives, Kew, SP 9/61.

lery, at the end of the main room, in the bottom of a large cupboard, he found transcriptions of Milton's tracts and letters from the years he had served Cromwell and the Council of State. They were covered in dust and wrapped in torn and dirty brown paper. Bundled together with them was Milton's heretical manuscript.

———

Of course, Milton's official approval of *The Racovian Catechism* does not square entirely with his argument for free speech in *Areopagitica*: just serving the Council of State as a licenser of the press, Milton was complicit in the type of prepublication regulation that he had excoriated in his earlier tract. When he defended divorce and opposed Charles I's absolutist policies, he wanted the right to express himself freely; when monarchy was temporarily overturned and he worked as secretary for a more republican form of government, he did not want critics to weaken the council or Cromwell's tenuous hold on authority.

In March or April 1673, the year before Milton died—blind, battling ill health, coping with terrible pain in his feet and joints—he dictated and published a final treatise, *Of True Religion, Heresy, Schism, Toleration*. The tract is fairly short (fourteen pages), the argument more straightforward, and the scope less ambitious. Gone is the vinegar and pepper that characterized so much of Milton's prose from his thirties and forties. Gone, too, is much of his richly metaphorical language from *The Doctrine and Discipline of Divorce* and *Areopagitica*. In this pamphlet, Milton was specifically objecting to the withdrawal on 8 March 1673 of the Declaration of Indulgence, a royal statute that had suspended all penal ecclesiastical laws and allowed Protestant nonconformists to apply for licenses to worship publicly. It also had permitted Roman Catholics to worship in private homes, a provision that provoked considerable controversy.[42] Milton in his tract replaces a fuller discussion of toleration with direct arguments against popery. Only Catholics, he reasoned, should be deemed heretical because they reject the sole authority of scripture (in favor of the church, the pope, and ritual), and so only they cannot be allowed.

Milton also uses the occasion to insist one last time on religious freedom and to make the case for free speech. He argues once again that "all sorts and degrees of men" should read the Bible and arrive at their own understanding, and he continues to propose that all believers "ought to be grounded in spiritual knowledge" (YP VIII: 434, 435). For all of Milton's temerity and egoism in defying church authority, for all of his confidence in his convictions as he published *Areopagitica* and later stared down the parliamentary commission, the search for truth remained foremost a collaboration—an ongoing, inclusive, difficult, and essential process, requiring many voices, much writing, and many opinions.

SIX

Arrogance
"Pride and worse ambition"

IT CANNOT BE COINCIDENCE THAT when around 1658 Milton finally sat down to dedicate himself to composing *Paradise Lost* he began with the story of a rebellion. As he turned from prose to poetry, he could not help thinking about England's recent political turmoil. When readers first glimpse the tyrant Satan in the epic's opening book—waking up in hell, chained on a burning lake—he is lying face down with his head lifted just above the waves, the same humiliating posture that Charles I was forced to endure at the moment of his execution.

But Milton did not reduce the devil into a version of the late king. The character of Satan in *Paradise Lost* is compelling and vital because Milton also channeled into his antihero his understanding of the desire to rebel and the need to be right. In the midst of a poetic work based on the first three chapters of Genesis, Milton explores his own story: consciously or unconsciously, he was questioning the ambition that drove him—first to challenge the church's hierarchy, then to oppose his nation's marriage laws, then to dethrone an autocratic king. Now he would try to write an

135

epic that would out-Homer Homer, and in a possibly stunning self-rebuke he placed at its center a character undone by the sin of hubris. Ultimately, Milton was confident that his actions were righteous, that his poem was divinely inspired, and that Charles's trial and execution had been the correct course. But in creating the rebel Satan, he seems to have paused to wonder whether he was utterly justified and whether England's revolution had been purely motivated. Certainly the nation was better off without a king, but on some level Milton was reconsidering the man he was at the start of the civil war—his insistence and his high self-regard. Could ambition be corrupting? What was the difference between dauntless courage and damning pride?

Yet, Milton also did not want to limit the grand scope of his story by writing a veiled memoir or mere allegory. For more than a decade, he had been planning to "leave something so written to aftertimes, as they should not willingly let it die" (YP I: 810), and he had set his sights much higher. He wanted not just to meditate on the nature of rebellion and the perils of ambition, but to vindicate God in the face of the existence of evil—to "justify the ways of God to men," as he audaciously put it (Book 1, line 26). In the eighteenth century, the German philosopher Gottfried Leibniz would coin the term *theodicy* to describe such a work. If there is a god, and if that god is good, then how can there be evil? How can there be so much grief and agony?

Milton set out to answer these questions, and he decided the best way was in verse. At that time, epic was considered the highest and most difficult type of writing: a long narrative poem about a heroic subject, written in an elevated style.[1] Virgil and Homer, the two greatest poets, had written epics. That is with whom Milton wanted to compete, with the writers he and Diodati had first studied together back at St. Paul's. But Milton would write an epic in his native tongue, not in Latin or Greek, and he would not settle for yet another epic about warfare—"long and tedious havoc," with "fabled knights / In battles feigned," as he summed up the tradition (Book 9, lines 30–31). Milton would include a battle, but his epic would instead focus on the "better fortitude / Of patience and heroic martyrdom" (Book 9, lines 31–32). His poem would be "not less

but more heroic" than the *Iliad, Odyssey,* and *Aeneid* (Book 9, line 14).
He would defend God, rewrite the Bible, and retell the story of creation
and the first sin.

In October of 1658, around the same time that Milton's thoughts were
turning to this massive new project, he published a revised version of his
widely successful *Defense.* Oliver Cromwell had died in early September—
from natural causes, probably a urinary tract infection—leaving the still
newly formed republican government in a precarious state. Cromwell's
son, Richard, inherited an unsettled foreign policy, a vague strategy for
the nation's church, and an expensive standing army. Without Oliver's
strong personality and without the deep loyalty that he had cultivated
among so many officers and soldiers, the new Protectorate was destined to
falter. Some republicans objected because the son's succession smacked of
monarchy.[2] Richard Cromwell would remain in power only seven months,
and when Charles II ascended to the throne in May 1660, the revolution
would be officially a failure. Milton had planned a more extensive revision
of his *Defense,* but the rapid unraveling of the commonwealth in these
years prompted him to hurry the second edition to print. It was a timely
reminder of both his service to the nation and the reasons for opposing
a king.

In the final pages of the new *Defense,* Milton explained that he was
now planning "greater things" dedicated "to the cause of Christendom
above all."[3] This might have been a reference to his theological treatise,
already in progress; but more likely it alluded to the epic that he had conceived eighteen years earlier and that he was, at last, starting to write.[4] He
had first begun work on the poem that became *Paradise Lost* after returning from Italy and settling into his spacious rooms in Aldersgate Street,
the quiet, handsome house situated back from the street where he opened
his school and started teaching his two nephews.[5]

But Milton had initially considered various other approaches and
topics. His surviving notes from this earlier period contain close to
100 titles for poems or plays based on either biblical stories or British
history—subjects such as John the Baptist, Abraham from Moreh, Ofbert
of Northumberland, and the Slaughter of the Monks of Bangor.[6] The one

idea that he seems to have instinctively preferred over all the rest was a
tragedy based on the narrative in Genesis; he sketched out four possible
versions of a play about the fall of humankind. He titled one of the versions, "Adams banishment," which he struck out, adding below it in the
same neat hand, "Adam unparadiz'd." Another five-act drama he called
"Paradise Lost." All of these ideas for plays differ greatly from the heroic
poem that he would eventually write. Satan has a smaller role in all of
these versions, and allegorical characters such as Justice, Labor, and Igno-
rance crowd the stage with the devil and first humans.

Milton must have realized early on the importance of developing Satan's character; even the first lines he wrote were from the devil's perspective. He shared these early verses with his eldest nephew, Edward Phillips,
and ended up using them years later in the fourth book of *Paradise Lost*,
at the start of the devil's first soliloquy.[7] Escaping from hell, alighting on
Earth, and perching on the mountain Niphates, the devil addresses the
sun:

> O thou that with surpassing glory crowned,
> Look'st from thy sole dominion like the God
> Of this new world; at whose sight all the stars
> Hide their diminished heads; to thee I call,
> But with no friendly voice, and add thy name
> O Sun, to tell thee how I hate thy beams
> That bring to my remembrance from what state
> I fell, how glorious once above thy sphere;
> Till pride and worse ambition threw me down
> Warring in Heav'n against Heav'n's matchless King.
>   (Book 4, lines 32–41)

Satan in this moment feels both hatred and despair as he gazes at God's
new creation and remembers how he, too, had once shined brightly. No
doubt he is transferring his animosity toward God's Son onto the "full-
blazing sun" (Book 4, line 29)—just as Milton in imagining a character
warring against "Heav'n's matchless King" might have been transferring
his own aversion to England's late monarch. Surely Milton's recent ex-

periences in England's failed rebellion provided some of the depth and force in Satan's truculence, but the archfiend also helped Milton. The poet could examine on a heavenly scale whether his own choices had even a little of the dishonorable, self-serving motive that the devil embodies.

Of course, as the narrator reminds readers immediately before Satan's soliloquy, the archfiend is unique: he cannot appreciate the splendor of any of God's creations,

> for within him Hell
> He brings, and round about him, nor from Hell
> One step no more than from himself can fly
> By change of place. (Book 4, lines 20–23)

Satan had boasted that he could be happy even in hell because he defines his own reality: "The mind is its own place," he reassures his chief companion, the second-in-command Beëlzebub, soon after they awake in hell, before they rise off the burning lake, "and in itself / Can make a Heav'n of Hell, a Hell of Heav'n" (Book 1, lines 254–55). Satan is right—but not in the way he thinks. Even as he leaves behind the black, sulfurous realm and flies away through chaos to reach Earth, he brings his hellish suffering with him. Yes, the mind is its own place, Milton's epic demonstrates, but Satan—who wants to repent and cannot—is trapped in a hell of his own making, regardless of where he travels.

Clearly, Satan is the most remarkable character in Milton's poem. If modern readers know anything about *Paradise Lost*, they know Milton's Satan, and often they find themselves pitying or admiring him. And why not? Satan in *Paradise Lost* is smart, dynamic, vulnerable, and articulate. He is also the ultimate underdog, daring to challenge an all-knowing, all-powerful divinity.

Helping Satan's case in this regard is that Milton follows scripture and insists on God's unknowableness. He renders his Deity as more of a theological construct than a rounded character, a figure who remains mostly invisible, a voice from a cloud that even angels approach timidly, shielding their eyes with their wings against his dazzling brilliance.[8] When God speaks, he often sounds harsh and bluff, delivering absolute pronouncements without doubt, justification, or even much personality. He may seem a version of the capricious autocrat whom Milton so thoroughly despised—the aloof monarch or pampered cleric claiming extraordinary power and sitting across an unbridgeable divide—but as a truly omnipotent, omniscient deity, Milton's God is singularly justified. At one point (in Book 5, through a long flashback), he assembles the angels and announces that he has decided to exalt his Son, to anoint him as the angels' leader—and he never explains why. The angels jubilate, but Satan is jealous: "All seemed well pleased, all seemed, but were not all" (Book 5, line 617). Curious readers might sympathize with the archfiend here and want to know what prompted God's decision. But God, of course, needs no reason for anything.

In contrast, Milton's Satan repeatedly grapples with doubt and struggles to rationalize his actions. He comes on strong at the start, especially in the poem's first two books. The devil delivers rousing, heroic speeches and exhibits a realistic psychology of personal vengeance and hurt pride. When the poem opens, Satan and his followers have already taken up arms against God, and (not surprisingly) they have been thoroughly smashed. They fell from heaven for nine days and spent another nine days unconscious, in hell, lying chained and vanquished on a burning lake. But does Satan, after he comes to, consider quitting? Never.

On the contrary, Satan overcomes his initial confusion as he awakens in Hell and reaffirms his opposition to God:

> What though the field be lost?
> All is not lost; the unconquerable will,
> And study of revenge, immortal hate,
> And courage never to submit or yield:
> And what is else not to be overcome?
> That glory never shall his wrath or might
> Extort from me. To bow and sue for grace
> With suppliant knee, and deify his power,
> Who from the terror of this arm so late
> Doubted his empire, that were low indeed,

FIGURE 22. Michael Burgesse, illustration opposite page 1,
in Milton, *Paradise Lost* (London, 1688)

Source: Robert J. Wickenheiser Collection of John Milton, Irvin Department of Rare Books
and Special Collections, University of South Carolina Libraries, Columbia, S.C.

That were an ignominy and shame beneath
This downfall; since by fate the strength of gods
And this empyreal substance cannot fail,
Since through experience of this great event
In arms not worse, in foresight much advanced,
We may with more successful hope resolve
To wage by force or guile eternal war
Irreconcilable, to our grand foe,
Who now triumphs, and in th' excess of joy
Sole reigning holds the tyranny of Heav'n. (Book I,
    lines 105–24)

The defiance that Satan exhibits in this speech is difficult to resist, especially when rendered in such exquisite pentameter. The doubling of the "since" clauses near the end—"since by fate " and "since through experience"—builds a rousing sense of momentum, dramatizing Satan's claim that he and his army are justified in continuing to oppose God. We are down, the fiend says, but now we have experience fighting God, we still have great strength, and so we can hope for success next time. The repetition in the stack of "and" phrases at the start foregrounds the devil's intransigence. Milton often stretches his sentences from one line of verse to the next, but here at the start of Satan's speech, the discrete phrases are separated by line breaks, enhancing the sense that the devils still have much to fight for. If Satan were a football coach at half-time, or a general leading the Allied forces during World War II, his passionate speeches would almost certainly have inspired and encouraged his team or battalion. Milton may have even projected a version of his own personal commitments in the fiend's insistence and his enmity toward a monarchical power structure. The problem, of course, is that *the devil* says these words, and he wants to muster his troops to fight God, not to kill Nazis, challenge a rival team from across town, or resist an unjust English monarch. Readers cannot entirely trust Milton's Satan (again, not surprisingly) so that, for example, he refuses to use God's name, as in this passage, and instead tries to make his own cause sound righteous by consistently pretending that there are multiple gods and referring to the Deity as a foe and tyrant. This is similar to the strategy that Milton himself had deployed when making the case for holding Charles I accountable in *The Tenure of Kings and Magistrates*: Milton had never used Charles's name and had concentrated his argument on opposing tyrants in general. The subtle resemblance between Milton and his devil, though perhaps unconscious, may be another indication that the poet was examining his own earlier actions and recognizing on some level his own temerity.

FIGURE 23. John Martin, illustration for book I, line 314, in *The "Paradise Lost" of Milton with Illustrations, Designed and Engraved by John Martin* (London: Septimus Prowett, 1825–1827)

With Satan, Milton makes the devil's show of resolve even more compelling by exposing how hard it is earned. Initially, the force and eloquence of Satan's speeches are disarming, and he sounds powerful and noble. "Better to reign in Hell, than serve in Heav'n" (Book 1, line 263), he defiantly asserts, and this degree of willfulness is astonishing. Of the heroes from ancient epics, he sounds most like Achilles as he inspires his comrade Beëlzebub, then summons his followers to get off the burning lake and build the palace of Pandemonium:

> O myriads of immortal spirits, O powers
> Matchless, but with th' Almighty, and that strife
> Was not inglorious, though th' event was dire,
> As this place testifies, and this dire change
> Hateful to utter: but what power of mind
> Foreseeing or presaging, from the depth
> Of knowledge past or present, could have feared,
> How such united force of gods, how such
> As stood like these, could ever know repulse?
> For who can yet believe, though after loss,
> That all these puissant legions, whose exile
> Hath emptied Heav'n, shall fail to reascend
> Self-raised, and repossess their native seat? (Book 1,
>   lines 622–34)

The devil begins by acknowledging their defeat and terrible new surroundings, but he also emphasizes the demons' power with words such as "myriads," "immortal," and "matchless." He then quickly changes tactics with a disruptive, mid-line "but"—"but what power of mind"—and begins persuading his followers that they can still return to heaven and get revenge on God. Who could have predicted, he says, who would have feared—standing with the "united force of gods"—that they could ever be conquered?

Of course, just Satan's use of the plural "gods" in this speech is blasphemous and false, as is his exaggeration that they "emptied Heav'n" in their rebellion: God tells the Son that "far the greater part" of his host remained loyal during the war (Book 7, line 145), and in other places Milton uses the number from the Book of Revelation and writes that only one-third of the angels fell.[9] Satan is also wrong in his boast that the bad angels raise themselves off the burning lake; the narrator explains that it is only "the will / And high permission of all-ruling Heaven" that releases the devil from the fiery lake so that "with reiterated crimes he might / Heap on himself damnation" (Book 1, lines 211–15).

But part of what makes Milton's devil such a fascinating character is that he is not just wrong and not just dishonest. Gradually, Milton shows the despair and pain behind the fiend's swagger. Like a camera panning back from a close-up, the poem's focus expands slowly in the opening book from Satan's stirring speech to his humiliating posture. The bold threats that he has been shouting—his daring insistence, his refusal to relent—suddenly seem both ridiculous and more audacious as readers discover that all this time the devil has been lying face down, in chains, just raising his chin above hell's flames.

And Satan, Milton eventually reveals, feels bad about himself. First, the devil begins to cry when addressing his troops in hell. He looks out on "the fellows of his crime"—assembled in perfect squadrons, their shields close together, their spears rising like a huge forest—and he admits to himself that they are his "followers rather" (Book 1, line 606). He tries to speak three times and weeps, remembering how he beheld them "far other once" in heaven. He realizes that they are

> condemned
> For ever now to have their lot in pain,
> Millions of spirits for his fault amerced
> Of Heav'n, and from eternal splendors flung
> For his revolt. (Book 1, lines 607–11)

Satan's sense of guilt increases as he later confronts his own conflicted impulses. On his way to tempt Adam and Eve—in the same soliloquy that contains the first lines that Milton wrote for the poem—the devil tries to assess honestly the injustice of his defying God's authority. He may subtly deflect some of the responsibility for his fall on "pride" and "ambition" (instead of directly blaming himself), but here he sounds painfully self-aware of his flaws and error:

> pride and worse ambition threw me down
> Warring in Heav'n against Heav'n's matchless King:
> Ah wherefore! He deserved no such return
> From me, whom he created what I was
> In that bright eminence, and with his good
> Upbraided none; nor was his service hard. (Book 4,
>   lines 40–45)

Satan recognizes that he is wrong to war against God, that God does not deserve his animosity, and that serving God was not difficult. Milton may have had his own painful, deep-seated admissions after the failure of England's revolution in 1660. Had he himself gone too far a decade earlier in defending the king's execution and thus supporting political violence? Or, as the war against Charles I was collapsing—the war that Milton had so passionately defended—did he question the pride or worse ambition behind his own and some of its leaders' actions? England's lost revolution, as with Satan's failed rebellion, must have invited its fair share of guilt, introspection, and second-guessing. Oliver Cromwell, in particular, had compromised the war's republican ideals by accepting the title of Lord Protector of England, Scotland, and Wales, a lifetime position superseding the Council of State and granting Cromwell "the chief magistracy and administration of government."[10] The exclamation "Ah wherefore!" that Satan utters here would have been on the lips of all the English rebels as they tallied up their losses and the nation reverted to an absolute monarchy more rigid than the one that they had temporarily displaced.

In the case of the archfiend, Satan's acute self-awareness is admirable, but he ultimately cannot act on it because he cannot accept his debt to God and relinquish his anger. He resembles an addict who wants to quit but keeps caving in to the drug: he regrets his bad behavior but cannot bring himself to stop and ask for forgiveness and help.[11] Even if he were to repent, he reasons, he would eventually fall again. He could promise to be good because he is in pain, but as soon as he felt better, as soon as he glimpsed his former glory, he would recant and relapse:

But say I could repent and could obtain
By act of grace my former state; how soon
Would highth recall high thoughts, how soon unsay
What feigned submission swore: ease would recant
Vows made in pain, as violent and void. (Book 4,
    lines 93–97)

All Satan can do, he concludes, is to double down on his rebellion and remain dauntless—not in itself, as Milton personally knew, a bad choice, but for Satan thoroughly the wrong one. Milton may be exorcising the guilt or uncertainty he felt about his actions leading up to and during the violent war years. However much he identified with the devil's excessive pride or desire to rebel, he could also separate himself from those qualities by associating them with Satan; Milton could reassure himself that, despite any presumption in his prose tracts, he had written according to his conscience, the king had genuinely been disloyal, and his own commitment was to personal liberty and a more representative form of government, not to anything diabolic. Satan, in contrast, is thoroughly self-interested. He bids farewell to hope, fear, and remorse by the end of his speech. "All good to me is lost," he defiantly announces (Book 4, line 109), then takes flight to Paradise to destroy Adam and Eve and all of their descendants.

———

Milton had first written about Satan at age seventeen in a Latin poem on the Gunpowder Plot. Three years before he was born, in 1605, a group of religious radicals had attempted to assassinate James I by blowing up one of the houses of Parliament. The conspirators—a group of extremists led by the handsome and charismatic Robert Catesby—were incensed by the Protestant king's denunciation of the Church of Rome and his order that all Catholic priests leave the country. Over the course of the spring and summer, the group secreted thirty-six barrels of gunpowder into the ground-floor cellars that extended the length of the Lords Chamber in the Palace of Westminster. Their plan that fall was to set off the nearly one ton of explosives just as James entered the House of Lords to open the new session of Parliament.

The anniversary of this failed terrorist attack was celebrated annually throughout the seventeenth century with fireworks, bell ringing, and
bonfires.[12] Milton, while still a teenager, composed five Latin poems condemning the plot—more poems than he would compose about any other
single subject. He called the attempt an act of "unspeakable evil" and
denounced the men who had planned it as beasts and monsters.[13]

In the longest of Milton's poems on the plot, "In Quintum Novembris" ("On the Fifth of November"), he attributes the conspirators' act
of treason directly to Satan. Here Milton presents a horrible, but conventional portrait of the devil. He is "the black lord of the shadows, the ruler
of the silent, the predator of men" ("Cum niger umbrarum dominus, rec-
torque silentum, / Praedatorque hominum," lines 78–79). He has black
wings, blazing eyes, and a ferocious mouth: "The adamantine array of his
teeth grinds with a noise like that of arms and of spear struck by spear"
("Ignescunt oculi, stridetque adamantinus ordo / Dentis, ut armorum
fragor, ictaque cuspide cuspis," lines 38–39). Milton's devil is committed
to disguise, deception, and malice against England, but the character's
rich psychology is manifestly missing in this early poem. He is more of a
stock figure, terrible but lacking the complexity that Milton would add to
the version of Satan in his epic.

This complexity is also missing in the Bible, which has little to say
about the devil in general. In a few places, the scriptures refer passingly
to Satan or to a fallen angel, such as when Jesus tells his apostles that he
"beheld Satan as lightning fall from heaven" (Luke 10:18), when a Baby-
lonian ruler is compared to a "morning star"—in Latin, *Lucifer*—that fell
from Heaven and was felled like a tree (Isaiah 14:12), or when as part of
a warning against false prophets we learn that "God spared not the angels
that sinned, but cast them down to hell, and delivered them into chains
of darkness" (2 Peter 2:4).

But even when the devil plays a more prominent role in the Bible—
testing Job's faith, for example, or tempting Jesus in the wilderness—
readers learn nothing about the devil's history and character.[14] And
probably the most well-known story about Satan, that he took on the
serpent's form to tempt Eve, is not in scriptures. Instead, the author of

Genesis refers only to a snake. That the serpent was Satan in disguise is an interpretation that primarily comes from a passage written centuries later in the Book of Revelation, which describes "the dragon, that old serpent, which is the Devil, and Satan" (20:1–2). Commentators have also used Revelation's apocalyptic prophecy of an angelic conflict (1:7–9) to infer that an earlier war in heaven must have led to Satan's banishment.

The depiction of Satan in *Paradise Lost* is largely of Milton's own making. Working from these few scriptural texts as well as some apocryphal ones, here is Satan's backstory, as Milton writes it: Long ago in heaven, before the creation of the universe, Satan was important, "If not the first Archangel, great in power, / In favor and in pre-eminence" (Book 5, lines 660–61). Milton also explains that Satan originally had a different name. He became Satan—literally, "the Adversary"—only when he decided to wage war against God. Before that point, he was called something else, but his momentous mistake literally redefined him. God permanently blotted out the rebels' original names from the Books of Life. Lucifer can be used to refer to Satan before the war, as the angel Raphael explains to Adam and Eve, but Lucifer was not actually the devil's name; it just figuratively describes how, before he rebelled, he resembled a morning star and shined more brightly than those around him.

How did this once great angel become Satan? Raphael again explains that the transformation began when God promoted the Son as the angels' "head" (Book 5, line 606). Satan "could not bear / Through pride that sight, and thought himself impaired" (Book 5, lines 664–65). We saw in the preceding chapter that Milton in his later years took the heterodox position of denying the Trinity, so that the Son—even after the exaltation—is never equal to God. Milton was not as radical as some seventeenth-century theologians, such as the author of the heretical *Racovian Catechism*, who posited that Christ was not divine and was only a man. But Milton still came to believe that the "begotten" Son was not also God—was not co-eternal, co-essential, and self-existent.[15] As Milton repeatedly asserts in his theological treatise, "It is impossible for things to be said about the one God which are inconsistent with his unity, and which make him one and not one."[16] In *Paradise Lost*, God similarly tells

Adam that he has been "alone / From all eternity, for none I know / Second to me or like, equal much less" (Book 8, lines 405–407). The Son in *Paradise Lost* distinguishes himself from the other angels not because he is divine but because God created him first and because of his merit—as God announces, he "hast been found / By merit more than birthright Son of God" (Book 3, lines 308–09). This statement underscores the Son's natural capabilities by breaking midthought so that "by merit" is foregrounded at the start of a new line. And, as the narrative unfolds, the Son goes on to assemble an impressive résumé: he helps in creating the universe, dispels the bad angels from heaven, and volunteers to become a man and die.

The absence of the Trinity in the poem does not justify Satan's reaction to the Son's new status. But it provides important psychological support for the devil's jealousy. Given that the Son is not God and is not eternal, Satan could reasonably be surprised by the announcement of the Son's sudden promotion, and he could reasonably feel that he and the other angels have suddenly been demoted. That night, frustrated and unable to sleep, he wakes up his companion, whose original name God has also erased; one day on earth people will call him Beëlzebub (literally, "Lord of the Flies"). Satan nudges him awake, "Sleep'st thou companion dear?" (Book 5, line 673). He then asks Beëlzebub how he can sleep at a time like this:

> Both waking we were one; how then can now
> Thy sleep dissent? New laws thou seest imposed;
> New laws from him who reigns, new minds may raise
> In us who serve, new counsels, to debate
> What doubtful may ensue, more in this place
> To utter is not safe. (Book 5, lines 678–83)

Satan is clearly bothered by the Son's new status because he impresses on Beëlzebub how much things have changed by repeating the word *new*—"new laws," "new minds," and "new counsels." He then asks Beëlzebub to assemble all of the angels under his command and to meet at his palace in the north of heaven. He says he wants to plan a reception and entertainment to celebrate the Son's new position. But Satan is lying, and once the angels have gathered, he reveals his true intentions and begins to sway the host to follow him. The gist of Satan's argument: it is vile for us to prostrate ourselves before God, and now we also have to do it before the Son, his image. He urges them to join him in waging an unholy civil war.

It is during the war that Satan creates gunpowder. Milton might have been thinking back to his youthful "In Quintum Novembris," where he blamed the devil for the treasonous Gunpowder Plot. Here, though, he was directly tackling Homer and Virgil on their own terms; he would include his own epic war, but his would be grander—a heavenly battle between good and bad spirits—and he would need only two of the poem's books to recount it. On the first day of the conflict in heaven, the rebels are soundly defeated by the good angels, led by Gabriel and Michael. The two battalions meet each other in midair, each in the formation of a quadrate, armed with only swords, spears, and shields. Michael strikes Satan, shearing the devil's weapon in two; then with a quick backhanded upstroke, he slices off Satan's entire right side. Satan feels pain for the first time, but he is still more ethereal than hardened matter, so his body heals quickly, the wound knitting itself back together, like a zipper. With nightfall, a truce is called, and Satan addresses his council, insisting that they need only better arms to fare better and win the next day. He proposes that they dig "deep under ground, materials dark and crude, / Of spiritous and fiery spume" (Book 6, lines 478–79). On the second day of battle, the rebels hide their new combustible weapons within their phalanx. As Satan flies ahead, leading his troops toward the good angels' battalion, he calls out to assure God's army that he now comes seeking peace. But his language reveals his true motives; he slyly alludes to the newly created guns with words such as "propound" and "discharge" (Book 6, lines 564, 567). This is the invention of punning: words no longer necessarily mean what they say. The rebels divide their flanks and open fire, and the good angels fall by the thousands and flee. Some begin hurling mountains and rocks in retaliation, and the second day ends in a stalemate.

It is on the third day that God finally intervenes. He sends his Son to drive out the rebels in his chariot, and the Son chases them to Heaven's

FIGURE 24. Frontispiece illustration of the War in Heaven by Gustave Doré from *Milton's "Paradise Lost"* (London: Cassell, 1870)

Source: Photograph by Lori Howard, Georgia State University.

crystal wall, where a spacious gap yawns. The choice for Satan and his followers is to face the Son in his fury or to throw themselves headlong from heaven "into the wasteful deep" (Book 6, line 862). The rebels are "drained, / Exhausted, spiritless, afflicted, fall'n" (Book 6, lines 851–52), so they leap into the void, choosing to drop all the way to hell rather than feel God's wrath—a crucial detail, consistent with the emphasis on free will in Milton's theodicy. Evil is freely choosing to turn away from God's goodness; no one forces Satan and his followers to leave heaven.

The story of the war in heaven and Satan's rebellion is recounted largely through flashback in *Paradise Lost* when God sends Raphael to warn Adam and Eve, and the archangel tells them of the fiend's origin. As the epic opens, Satan and his damned crew have already failed in their military enterprise, and they find themselves in hell, immersed in "darkness visible," an absence of light that seems palpable (Book 1, line 63). The phrase conveys the impenetrability of the devils' surroundings and underscores how far they have fallen from divine resplendence. The American novelist William Styron aptly chose this phrase in 1990 for the title of his memoir on depression and mental illness.

Then, in a stunning flashforward, the epic narrator explains that all of the devils will one day follow Satan to Earth and be worshipped— "adorned / With gay religions full of pomp and gold, / And devils to adore for deities" (Book 1, lines 371–73). Milton is including and outflanking his classical predecessors. How is it that ancient authors did not know about the one true God and prayed instead to figures like Jupiter, Athena, and Neptune? The gods that Virgil and Homer worshipped and wrote about are given a clever, Christian origin: they were not deities, but demons with some supernatural powers, mistaken for gods by pagan writers between the time of Adam and Eve and the age in which Milton lived.

Here is how this narrative strategy works. After Satan urges his followers to get off the burning lake in hell, he calls for a council so that they can decide what type of war now to wage, an open or covert campaign against God. A brigade of bad angels flies to a nearby hill and begins violently mining it for gold to construct Pandemonium to hold their meeting. Even the act of making something in hell sounds like a violation: Milton describes how the crew of bad angels "Opened into the hill a spacious wound / And digged out ribs of gold" (Book 1, lines 689–90). He then writes a beautiful, elegiac origin story for the building's architect:

> his hand was known
> In Heav'n by many a towered structure high,
> Where sceptered angels held their residence,
> And sat as princes, whom the supreme King
> Exalted to such power, and gave to rule,
> Each in his hierarchy, the orders bright.
> Nor was his name unheard or unadored
> In ancient Greece; and in Ausonian land
> Men called him Mulciber; and how he fell
> From Heav'n, they fabled, thrown by angry Jove
> Sheer o'er the crystal battlements; from morn
> To noon he fell, from noon to dewy eve,
> A summer's day; and with the setting sun
> Dropped from the zenith like a falling star,
> On Lemnos th' Aegean isle: thus they relate,
> Erring; for he with this rebellious rout
> Fell long before. (Book 1, lines 732–48)

Milton is appropriating the myth of Mulciber, the god of the forge, known more commonly as Hephaestus (in ancient Greece) and as Vulcan (in "Ausonian land" or Italy). The poet explains that this angelic architect actually got his start much earlier, designing palaces in heaven. Ancient writers may claim that Mulciber landed on the island of Lemnos in the north Aegean Sea when Jove angrily threw him from Mount Olympus for siding with Hera. In fact, Milton says, that is a fable, and Mulciber was one of Satan's followers, cast out of heaven with the rest of the devilish crew.

Milton, though, is not content with simply appropriating the story of a classical god to flesh out the narrative of the bad angels' failed rebellion. He dramatizes Mulciber's slow descent by repeatedly wrapping his sentences across line breaks—"how he fell / From Heav'n," "thrown by angry Jove / Sheer," and "with the setting sun / Dropped." The repetition of "noon" to mark the passage of time—"from morn / To *noon* he fell, from *noon* to dewy eve"—also makes the angel's fall sound more gradual, as does the poignant detail of a long "summer's day" to measure his descent. Then, abruptly, all the lyricism of this description ends with the sudden reminder that the story he has been recounting is false—"thus they relate, / Erring." The jarring disruption of "erring," stressed on the first syllable, sunders the poem's iambic rhythm and evokes the violent impact of Mulciber's falling body. The whole passage is a virtuoso performance, all the more remarkable because it almost seems a throwaway, a long digression about a minor character who will never reappear in the epic's remaining eleven books. But this is how Milton repeatedly gets things both ways: he simultaneously repudiates and relishes the stories of his classical forbears. He does not reject the writers he had first studied at St. Paul's; he finds a way to use and redeem them.

The final scene of the bad angels in *Paradise Lost* occurs near the end of the poem, and like the devils' first scene, it also takes place in hell. Satan triumphantly returns from Earth after seducing Eve to eat the Forbidden Fruit. Disguised as a plebian angel, he sneaks back into the ornate palace of Pandemonium. Like Odysseus's returning incognito to his hall in Ithaca, Satan wants to surveil what has happened in his absence and to make a dramatic entrance when he suddenly shows himself. Milton is also suggesting that Satan in going back to hell is going home, like the famous wandering Greek hero. But as the archfiend announces himself and boasts of his success, expecting applause and adulation, he is instead received with hisses, the sound of scorn. God in that instant has turned all of Satan's followers into serpents. Satan, too, suddenly falls on his belly, feels his arms cling to his ribs and his legs entwine. He mutates into a giant snake. Overcome by a fierce hunger and scalding thirst, the snaky devils roll in heaps up the multitude of fruit trees that just then spring up—only to find, again and again, that the fruit turns to ashes in their mouths. The narrator speculates that they will undergo this terrible transformation each year.

FIGURE 25. Illustration of Satan's return to hell by Gustave Doré
from *Milton's "Paradise Lost"* (London: Cassell, 1870)

Source: Photograph by Lori Howard, Georgia State University.

If Satan in *Paradise Lost* initially seems heroic for his determination, in the end Milton has unequivocally cast the fiend and his followers as monsters, and he has unequivocally distanced himself from his poem's proud and overly ambitious leader. The delay of the devils' disfigurement communicates part of the epic's moral message: challenging an omnipotent God is less grievous than intentionally injuring one of God's creatures. Satan and the other bad angels are punished less for the war that they start than they are for their crimes against humanity.

———

Deferring Satan's diminished appearance also helps to make him sympathetic. The artists who have illustrated Milton's poem often resort to traditional iconography—horns, hoofs, and a tail—but Milton would not have wanted readers of *Paradise Lost* to be repulsed at the start by such images. We need to remember that for many early modern readers, the devil and his subordinate demons were a literal reality, and their well-known diabolic features from the medieval period were kept alive in carvings and other religious artwork. The seventeenth-century preacher John Rogers, for one, wrote that he was deathly afraid of not just hell but the devils he sometimes witnessed: "I thought I saw every foot in several ugly shapes and forms, according to my fancies, and sometimes with great rolling flaming eyes like saucers, having sparkling firebrands in one of their hands, and with the other reaching at me to tear me away to torments."[17] Milton's contemporaries might blame Satan for anything from erotic dreams to bad storms; the devil might afflict a child while its mother was still pregnant or appear suddenly, grab a sinner who was drunk, and fly off with him out a window. Charles I's father, King James, wrote a whole book on divination and magic, *Daemonologie* (1597), in which he examined various ways that demons could harm people, and William Prynne, in his long tract attacking the theater, recorded that during performances of Christopher Marlowe's *Doctor Faustus* the "visible apparition of the Devil" was sometimes reported on stage, "to the great amazement both of the Actors and Spectators," right alongside the performers who were playing the characters Mephistophilis and Lucifer.[18] Many of Milton's contemporary readers would not have doubted the devil's immediacy nor his role as a tempter and instrument of divine justice.[19]

Milton was both endorsing and defying these expectations in his epic by refusing to describe the devils. He could assume that his readers already knew what the bad angels would look like, so he need not initially portray them. But by including very few details of Satan's horrific appearance, Milton also allows readers to be beguiled by the devil's heroic rhetoric and conflicted feelings, and permits himself initially to see a possible resemblance between his own actions and the devil's vaunting ambition. Of course, Milton also had to make Satan seem attractive at the start. If the epic were going to dramatize free will, if Milton wanted to write a theodicy, he had to make Satan a seductively commanding character. Evil has to appear appealing and credible if doing good is a genuine choice, as opposed to a foregone conclusion.

A long history of readers have argued that Milton himself had sympathy for his devil. Surely a writer who had sacrificed his sight in support of rebellion against a king—who suffered daily from his own "darkness visible"—identified, if only unconsciously, with a character who zealously wars against the monarchy of heaven. Satan is too vigorous and speaks too eloquently for Milton to have simply dismissed him. The Romantic poet Percy Shelley declared that "nothing can exceed the grandeur and the energy of the character of the Devil" in *Paradise Lost*, and the poet and artist William Blake more emphatically concluded that Milton "was a true Poet and of the Devil's party without knowing it."[20] Blake, who also created a series of extraordinary watercolor illustrations for Milton's epic, thought that Milton in his poem was engaging in an internal debate. The author's staunch commitment to Christian theology was in conflict with his desire to explore his personal religious ideas. For Blake, the latter had the upper hand, so that *Paradise Lost* expressed Milton's own beliefs, his unconscious attraction to Satan's heroism and rebelliousness.

Another group of commentators—led by the novelist and scholar C. S. Lewis—argued with equal vehemence that Milton's theodicy was sincere and successful. Instead of sympathizing with the devil, Milton was thoroughly on the side of God and the Son, and the poem enacts Christianity's "great central tradition."[21] Only readers who already object to the Christian God, Lewis believed, could find fault with Milton's supreme deity and think the devil offered a viable alternative.[22]

In 1967 a young literature professor from the University of California at Berkeley devised a clever solution for reconciling the two camps. Stanley Fish argued that they were both right: Milton deliberately ensnares readers with passages that make Satan seem heroic and God seem unfair—only so that Milton can then correct this mistake by underscoring divine justice.[23] Readers are repeatedly forced to rediscover their own fallenness, and then are admonished for not simply accepting divine obedience by one of the epic's authoritative voices.

Fish's reading is still taught today in some classrooms, in part because it creates an appealing consensus. And, in some places, as in the opening pages of Milton's epic, Fish's thesis holds. Satan sounds strong and heroic as he awakens and determines to continue resisting divine authority—until Milton reveals the archfiend's abject posture. Fish is also helpful in explaining Milton's depiction of life before the Fall. When the angel Raphael describes the serpent to Adam, he calls it the

> subtlest beast of all the field,
> Of huge extent sometimes, with brazen eyes
> And hairy mane terrific, though to thee
> Not noxious, but obedient at thy call. (Book 7,
>   lines 495–98)

Fish argues convincingly that many readers will struggle to see beyond their own fallen knowledge and will interpret the prelapsarian serpent as a threat—"huge," "brazen," and "terrific"—even though snakes are innocent at this point in the poem.[24] The subtitle of Fish's book is "The Reader in *Paradise Lost*" because, he argued, the epic finds its unity in the reader's experience. We are repeatedly forced to discover our own corrupt natures; we are gulled by Milton's language into seeing how our own fallenness colors everything we encounter in the poem.

But for Fish's deft reading to work throughout the epic, readers would have to be a little dumb, falling for this same trick, verse after verse, over twelve books, over more than 10,000 lines. The consensus reading also potentially reduces Milton into a one-trick poet, a finger-wagging pedant, taking almost sadistic glee in successively trapping his readers.[25] Nothing in Milton's life or writings supports such a caricature of the author. He wanted to surpass—to "soar / Above" (Book 1, lines 14–15)—Virgil and Homer, not to flatten his heroic poem into a single didactic maneuver. For readers, he expected them to work hard and to use their reason. In *Paradise Lost*, he wanted a "fit audience," not simpletons whom he could entrap repeatedly (Book 7, line 31).

Another problem with the consensus reading is that it overlooks the way that the proud fiend reflects a version of Milton's own striving and combativeness. Maybe the internal debate that Milton was rehearsing in the epic was not, as Blake proposed, theological but instead personal. As the author meditated on England's recent history, as he worried about his grand literary aspirations, he created a corrupt but not entirely contemptible version of the ardor that drove him. The ambition and intransigence that Satan represented were not, Milton seems to have eventually realized, either inherently good or inherently bad. The value depended on how these traits are used.

Ultimately, Milton's bad angels are not without admirable qualities. When Satan and his followers hold their council in Pandemonium, they agree to attack Earth instead of undertaking another open war against God or doing nothing and making the most of their horrible predicament. Satan calls for an emissary to travel alone to find the new world, and all of the bad angels sit silent: "All sat mute, / Pondering the danger with deep thoughts; and each / In other's count'nance read his own dismay / Astonished" (Book 2, lines 420–23). So Satan himself volunteers. If he is going to lead, he says, he should be the one to accept the greatest hazard.

Satan has manipulated the council: he fails to mention that they could ask for forgiveness, he uses his companion Beëlzebub to introduce his own plan of attacking God's new creation, and he discourages anyone else from volunteering to go to Earth by impressing on his followers the enormity and danger of the expedition. He also announces that he will go alone: Satan does not want anyone to share his glory, and he does not want anyone after him to volunteer and then be refused—as the narrator explains, "winning cheap the high repute / Which he through hazard huge must earn" (Book 2, lines 472–73). But, Satan does volunteer. When no one else will stand up to accept the responsibility, Satan does. His volunteering appeals to readers' sense of justice—and it is in stark contrast to Agamemnon's famously less daring behavior, standing apart from the battles, as Achilles accuses him near the beginning of the *Iliad*.

The Son in the epic's next book will also volunteer. God predicts that humankind will disobey his one edict and so, according to his decree, must die—unless, God adds, someone were to take on this death for Adam and Eve: "Unless for him / Some other able, and as willing, pay / The rigid satisfaction" (Book 3, lines 210–12). Once again, an invitation is met with silence; all the good angels sit mute, just as the bad angels had in hell, and no intercessor initially steps forward. Then the Son, full of divine goodness, offers to sacrifice himself:

> Behold me then, me for him, life for life
> I offer, on me let thine anger fall;
> Account me man; I for his sake will leave
> Thy bosom, and this glory next to thee
> Freely put off, and for him lastly die
> Well pleased, on me let Death wreck all his rage. (Book 3,
>   lines 236–41)

This is the single most heroic moment in the epic, and it is not an act of slaying but one of subjection. How much does the Son love humankind? So much that he is willing to become mortal and sacrifice his life. Clearly, the two scenes of volunteering, appearing back-to-back in Books 2 and 3, offer a striking parallel. But the difference is also crucial: the Son volunteers to die to save humankind; Satan volunteers to commit murder.

But again Milton complicates a straightforward contrast between heaven and hell. Not only is Satan's offer to fly to Earth valiant, but the narrator then steps forward to compliment the fallen angels as a group for backing Satan's plan and reaching a swift general agreement:

> O shame to men! Devil with devil damned
> Firm concord holds, men only disagree
> Of creatures rational, though under hope
> Of heavenly grace: and God proclaiming peace,
> Yet live in hatred, enmity, and strife
> Among themselves, and levy cruel wars,
> Wasting the earth, each other to destroy. (Book 2,
>   lines 496–502)

Milton, fresh from the terrible experience of Britain's years of conflict, uses the scene to chastise his fellow countrymen for failing to reach their own accord. He knew all about the waste and destruction that come from civil "strife" and "cruel wars." The English, he suggests, have been behaving worse than devils.

The larger lesson of Milton's bad angels is that being strong is not the same as being good. Satan demonstrates tremendous resolve in the face of overwhelming obstacles—but to what end? He may be right that God has absolute power, and he may be sympathetic for his suffering, but in corrupting God's new creations the devil is motivated by revenge, jealousy, and pride. *Paradise Lost* shows that standing fast is not by itself heroic, and that true grit requires a commitment to what is true, not just being committed. As Adam and Eve will illustrate after they fall, their future happiness depends on both their resolution and their willingness to admit and atone for their errors. In the case of Satan, he is strong— courageous, determined, and relentless—but he is never good and never makes amends for his wrongs. His tenacity seems commendable, but it is this very quality that damns him, again and again.

Milton finally sees Satan in part as a counterexample to himself and a warning against charismatic leaders who overpromise what they can achieve through sheer will. Blake might have been right, and Milton might have been "of the Devil's party without knowing it"—but only to a point. Milton could admire and identify with his devil's courage but never his cause. When another of Milton's tragic characters, Samson— blind, imprisoned, and betrayed—confronts his own tremendous losses at the start of *Samson Agonistes*, he laments the limitations of his abilities: he asks, "what is strength without a double share / Of wisdom?" (lines 53–54). Samson is referring to his physical prowess, which lies in his un-shorn hair, and his foolish decision to reveal this secret to Dalila. But the relation he offers between strength and wisdom also applies to Milton's archfiend. Satan repeatedly demonstrates great strength of character, but, without the wisdom to repent, he repeatedly succeeds only in heaping more suffering and pain on himself and all of his followers.

SEVEN

Forgiveness

"Hand in hand with wand'ring steps"

BY THE 1650S, BY THE time that Milton was hard at work on *Paradise Lost*, his first wife, Mary, had already died. He had already remarried and been widowed a second time, and four years before the epic was published, he married a third time and was apparently happy. But it was in Milton's tumultuous first marriage that he seems to have discovered the intense emotions that shaped his ideas about romantic love. He learned firsthand about the pain of separation and the joy that can come with reconciling. Even if Milton were not consciously thinking of his first marriage—the hurt feelings, the mutual recriminations, and the solace found in forgiveness—these indelible early experiences seem to have seeped into his poem's depiction of the world's first couple.

Little is known about the circumstances leading up to Milton's marriage to Mary Powell. In June 1642, three years after returning from his Continental journey, Milton traveled to Forest Hill in Oxfordshire, a small town in a large county west of London. The area was dotted with hamlets and villages, and dominated by juniper scrub and flowered meadows. The overworked teacher/writer probably needed some time away from his school, his live-in students, and the noise of the city.

Fifteen years earlier, Mary's father, Richard Powell, a justice of the peace in Forest Hill, had borrowed £300 from the senior John Milton, who commonly lent money in his official capacity as Scrivener. Milton most likely traveled to Oxfordshire to collect the semiannual payment of interest. Maybe he also hoped to visit Oxford University and see where his boyhood companion, Charles Diodati, had lived and studied while at Trinity College. Four years later, in 1646, Milton would give inscribed copies of eleven of his prose tracts and his first volume of poems as gifts to the university's librarian, James Rouse.[1] When the book of verse that he sent Rouse went missing, Milton provided a replacement copy and penned an affectionate Latin poem to the librarian in which he complimented him as "the faithful guardian of eternal works" ("Aeternorum operum custos fidelis," line 54). In his volume of prose tracts, Milton had written, "to the most excellent judge of books."[2]

But whatever Milton's motives for traveling to Oxford in the summer of 1642, this much is definite: he returned to London a month later with a new bride. Milton was thirty-three. Mary Powell was seventeen.

Given the couple's age difference and their courtship's brevity, it is not surprising that their marriage soon experienced difficulty. That summer, some of Mary's immediate family traveled with her from Oxford to London to celebrate her nuptials; her family stayed for a few days at Milton and Mary's home in Aldersgate Street in the northwest part of the city.[3] Then, sometime in the next two months, Mary took a coach back to Oxfordshire to see her parents and ten siblings. Milton expected it would be a short visit. She did not return to London for almost four years.

In the first months after Mary left, Milton seems to have written often to his young bride, urging her return. But when his letters went unanswered—on one of the rare occasions his writing proved ineffectual—he must have started to panic. Trying to save face but growing more desperate, he sent a messenger to Oxfordshire to ask Mary to come home. The messenger was rudely rebuffed—"dismissed with some sort of Contempt," according to Milton's nephew.[4]

The outbreak of the civil war made things worse. In March 1642, Parliament had passed, without Charles I's approval, an ordinance claiming executive power. The king was outraged and probably fearful. He immediately assembled a militia for his defense, and by October Charles had left London and set up an alternative government that eventually settled in the city of Oxford. As the surrounding area became a Royalist stronghold, travel between Oxford and London grew dangerous; the king's forces regularly marched and trained in the streets and parks. Although most Oxford residents sided with Parliament, the Powells remained loyal to the king. The explanation favored by Milton's nephew is that Mary's parents prevented their daughter from returning to London because they now disapproved of her marriage to an outspoken supporter of Parliament.[5]

Also at issue was probably that Mary was so young. In the seventeenth century, the average age for women at marriage was more than six years older, almost twenty-four.[6] Had Mary's family pushed her to wed, and she then discovered that she and her much older husband had little in common? Given Milton's sense of himself as a divine spokesperson, Mary might have simply found him vain and disagreeable, ill-equipped for married life. One early biographer suggests that she was lonely in London. She was, he writes,

> brought up & lived where there was a great deal of company & merriment, and when she came to live with her husband . . . she found it very solitary: no company came to her, often-times heard his Nephews cry, and beaten. This life was irksome to her; & so she went to her Parents.[7]

At least one of these additional details rings true: the tradition of whipping of boys in grammar school, in particular in teaching young men Latin. Mary, as a woman, would have been cut off from this common practice. For her to move in with her new husband and to hear him doling out corporal punishment to his young nephews must have been unnerving and upsetting.

Regardless of why Mary stayed away for so long, Milton had to have felt hurt and embarrassed, especially given seventeenth-century assumptions about patriarchal authority and the legal doctrine of coverture, by which, upon marriage, a woman was thought to relinquish all her legal rights to her husband. Milton responded to his humiliation by taking comfort in words, by putting pen to paper and trying to master his feelings in prose. It was in these years, without ever mentioning his own difficulties—and without saying much about the subject of desertion—that he published his four tracts defending divorce. He had privately held this position for a long time, but now, spurred by his own heartache, he decided to air it in public.[8]

The question for Milton and his young wife in the 1640s was whether their differences were reconcilable. Could the couple overcome their conflict and separation, whatever the causes? Could they achieve the kind of emotional and intellectual rapport—the "apt and cheerful conversation" (YP II: 235)—that Milton in his prose held up as the ideal of wedded life? After so much time apart, the two must have at least agreed that both of them would need to make concessions. They would have to work hard and act with compassion if they were to reconcile and save their troubled marriage.

———

In *Paradise Lost*, Adam and Eve, of course, do reconcile after the Fall, first forgiving each other and then striving to obtain God's pardon. Milton foregrounds this point at the start of his epic. In the opening lines, he quickly sets out the broad outline of the couple's biblical narrative:

> Of man's first disobedience, and the fruit
> Of that forbidden tree, whose mortal taste
> Brought death into the world, and all our woe,
> With loss of Eden, till one greater man
> Restore us, and regain the blissful seat. (Book 1, lines 1–5)

As Milton's readers knew well, Adam and Eve will both fall and be saved. The Son, the "one greater man," will volunteer to redeem humanity's crime by dying on their behalf—"death for death," as God later explains, the "just th' unjust to save" (Book 3, lines 212, 215).

But Milton in *Paradise Lost* also emphasizes the other side of divine beneficence: the prevenient grace purchased by the Son must be actively sought. Forgiveness is a process, not an event, and must be earned, not passively accepted. A person who commits a wrong needs to own up to the mistake and sincerely feel contrite. This is what Satan never achieves, what Milton learned from his first marriage, and what Adam and Eve are ultimately able to accomplish, together.[9]

Adam and Eve are not the heroes of *Paradise Lost*. For that to have been true, they would have had to resist Satan's temptation and continue to keep God's single commandment and not eat the Forbidden Fruit. But, even in their flaws and failure, they are a model of a deep, abiding affection. What continues to hold them together after breaking God's law—after losing Paradise, after damning themselves and all of their descendants—is the act of forgiveness.

Immediately after Adam and Eve commit the first sin, though, they do not hurry to make amends. After they disobey God's sole command, they feel intoxicated—their heads "swim in mirth"—and they are overcome with sudden lust:

> [they] fancy that they feel
> Divinity within them breeding wings
> Wherewith to scorn the earth: but that false fruit
> Far other operation first displayed,
> Carnal desire inflaming; he on Eve
> Began to cast lascivious eyes, she him
> As wantonly repaid; in lust they burn. (Book 9,
>   lines 1009–15)

The description of Adam and Eve's imagined flight as *scorning* the earth tarnishes any newfound pleasure they feel and recalls Satan's earlier journey when he "spurns the ground" to fly through chaos (Book 2, line 929). The couple's reciprocal gaze—"he on Eve" and "she him"—suggests their mutual blame, and the images of heat—"inflaming" and "burn"— anticipate the hellish consequences that they will also share. Overcome with desire, Adam then seizes Eve by the hand and leads her willingly to a shady bank and a bed of violets, pansies, asphodels, and hyacinths.

This is not the first time that Adam and Eve have sex. Milton took the unconventional view that the pleasures of Paradise before the Fall

extended beyond the lush vegetation—the flowers of every color, the
groves of sweet-smelling trees—and beyond the herds of sportive animals,
the gamboling tigers, leopards, and bears. Before the Fall, Adam and Eve
eat, pray, and garden. They also daily make love.[10] When at sunset they
finish their evening worship, they retire hand-in-hand to their flower-
decked bower. The narrator interrupts to explain that the two

> Straight side by side were laid, nor turned I ween
> Adam from his fair spouse, nor Eve the rites
> Mysterious of connubial love refused:
> Whatever hypocrites austerely talk
> Of purity and place and innocence,

FIGURE 26. *As They Thirsted* by Gustave Doré from *Milton's*
"Paradise Lost," edited with notes and a life of Milton by Robert
Vaughan (London: Cassell, Petter, and Galpin, 1866)

Defaming as impure what God declares
Pure, and commands to some, leaves free to all. (Book 4,
    741–47)

Milton did not often write about sex, but clearly he did not think physical
pleasure was immoral, as did some of his contemporaries. Elsewhere in the
poem he lingers on the first couple's innocent erotic play, so that when Eve
concludes her story about first meeting Adam, she "half embracing leaned
/ On our first father, half her swelling breast / Naked met his under the
flowing gold / Of her loose tresses hid" (Book 4, 494–97). Living at a time
when many male writers seem baffled by female sexuality, Milton shows
that Eve in her innocence can rightfully express her own desire.

But, after the Fall, after Adam and Eve disobey God, everything
changes, including sex. Now it is urgent and immoderate, and leaves the
couple worn out but no longer able to sleep well. They awaken feeling guilty
and shameful. Soon they start to squabble.

It is important to recall that almost none of these details are in the
Bible. The account in Genesis of Adam and Eve's fall is comparatively terse:

Now the serpent was more subtil than any beast of the field which
the LORD God had made. And he said unto the woman, Yea, hath
God said, Ye shall not eat of every tree of the garden? And the
woman said unto the serpent, We may eat of the fruit of the trees
of the garden: but of the fruit of the tree which *is* in the midst of
the garden, God hath said, Ye shall not eat of it, neither shall ye
touch it, lest ye die. And the serpent said unto the woman, Ye shall
not surely die: for God doth know that in the day ye eat thereof,
then your eyes shall be opened, and ye shall be as gods, knowing
good and evil. And when the woman saw that the tree *was* good
for food, and that it *was* pleasant to the eyes, and a tree to be desired to make *one* wise, she took of the fruit thereof, and did eat,
and gave also unto her husband with her; and he did eat. And the
eyes of them both were opened, and they knew that they *were*
naked; and they sewed fig leaves together, and made themselves
aprons. (3:1–7)

Milton extrapolates the single phrase "knew that they *were* naked" into the scene of lascivious lovemaking, followed by shame, regret, and bickering. It is just one instance of how he adapts a story that fits neatly into three short chapters of scripture, and develops and expands it into twelve books of roughly 700 to 1,000 lines each.

Biblical commentators across several centuries had taken the same brief verses in Genesis and concluded that Eve was entirely to blame for the Fall because she allowed the serpent to trick her and then gave the fruit to her husband. This reading is part of a long misogynist tradition of treating women and matter as intrinsically corrupt. Humanist, patristic, and Puritan writers interpreted the Genesis narrative as an allegory: Adam was a symbol of the mind, and Eve a symbol of lesser, sensory experience.[11] The story of eating the fruit was thus a warning not to allow feminine feeling to seduce and overpower manly contemplation and spirituality. This way of reading Genesis continued well into the seventeenth century, especially in the commentary of some Continental thinkers.

Milton would have none of it. First, he was a monist and a materialist. That is, he did not think in terms of spirit and matter, and he did not think matter was inherently base. Instead, he took the heterodox position that there was a single, original substance out of which everything was made—animals, people, plants, and minerals. "One first matter all," as Raphael succinctly explains to Adam and Eve in *Paradise Lost* (Book 5, line 472). The angel adds that the refinement of this one material determines how each type of being or thing fits into God's existential hierarchy. Angels are on top, then humans below them, then animals below humans, then plants below animals, and so on. As the most ethereal creatures, Milton's angels are virtually fluid. They communicate mostly through intuition, can assume both or either sex, and make love by completely interpenetrating each other.

Humans, both male and female, are just below angels, according to Raphael. The angel is one of the most overtly patriarchal voices in the poem, but that he here does not treat one sex as higher than the other further separates Milton from traditional readings of Genesis. The poet, despite the biases he personally harbored, offers a much more complex picture of the first parents than had his peers and forbears. For Milton, both Adam and Eve have free will, and both fall, and neither is more culpable than the other. A sin is a sin is a sin. What matters who sins first?

Milton begins complicating Adam and Eve with their physical appearance. Unlike the appearance of Satan and the other fallen angels, which Milton reveals only near the end of the poem when God turns them into monstrous snakes, Adam and Eve's physical shapes are front and center as soon as they stride into the epic:

> His fair large front and eye sublime declared
> Absolute rule; and hyacinthine locks
> Round from his parted forelock manly hung
> Clust'ring, but not beneath his shoulders broad:
> She as a veil down to the slender waist
> Her unadornèd golden tresses wore
> Dishevelled, but in wanton ringlets waved
> As the vine curls her tendrils, which implied
> Subjection, but required with gentle sway,
> And by her yielded, by him best received,
> Yielded with coy submission, modest pride,
> And sweet reluctant amorous delay. (Book 4,
>   lines 300–11)

Milton leans on traditional assumptions about anatomy to sketch the couple—Adam has "shoulders broad," Eve has a "slender waist"—then turns to Western ideas about a man and woman's appropriate hair length to distinguish the two sexes more fully.[12] Comparing Adam's hair to hyacinth petals is no doubt an attempt to make him seem heroic. It is an allusion to Odysseus after Athena gussies him up and teases his curls like tendrils of wild hyacinth so that he can favorably impress King Alcinous.[13]

Eve's waving ringlets are even more luxurious; Milton depicts them as robust, amorous, and unrestrained. This last detail is most important. Seventeenth-century love poetry frequently described women's hair as containing a trap or snare—an expression of the moral danger allegedly posed by women's alluring sexuality.[14] So Edmund Spenser in his sonnet sequence *Amoretti* (1595) emphasizes the dangers of the "golden snare" on his beloved's head; he worries that these "fayre tresses" will "tye" his heart "with servile bands," and he fears her locks will "craftily" and "cunningly" "entangle" his affection.[15] In *Paradise Lost*, Eve's hair is striking for being entirely free—unlike the fashion at court—and containing no fetters. To some commentators, the specific account of her curls as "wanton" and "dishevelled" has implied that Milton might be going along with the humanist and patristic tradition and hinting that Eve before the Fall is somehow immoral.[16] But any whiff of corruption in these words comes from Satan's influence. Readers encounter this first description of Adam and Eve over the devil's shoulder, as he alights in the Garden of Eden and surveys with disdain all of God's new creation.[17]

Satan's voyeurism also contributes to the epic's most emphatic assertion that Eve is inferior to Adam. As part of the couple's introduction, Satan perceives a rigidly hierarchical relationship:

> For contemplation he and valor formed,
> For softness she and sweet attractive grace,
> He for God only, she for God in him. (Book 4,
>   lines 297–99).

These lines seem to settle the couple's relative authority, and they may reflect Milton's own prejudices, as revealed more plainly in, for example, his divorce tracts. Yet almost immediately the details of Adam and Eve's physical appearance in *Paradise Lost* begin to chip away at the hierarchy that Satan supposes. Even Adam and Eve's hair sounds balanced and reciprocal, especially the echoing phrasing that Adam's "forelock manly hung / Clust'ring, but not beneath his shoulders," while Eve "her unadornèd golden tresses wore / Dishevelled, but in wanton ringlets." By the time that Milton finishes describing the couple's appearance, he relegates the idea of subjection to their hair—Eve's curls resemble a vine's curling tendrils—and, he says, the "subjection" is not real, only "implied."

Regardless of what Milton personally believed or intended, his account of the first couple across the poem's remaining books ultimately transcends the ugly patriarchal assumption of "He for God only, she for God in him." In places, Adam or Eve will still assert or imply that he is her superior; but other passages, such as the couple's introduction, suggest that their authority is more flexible. Only after the Fall does the Son tell Eve that because of her sin she must now submit to her husband: "He over thee shall rule" (Book 10, line 196).

Yet even this terrible injunction is not entirely fulfilled in the poem. Both before and after the Fall, Milton's Eve proves remarkably powerful. She is smart, independent, and assertive. Milton was living at a time when women (except for Quakers) were not allowed to speak up in religious services and when their labor was often limited to the domestic sphere. In *Paradise Lost*, Eve and Adam pray unanimously and work side-by-side, and when Satan first confronts Eve alone in the garden, her beauty so overwhelms him that for just a moment he again becomes good:

> Her graceful innocence, her every air
> Of gesture or least action overawed
> His malice, and with rapine sweet bereaved
> His fierceness of the fierce intent it brought:
> That space the evil one abstracted stood
> From his own evil, and for the time remained
> Stupidly good, of enmity disarmed,
> Of guile, of hate, of envy, of revenge. (Book 9,
>   lines 459–66)

Sometimes Eve asks Adam for help, as when she questions why the stars still shine if she and Adam are asleep; and sometimes she corrects Adam, as when he asks her to take food out of storage to share with the arch-angel Raphael. Adam's explanation of the stars sounds speculative, but Eve's reply about the food is based on firsthand knowledge. She kindly points out that storing food is unnecessary in Paradise. (Adam and Eve are vegetarians before the Fall, according to Milton.) When Eve recalls meeting Adam for the first time, she says that she found him "less fair, / Less winning soft, less amiably mild" than the reflection of herself in the smooth lake next to where she was created (Book 4, lines 478–79). She takes one look at Adam and turns away, hurrying back to the lake. She says that he followed, crying "return fair Eve," and only after his "gentle hand / Seized mine" did she yield and decide to stay with him (Book

4, lines 481, 488–89). Milton is anticipating here the moment after the Fall when a suddenly lustful Adam will again "seize" Eve's hand, and his touch is no longer gentle (Book 9, line 1037). But the scene also alludes to—and corrects—the story of Narcissus, the beautiful young hunter from mythology who pines in vain for his own reflection in a pool and is ultimately turned into a white flower that often grows beside lakes. With Eve, God's grace prevents her from repeating Narcissus's self-destructive mistake—it is the divine voice that calls Eve away from her image in the first place—but Milton's version also emphasizes that Eve makes her own choices and decides freely whether to accept Adam.

When Milton imagines Adam earlier, alone among the animals, asking God for a companion, the first man sounds less independent than Eve. He stresses that, above all, he wants an equal:

> Among unequals what society
> Can sort, what harmony or true delight?
> Which must be mutual, in proportion due
> Giv'n and received. (Book 8, lines 383–86)

The Bible refers to Adam and Eve as "one flesh" (Genesis 2:24), but Milton expands this phrase to underscore again the couple's mutuality: Adam tells God that Eve and he share "one flesh, one heart, one soul" (Book 8, line 499). It is a physical, emotional, and intellectual connection that supersedes the story of Eve's creation from Adam's rib (Genesis 2:21–22). In *Paradise Lost*, Milton imagines two fully developed, mutually affectionate characters—each with dreams, fears, and hopes—who have to fall and fall apart before they discover that they are stronger together and that the earthly Paradise they forfeit can be surpassed by finding a paradise within.

―――――

Still, Milton could not contradict the Bible. He could embellish, explain, and extrapolate Adam and Eve, but he could not invent a new story for them. His challenge as narrator was accommodating his readers' confident knowledge of scripture while providing plausible motives for the first couple. The author of Genesis had recounted the details of Adam and

Eve's sin in plain terms: the serpent first tricks Eve, who then shares the fruit with her rash husband. But if Eve is so good and strong, why would she disobey God and fall for a talking snake? And why would Adam—also noble, good, and intelligent—then eat the fruit that Eve offers him?

Milton rejected the Calvinist answer that Adam and Eve were pre-destined to sin. He also did not think the pair was unaware or stupid. Instead, he explains the cause of the Fall by inventing an extra scene, not included in Genesis, in which the couple begins another day in Paradise and discusses the best plan for gardening. Milton again differed from many commentators: he believed that Adam and Eve's work preceded their sin and banishment from Eden. Before the Fall in *Paradise Lost*, the pair already gardens, but their labor is thoroughly pleasurable: no sweat, no thorns, and no thistles.

One morning Eve proposes to Adam that they should divide their work until noon because, when they garden side-by-side, they get dis-tracted and get less done. As she puts it,

> while so near each other thus all day
> Our task we choose, what wonder if so near
> Looks intervene and smiles, or object new
> Casual discourse draws on, which intermits
> Our day's work brought to little, though begun
> Early, and th' hour of supper comes unearned. (Book 9,
> lines 220–25)

Adam replies that God has not so strictly imposed their labor that they cannot enjoy each other's company. They can easily keep the paths and bowers from becoming overgrown even if they sometimes pause to talk or flirt. He also reminds Eve that Raphael warned them of a malicious foe still at large.

This is the first argument in Paradise—never heated and entirely free from enmity because Adam and Eve are still unfallen. And yet they dis-agree. As the couple's conversation unspools, Eve notes that Adam is not afraid of Satan's violence but apparently thinks she will be susceptible if she is alone; Adam counters that they should not underestimate Satan's malice and guile. Eve then replies that they cannot live in fear and that virtue must be tested—the very position that Milton himself had taken in *Areopagitica* when writing against censorship. There he wrote, "I cannot praise a fugitive and cloister'd virtue, unexercised & unbreath'd, that never sallies out and sees her adversary" (YP II: 515). Only a person who knows about both good and evil, who confronts temptation head on and still chooses good is truly righteous, like the Lady who refuses Comus in *A Masque Presented at Ludlow Castle.*

Armed with this insight, Eve in *Paradise Lost* wins the day and eventually goes off to garden separately from Adam. Of the two, Eve gets the best lines in the poem, and in this exchange Adam has to concede that Eve is right and that she is free to do as she wishes: "Go; for thy stay, not free, absents thee more," he realizes (Book 9, line 372). Milton concludes the scene by focusing on the couple's hands: Eve promises that she will be fine, and "from her husband's hand her hand / Soft she withdrew" (Book 9, lines 385–86). The inverted syntax seems to dramatize the pair's undoing, like a film clip run backward; the abrupt line break that rends the sentence hints at the dire rupture that this simple decision anticipates.

The added scene also provides the crucial justification for the barebones biblical narrative: because the couple agrees to work apart, Satan in *Paradise Lost* will find Eve alone when he seduces her into disobeying God. If readers were to judge the new conversation by its outcome, Eve might seem all the more blameworthy: she should not have wanted to work on her own because it is shortly afterward that she falls for Satan's specious argument and breaks God's one commandment. For Milton, though, the exchange highlights how both Eve and Adam make their own choices. Each has free will and can decide whether to work together or alone, just as each must decide individually whether to obey God's stricture about the Forbidden Fruit. Eve's sin is disobeying God's one law, not wanting some independence.

Milton builds in a further defense of Eve—but not an exoneration—by emphasizing Satan's cunning. Earlier, the poet had invented a scene in which the devil, disguised as a young cherub, was able to fool the archangel Uriel, who gave Satan directions to Earth and Paradise:

FIGURE 27. William Blake, Illustration to Milton's *Paradise
Lost: The Temptation and Fall of Eve*. Watercolor.

Source: Huntington Art Museum, San Marino, California.

> For neither man nor angel can discern
> Hypocrisy, the only evil that walks
> Invisible, except to God alone,
> By his permissive will, through Heav'n and Earth. (Book
>   3, lines 682–85)

Now, disguised as a serpent, the fiend approaches Eve, and she is surely
not to be faulted for failing to see through his dissembling if Satan was
even able to fool one of the seven angels nearest God's throne. The devil
as serpent does not wriggle on the ground, but springs on his coiled tail.
Part of the serpent's punishment for its role in seducing Eve will be crawl-
ing on its belly in the dust and dirt (Genesis 3:14), so Milton imagines
that snakes before the Fall must have moved differently—"on his rear,

/ Circular base of rising folds, that tow'red / Fold above fold a surging maze" (Book 9, lines 497–99).

Satan begins his seduction of Eve by praising her beauty and licking the ground where she treads. Naturally, she distrusts such gross flattery, but she wonders how a snake came to speak. Satan is ready with a story about the aroma of a tree, far distant, that quickened his hunger. He insinuated himself among its mossy branches, ate his fill, and felt a strange alteration, miraculously becoming more human. This is Milton's most striking revision of Genesis and the key to Satan's devious rhetorical strategy. The serpent in the Bible does not attribute his speech and reasoning to the fruit.

Eve then asks where this tree is, and the serpent, having won her confidence, now takes her to the Forbidden Fruit. There he presses home how the fruit will elevate her to a god since it has raised him from a brute to human intelligence. When Eve explains that she may not touch or taste this tree and that the punishment is death, Satan has another ready answer:

> ye shall not die:
> How should ye? By the fruit? It gives you life
> To knowledge. By the threat'ner? Look on me,
> Me who have touched and tasted, yet both live,
> And life more perfect have attained than fate
> Meant me, by vent'ring higher than my lot.
> Shall that be shut to man, which to the beast
> Is open? Or will God incense his ire
> For such a petty trespass, and not praise
> Rather your dauntless virtue, whom the pain
> Of death denounced, whatever thing death be,
> Deterred not from achieving what might lead
> To happier life, knowledge of good and evil;
> Of good, how just? Of evil, if what is evil
> Be real, why not known, since easier shunned?
> God therefore cannot hurt ye, and be just;

Not just, not God; not feared then, not obeyed:
Your fear itself of death removes the fear. (Book 9,
    lines 685–702)

Satan's temptation is, of course, based on the lie that he is a serpent and that he obtained speech by eating the fruit. But beyond this false premise, the devil spins a masterfully fallacious argument of dizzying illogic, peppering Eve with a quick series of questions and holding out the possibility that she can improve her place in the hierarchy of creation by daring to touch and taste the fruit. He first diminishes sin into a "petty trespass," then elevates it into a courageous act, then subtly questions the reality of evil, God, and death. The devil is upending God's sole commandment not to eat the fruit: on the contrary, Satan says, God will praise you for risking death in the pursuit of knowledge. Eve is hungry, the fruit looks and smells delicious, and Satan's argument about the fruit's intellectual power sounds reasonable. She plucks and eats and falls.

Adam's reason for disobeying God in *Paradise Lost* is entirely different but just as culpable. When Eve returns to her husband dragging behind her a whole bough of the Forbidden Fruit, he quickly realizes what she has done. He wonders silently and sadly, "How art thou lost, how on a sudden lost, / Defaced, deflow'red, and now to death devote?" (Book 9, lines 900–901). The alliterative *d* sounds are dolorous and foreboding, underscoring the first man's baleful choice. Milton also returns here to an image of hands. Adam had been making a coronet of flowers for Eve while they worked apart, and as she holds out the Forbidden Fruit to him, he is horrified: "From his slack hand the garland wreathed for Eve / Down dropped, and all the faded roses shed" (Book 9, lines 892–93).

Adam decides to defy God with clear and full knowledge. He would rather die with Eve than live without her, a choice that sounds grand and noble, the type of sentimental gesture typically found in pop ballads and romance novels. But, like Satan's seemingly heroic resolution to persist in his defiance, or Eve's seemingly laudable desire for more knowledge, Adam's sacrifice is in no way honorable. It might seem selfless, but he only completes Eve's sin. Milton's point is that doing the wrong thing, even for a good reason, can never be justified. The only way to be a good husband or wife is, first and foremost, to be virtuous.

———

It is unclear whether Milton himself was a good husband especially in his first years of marriage, but it is interesting to speculate that in *Paradise Lost* he was drawing on some of his own experiences to portray the first couple. Did he, on some level, identify with Adam? The first man's hair does not just resemble a hyacinth but hangs to his shoulders, a relatively shorter style that was favored in the civil wars by the king's opponents (whereas members of the king's party preferred more luxurious coiffures that reached much lower). Adam's hair is also parted in the middle. The only two figures in the seventeenth century whose portraits include a "parted forelock" are Oliver Cromwell and Milton.[18]

Also, like Adam, Milton ultimately found contentment and consolation after being separated from his spouse. Mary decided to rejoin her husband in London. And Milton? He took her back. It was a generous gesture for a wronged man in the seventeenth century, and it was a brave choice by Mary after having stayed away for years. She must have found it particularly difficult to return to a husband who had written so vehemently in favor of divorce. Maybe the couple was pressured by family, or maybe, with time, the pair felt the pull of a burgeoning affection. Mary's family certainly had incentive to see their daughter and son-in-law reunited: the king's cause in the civil war was rapidly declining. Charles I commanded his troops in person, and at the Battle of Naseby on 14 June 1645 he suffered a tremendous loss to Parliament's better-disciplined New Model Army. The Parliament's forces were led by Oliver Cromwell and its first Commander-in-Chief, the formidable Thomas Fairfax, to whom Milton would also later address a sonnet, praising Fairfax's "firm unshaken virtue" (line 5). Roughly 5,000 of the king's men were captured at Naseby, including officers and significant artillery.[19] The Powells must have seen the writing on the wall. Maybe they could flee Oxford for London and appeal for help to their estranged son-in-law—no doubt a further humiliation for Mary.

FIGURE 28. *Cromwell in the Battle of Naseby in 1645*
(1851) by Charles Landseer. Oil on canvas.

Source: Alte Nationalgalerie.

The Powells began to scheme.[20] In London, in the Lane of St. Martins
Le Grand, lived one of Milton's relatives, William Blackborough. Almost
nothing is known about this man, but Milton evidently enjoyed visiting
him. Mary's acquaintances conspired with the author's friends to conceal
her in a room in Blackborough's house. When Milton went on one of his
regular visits, she suddenly stepped forward. Milton must have been astonished. No specific account survives of what the two said to each other that
day, sitting together, finally face-to-face. Milton's nephew reported that
Mary fell to her knees.[21] Certainly Milton, for airing his grievances (though
veiled) in his divorce tracts, also had need to ask forgiveness. Maybe, too,
he had been an unfit companion, preoccupied and self-involved. But whatever pain the couple had caused and suffered, whatever the accusations,
admissions, and appeals, in the end they apparently walked out of Blackborough's house together, reunited as wife and husband.

Milton and Mary made quick plans. They decided that she should remain in the city with one of her friends, Isabel Webber, a widow and the mother-in-law to Milton's brother Christopher. In the meantime, Milton would prepare their new home, a large brick mansion with two square bay windows, one above the other, facing the street.[22] It was not far from Aldersgate, where Milton had been living since the day Mary left, but it was in the densely populated area known as the Barbican. The neighborhood was known for its dissenters, writers, and actors (both Shakespeare and Jonson had once resided there). In this new home, the couple hoped, they could get a new start.

In 1646, the year after Mary finally returned, Charles I surrendered to the Presbyterians, and the king's headquarters in Oxford were disbanded. Mary's parents, dispossessed and in danger, moved in with their son-in-law and his newly reconciled wife. They also brought along at least five of her brothers and sisters. Milton took in all of them. He would never be paid the £1,000 dowry that Mary's father had promised him, and he would never comment in print on his embarrassment. He would also never outlive the derisive epithet "the Divorcer" that his writings on England's marriage laws earned him among his political opponents. But for a little while at least, Milton and his wife seem to have found peace, maybe happiness. On 29 July 1646, a month after Mary's family moved in with the couple, she gave birth to their first child.

In *Paradise Lost*, Milton dramatizes a version of the forgiveness that he and Mary Powell apparently forged. In the final books, after the Fall, Adam and Eve also reconcile. But regardless of whether Milton recognized himself and his first wife in the epic's biblical couple, it is notable that, when the Son confronts the pair and asks why they are hiding, Eve shows greater dignity than her husband. Adam sounds bitter and petulant, trying to foist all the blame on Eve and God. Adam says he ate the fruit only because of "This woman whom thou mad'st to be my help, / And gav'st me as thy perfect gift, so good, / So fit, so acceptable, so divine" (Book 10, lines 137–39). In contrast to Adam's contemptuous

tone—"*so* good, / *So* fit, *so* acceptable"—Eve sounds almost stately, responding succinctly to the Son in a single line, "The Serpent me beguiled
and I did eat" (Book 10, line 162).

The next time that we see the couple, Eve again seems more noble
than Adam. She breaks off from their quarreling and gracefully subdues
his anger by once more speaking simply and directly, both rescuing him
from despair and saving their marriage. She confirms her deep affection
for him—"witness Heav'n / What love sincere, and reverence in my heart
/ I bear thee"—and she selflessly exaggerates her fault: "On me, sole
cause to thee of all this woe, / Me me only just object of his ire" (Book
10, lines 914-16, 935–36). The repetition of "me" in the last line is not
a typo; Eve is trying to stress her mistake. She is echoing and amplifying
Adam's earlier request that "On me, me only, as the source and spring
/ Of all corruption, all the blame lights due; / So might the wrath."
But Adam had quickly dismissed this possibility as a "Fond wish!" (*fond*
meaning silly), and he had gone on to denounce his wife as a serpent, cruelly attributing all human misery to "female snares" (Book 10, lines 832–
34, 897). In both passages, to underscore the couple's sense of guilt, the
1667 and 1674 editions of the poem contain a more emphatic spelling,
"mee," so that Adam first entertains that he is solely responsible and then
Eve more humbly suggests that she alone should bear the blame.

Adam, moved by his wife's remorse and humility, at last relents and
responds in kind: "If prayers / Could alter high decrees, I to that place
/ Would speed before thee, and be louder heard, / That on my head all
might be visited" (Book 10, lines 952–55). Milton has the pair share responsibility. Both recognize their sinfulness, and both are willing to take
all of the blame. Eve feels so much self-loathing that for a moment she
wavers on the edge of despair: she proposes that they save their descendants from death by refusing to have children. Or, if she and Adam are
unable "to abstain / From love's due rites, nuptial embraces sweet" (Book
10, lines 993–94), then they could, she says, commit suicide. Adam responds with hope. He understands that they must put aside rancor and
pride and forgive both each other and themselves. Then, maybe, they can
together receive God's mercy and grace:

But rise, let us no more contend, nor blame
Each other, blamed enough elsewhere, but strive
In offices of love, how we may light'n
Each other's burden in our share of woe. (Book 10,
    lines 958–61)

Adam's use of "strive" describes the hard work that marriage entails and the difficulty the pair will no doubt have in letting go of their guilt and mutual recriminations. Only if they work together can they overcome their oppressive loss. Adam recommends that they go immediately to confess their faults and pray for help:

FIGURE 29. *Adam Resolved to Share His Fate with Eve* by Henry Fuseli from *The Poetical Works of John Milton*, 3 vols., ed. William Hayley (London, 1794–1797)

Source: Robert J. Wickenheiser Collection of John Milton, Irvin Department of Rare Books and Special Collections, University of South Carolina Libraries, Columbia, S.C.

What better can we do, than to the place
Repairing where he judged us, prostrate fall
Before him reverent, and there confess
Humbly our faults, and pardon beg, with tears
Watering the ground, and with our sighs the air
Frequenting, sent from hearts contrite, in sign
Of sorrow unfeigned, and humiliation meek. (Book 10,
    lines 1086–92)

Then, as if to emphasize the need to seek forgiveness actively, Milton has his narrator reiterate a few lines later the same process that Adam had proposed, step by step, as the couple carries out this exact plan:

forthwith to the place
Repairing where he judged them prostrate fell
Before him reverent, and both confessed
Humbly their faults, and pardon begged, with tears
Watering the ground, and with their sighs the air
Frequenting, sent from hearts contrite, in sign
Of sorrow unfeigned, and humiliation meek. (Book 10,
    lines 1098–1104)

Milton is borrowing from Homer, a master of artful repetition in epic, but the specific point here seems to be the equation of word and deed, the way Adam and Eve enact what they have just spoken. The egregious repetition and the string of active verbs—repairing, fell, confessed, begged, watering, and sent—highlight the effort needed to earn grace and the idea that forgiveness is above all an activity, not a passive event.[23] "Repairing" in particular captures the healing that comes with reconciliation: Adam and Eve must not just hurry but also re-pair, meaning be paired together again, if they are to repair, meaning remedy, their pain and sorrow.

Of course, Milton was not talking about himself in this scene, and of course he did not ally himself with a single character's point of view. But the mature perspective at the end of *Paradise Lost*, the ability to understand but not to define people by their shortcomings—the ability to let

FIGURE 30. William Blake, Illustration 5 to Milton's *Paradise Lost*: *Satan Watching the Endearments of Adam and Eve* (1807). Pen and watercolor.

Source: Huntington Art Museum, San Marino, California.

go and forgive—suggests a compassionate knowledge of human nature that Milton learned in part from the troubled years of his first marriage. He, too, was fallen, and he, too, needed to be forgiven and to forgive. The narrative of Adam and Eve in *Paradise Lost* suggests a poet who was questioning the relation between a person's character and actions and who came to recognize that grace and reconciliation are hard won. If even Adam and Eve could be wholly good but still make a horrendous decision, and if they could fatally disobey God and still find grace and love in their repentance and marriage—then, Milton seems to be saying, there is hope for all of us.

———

At the end of the epic, God sends Michael to instruct Adam and Eve about the enormity of their sin and to expel them from the Garden of Eden. Here again Milton deviates from orthodox Christian doctrine, as the angel banishes Adam and Eve but does not focus on posthumous compensation in a celestial realm. Instead, Michael reassures the pair mostly by describing the possibility of a better life on Earth, a real-world comfort that can be achieved here. Through hard work—through faith, virtue, patience, temperance, and love, as the angel enumerates—Adam and Eve can "possess / A paradise within thee, happier far" (Book 12, lines 586–87). Whereas Satan is trapped in a hell of his own making, Adam and Eve can bring with them an attitude of paradise as they listen to their conscience and try to do the right thing, regardless of where they together go.

Michael gives Adam and Eve a long lesson about their descendants and the terrible legacy of their disobedience; Adam's visions dominate the epic's final books, while Eve, off-stage, has been given a prophetic dream of her own (Book 12, lines 610–13). Michael then takes the couple to the eastern gate of Paradise—and disappears. Behind Adam and Eve, dreadful angels with flaming swords now stand guard, barring their return. But it is not a sad ending. It is not even properly an ending:

> The world was all before them, where to choose
> Their place of rest, and providence their guide:
> They hand in hand with wand'ring steps and slow,
> Through Eden took their solitary way. (Book 12, 646–49)

This final image describes Adam and Eve's freedom even as it intimates their future trials and missteps with words such as "wand'ring" and the description of their slow tread. The final lines dramatize the unclear moral circumstances that all people daily face. The emphasis, though, is on the fallen couple's reconciliation as Adam and Eve once again approach life together, literally and figuratively. One last time, Milton spotlights the couple's hands. They go forth, first holding on to the angel's hands, one on each side, then holding on to only each other, as they make their way tentatively to a new life and, they hope, a new and better world.

EIGHT

Resisting Temptation

"He who reigns within himself"

FOR MANY OF MILTON'S READERS, a new and better world must have seemed imminent as the civil war years finally came to an end. Some English men and women, especially those in rural areas, would have found that the demands of their daily lives eclipsed questions of high politics; they were not overly concerned whether the nation had a king or a Lord Protector. But other people had suffered immensely during the eleven-year military conflict: the army had recruited young men from villages across England, and many of those men returned home wounded and damaged. Many more never returned.[1] If only the king would come back! If only the natural order could be restored.

On the afternoon of 25 May 1660, these prayers were finally answered. The recently renamed *Royal Charles* completed a two-day journey from the Dutch city of Delft to the county of Kent. The ship was a formidable three-decker with banks of mounted guns jutting from both sides. On that sunny afternoon, as it dropped anchor in the shallow waters near Dover, the sheets were lowered, the topsail furled, and the thunderous guns fired. Thousands of people had reportedly swarmed the Dutch shoreline to see the ship's departure, but the reception in England was even larger and more exuberant. The white cliffs of Dover were covered with throngs of British men and women, shouting and waving to celebrate, at last, the return of their king.[2]

Four days later, exactly on his thirtieth birthday, the new monarch triumphantly entered London on horseback, surrounded by his infantry. Charles II—tall, slightly mustached, with a prominent nose, his dark hair framing his face in long curls—wore a silver doublet and a black wide-brimmed hat with a plume of red feathers. The royal procession traveled slowly across London Bridge, zigzagging through the city's narrow streets, arriving finally at the Banqueting House at Whitehall. Cheering crowds lined the way, many of them joining the military parade as it passed. Jugglers and dancers also joined the celebration, while ladies in

FIGURE 31. *Charles II Landing in Dover amid Popular Rejoicing*. Etching by W. Sharp after B. West.

gold and velvet watched and waved from balconies.[3] By one count, the procession surged to 20,000 on horse and foot, and needed some nine hours to wind its way through the capital. England was once again a monarchy, and the bonfires, fireworks, and toasting would continue unabated for weeks.

Milton by this time was already in hiding. He had not directly participated in Charles I's trial, and he had not signed the king's death warrant, but as a spokesperson for Oliver Cromwell's government, Milton had both defended Parliament's proceedings and repeatedly lambasted the late king. He had good reason to expect imprisonment or a more severe corporal punishment, and he must have been tempted to flee England. Just his argument for deposing a monarch in *The Tenure of Kings and Magistrates* was enough for Milton to fear for his life.[4]

That May, as Charles II assumed the throne that his father had occupied before him, the government's Excise Office collapsed, and Milton lost the £2,000 that he had managed to save from his salary as a secretary under the commonwealth.[5] He also saw himself mocked mercilessly in print. An anonymous broadside, "The Picture of the Good Old Cause," highlighted Milton's blindness as an example of God's righteous judgment[6]; a biography of the new king attacked Milton as a "blind Beetle that durst affront the *Royal Eagle*"[7]; a satiric poem put Milton in hell with other parliamentarians—"Traytors and Rebels . . . / King-killers"[8]; and still another poem suggested that Milton should just go hang himself.[9] Within less than three weeks, on 16 June 1660, Milton's arrest was ordered, and his books were removed from Oxford University. Parliament began to debate whether his writings against monarchy should be confiscated. Eventually, on 27 August 1660, several copies of two of his books—*Eikonoklastes* and the first *Defense*—were burned outside the Old Bailey by the public hangman.[10]

Milton took refuge in the home of a friend—we don't know whom—and sent his three daughters away, most likely to stay with their grandmother. He remained hidden for close to three months—"In darkness, and with dangers compassed round," as he describes in *Paradise Lost* (Book 7, line 27). Some of what Milton must have been feeling is expressed by

Samson at the start of *Samson Agonistes*, as he tries to get away from the loud celebrations of his enemies and cannot stop thinking about all of the mistakes that led to his current plight:

> Retiring from the popular noise, I seek
> This unfrequented place to find some ease,
> Ease to the body some, none to the mind
> From restless thoughts, that like a deadly swarm
> Of hornets armed, no sooner found alone,
> But rush upon me thronging, and present
> Times past, what once I was, and what am now.
>   (lines 16–22)

The Indemnity and Oblivion Act, which became law at the end of August 1660, was supposed to erase the Interregnum and forgive crimes committed during the preceding eleven years. Exceptions included anyone who had overseen the death of Charles I as well as rapists and murderers.[11] That summer, as Milton continued to work on *Paradise Lost* in hiding, he must have worried that he would join the ranks of the unforgiven. He could be betrayed by an inquisitive passerby, a careless servant, or a vindictive neighbor. When the regicides' sentences eventually came down, he was probably not surprised by the ferocity of the new government's justice. Prisoners condemned to death were hanged, then drawn and quartered. This last type of punishment required taking a man down from the gallows still alive, then tying each of his arms and legs to four different horses who, startled or whipped, bolted at once in four different directions. Milton knew many of these men; they were his friends and had been his collaborators.

Later that fall, probably in October, Milton himself was arrested. Nothing is known about the circumstances of his capture.[12] It was only through the intervention of friends—including the poet Andrew Marvell, who had also worked as a clerical assistant for the republic—that Milton was able to avoid worse punishment. The surviving details are sketchy, but his friends argued that the fine of £150 stipulated by the House of Commons was too steep, and they insisted that the blind author posed no

threat to the new monarch. Somehow after about a month Milton was released and pardoned; likely his friends had pledged his future cooperation
and called in a passel of personal favors.[13]

Milton's friends may have also downplayed his radical politics—in particular, his outright rejection of the divine right of kings in *Tenure*—and
tried instead to present the poet as a hired pen of the republic, a mercenary who had libeled the martyred king merely for money. In the long
term, this portrait of the author inspired passionate hatred. As Charles I
posthumously became a Christian hero, Milton's status plummeted. He
became Milton the unscrupulous, Milton the "knave," the writer who
"hath sworn service to prosperous villainy."[14] But, in the short term, the
strategy was an unqualified success. Milton not only escaped execution
and won release from custody; he seems to have been offered a job in
the new king's government. Charles II appreciated the value of a positive
public image. What better way for the young king to enhance his international standing if the man who had defeated Salmasius could be coaxed
into championing the Restoration? Three years after ascending to the
throne, Charles apparently sent a chief officer of state to visit the author at
his new home near Bunhill Fields, in Artillery Walk, so named because it
sat across from a large garden where a society of men regularly gathered
to fire their guns and practice military formations.[15] Milton and his third
wife, Elizabeth Minshull, had moved there shortly after their marriage in
February 1663.

Of course Milton said no to the king, and it is difficult to imagine that
he would have seriously considered compromising his principles to help
the new government. He could hardly have hoped to speak truth to power
under a hereditary monarchy, a form of government that he had publicly
excoriated and personally come to despise. According to both Milton's
widow and Henry Bendish, Oliver Cromwell's great-grandson, the author's response was emphatic. Milton told his wife that he "had never yet
employed his pen against his conscience," and he explained, "my aim is to
live and die an honest man."[16]

In the immediate aftermath of the civil wars, as England continued to
celebrate its new king, Milton seems to have found much more enticing

the proposition of simply giving up on public life and immersing himself in his studies. Why bother trying to help a nation that refused to accept a more representative form of government and that had betrayed his religious and political ideals? Well and good if the people wanted to welcome back as king the son of a man whom Milton deemed a traitor. Milton could return to the writers whom he and Charles Diodati had first enjoyed together at St. Paul's, and he could leave the nation's politics to others— the younger, the more energetic, and the sighted.

But whatever temptations Milton faced in the months and years after the return of a king, whatever opportunities he had for leading an easier or more comfortable life, he resisted. Instead of betraying his beliefs and defecting to the king's party—or, more likely, bowing out and burying himself in his library—he redoubled his efforts. As the nation reverted to monarchy, he continued to write and publish works that addressed directly his life-long commitments to liberty and toleration. Most often, he turned to verse. Perhaps, following the defeat of the commonwealth, he believed that poetry would rise above and outlast the more ephemeral genre of polemical prose. Or, perhaps he appreciated how poetry allowed for a more subtle or nuanced expression of his most controversial ideas as he turned his attention to the great work that he had anticipated many years earlier. Whatever the motive, long after the country returned to monarchy, Milton continued to write, creating during these years not just *Paradise Lost* but also his two other great long poems, *Paradise Regained* and *Samson Agonistes*.

———

How could Milton do it? The way to resist temptation, he knew, was not as simple as just saying no. Successful resistance required self-possession— that is, an understanding of his own character and principles, which could be achieved only with effort and time. During Milton's life, this virtue was sometimes called self-command or equanimity, and it could encompass both the ability to control one's emotions and the practice of taking control of and responsibility for one's actions and their consequences. Most simply, it is inner strength, the ideal, as expressed in Proverbs, that "he that is slow to anger, is better than the mighty: and he that ruleth his spirit, [is better] than he that taketh a city" (16.:32). Writing in the first century, the Roman Emperor Marcus Aurelius described self-possession as acceptance of a deterministic world: "A cucumber is bitter. Throw it away. There are briars in the road. Turn aside from them. This is enough. Do not add, 'And why were such made in the world?'"[17] Aurelius goes on to compare the self-possessed to a rocky bluff repeatedly pummeled by rough waves: it stands constant.

Yet for Milton, who held an uncompromising belief in free will, self-possession extended beyond the acceptance of bitterness or briars. It meant choosing to remain unflappable—confident and strong—in the face of sometimes overwhelming adversity, and it meant understanding that the most valuable possession of each person is the rational self. As the medieval philosopher Boethius explained—a writer whose popular and influential *Consolation of Philosophy* Milton almost certainly knew—happiness resides within everyone, not outside in the ever-changing world:

> Why seek ye, then, around you [for] the happiness which ye have placed within you by the divine power? . . . Canst thou now discover whether thou hast anything more precious to thee than thyself? I think, though, thou wilt say that thou hast nothing more precious. I know, if thou hadst full power of thyself, thou wouldest then have something in thyself, which thou never with thine own consent would relinquish, nor could Fortune take it from thee.[18]

The virtue of self-possession—of having "full power of thyself"—is also at the center of Edmund Spenser's allegorical masterpiece, *The Faerie Queene* (1590, 1596). Spenser's unfinished epic depicts a band of knights, each one associated with a different moral precept—holiness, temperance, chastity, friendship, justice, and courtesy. The poem's larger purpose, Spenser claimed, was to teach readers how to combine these virtues in the pursuit of becoming great in mind and heart. Spenser, following Aristotle, called this ideal "magnificence," and it seems to be closely allied with the virtue of self-possession; it can only be achieved by resisting worldly distractions and overcoming trials and tragedies. Milton must have been taken with Spenser's message: in *Areopagitica*, he wrote that Spenser was a "better teacher" than the medieval philosophers John Duns Scotus and St. Thomas Aquinas (YP II: 516), and in his own works Milton often returned to Spenser's theme of a Christian hero triumphing over temptation and persevering through constancy.[19] This is the ideal that Milton celebrates in Sonnet 9 to an unnamed lady, who (he says) faces adversities with honor, laboring "up the hill of heav'nly truth" and shunning "the broad way and the green" (lines 2, 4); it is the ideal that the angel Michael holds out to Adam and Eve at the end of *Paradise Lost* after describing the horrible results of the couple's sin; and it is again the virtue that Milton embraces at the end of his sonnet "When I consider how my light is spent," as he accepts that he can serve God even if he only stands and waits.

Self-possession is also the principle at the core of Milton's political and religious philosophy in his prose tracts. He opposed both monarchy and a top-down church hierarchy because, he argued, they make people into sheep—"softest, basest, vitiousest, servilest, easiest to be kept under; and not only in fleece, but in mind also sheepish-est" (YP VII: 460). Thus he also defended divorce, and opposed state-sponsored censorship; he expected the citizenry to take personal responsibility for making good, rational choices in everything from their marriages to the books they read.

Milton hoped that these habits could be instilled at an early age. In a brief treatise entitled *Of Education* that he published in 1644—and that he had reprinted in 1673, the year before he died—he calls for wholesale educational reform. He wished to inspire and challenge students, much more than the schools were doing at that time, and he set the bar high. Drawing on his own teaching, he describes how self-possessed students should become lifelong learners, "enflam'd" with education and virtue,

> stirr'd up with high hopes of living to be brave men, and worthy patriots, dear to God, and famous to all ages. That they may despise and scorn all their childish, and ill-taught qualities . . . [and] might in a short space gain them to an incredible diligence and courage: infusing into their young breasts such an ingenuous and

noble ardor, as would not fail to make many of them renowned and matchless men. (YP II: 385)

This language surely sounds idealistic, but for Milton the ultimate goal was practical. He expected self-possessed students, those who had learned to live courageously and virtuously, to use their education in perform-ing "justly, skillfully, and magnanimously all the offices both private and public" (YP II: 379). As Milton summed up in *Areopagitica*, God com-mits each person to manage their own mind, not to be "captivate under a perpetual childhood of prescription, but trusts him with the gift of reason to be his own chooser" (YP II: 513–14).

———

After the Restoration, near the end of his life, Milton continued to press the same point. In *Paradise Regained*, Jesus admonishes Satan for tempt-ing him with great wealth. Jesus explains that he needs neither realms nor riches:

> Yet he who reigns within himself, and rules
> Passions, desires, and fears, is more a king;
> Which every wise and virtuous man attains:
> And who attains not, ill aspires to rule
> Cities of men or head-strong multitudes,
> Subject himself to anarchy within,
> Or lawless passions in him which he serves. (Book 2,
>   lines 466–72)

This rebuke captures the dual sense of self-possession as both composure and self-knowledge. In contrast to a lawless tyrant, Jesus lauds the self-possessed citizenry, fit to govern cities because they learn first to govern "the inner man, the nobler part" (Book 2, line 477).

Milton's *Paradise Regained* offers his most sustained study of the difficulty of withstanding temptation and the necessity of following the "nobler part" of conscience. Decades earlier, his masque for the Earl of Bridgewater had dramatized the challenge of not giving in to sensual indulgence as the Lady boldly confronts the demon Comus and refuses to drink from his cup and join his crew of animal-headed hedonists. Also, in *Paradise Lost*, Milton expands the narrative of temptation from Genesis, as he depicts Satan, then Adam and Eve struggling unsuccessfully against their own selfish desires and impulses. But it is in *Paradise Regained*, wholly written after the failure of revolution and the return of monarchy,[20] that Milton focuses insistently on the theme of rising above and refusing to give in to temptation.

After the rich detail and complex structure of his earlier epic, Milton decided in *Paradise Regained* to scale back: he now preferred a much plainer style, better suited to the sublime simplicity of the Son's life, and he opted for a more straightforward narrative, more appropriate for depicting a series of long conversations between Satan and the Son. In *Paradise Lost*, Milton dared to retell the story of Adam and Eve from the opening chapters of Genesis; in this later, shorter poem—more of a complement than a sequel to his epic—he rewrites the story of Jesus's forty-day exile in the wilderness, as recounted in Luke (4:1–13), Mark (1:12–13), and Matthew (4:1–11). Milton once again deepens and expands the little information included in scripture, most closely following Luke's version of the Son's temptation, but also drawing on the copious biblical commentary that had grown up around the simple gospel story. In the Bible, Jesus is tempted three times; in Milton's poem, Jesus instead withstands nine separate temptations.

Because Milton took the heretical position that the Son was not God, the challenges that Jesus faces in the poem seem a genuine test of his virtue and wisdom. Of course, Milton's readers would know at the start that the Son will not succumb to the devil's offers, no matter how tantalizing they seem. But Jesus's heroism in *Paradise Regained* is not, as these same readers might have expected from the poem's title, an act of suffering and endurance. Milton wanted to write about regaining Paradise, but he was not interested in depicting the pain and horror of the Crucifixion.

Years earlier, probably in 1629, Milton had begun a poem called "The Passion" about Jesus's suffering and death on the cross. He never finished it. He said that he was not ready at age twenty to undertake such a serious subject—or, as Milton put it a decade later when he nevertheless had the incomplete poem printed, "This Subject the Author finding to be above the years he had, when he wrote it, and nothing satisfi'd with what was begun, left it unfinished."[21] But even later Milton seems to have been ill-suited, temperamentally or theologically, to bring to life the extraordinary sacrifice of the Crucifixion. In the incomplete "The Passion," he hems-and-haws for fifty-six lines, straining to find the right imagery and tone: "The leaves should all be black whereon I write, / And letters where my tears have washed a wannish white" (lines 34–35). Instead of supernatural suffering, Milton wanted a model of obedience that readers in their daily lives could emulate. Thus in *Paradise Regained* the Son resists temptation and stands up to Satan largely through an appeal to logic, scripture, and his own self-knowledge. This is the same method that Milton used to arrive at his convictions and that, *Paradise Regained* implies, remains available to everyone.

Satan in the poem starts small. At the outset, he tries three times to get the Son just to break his fast and distrust God's providence. As in Matthew and Luke, Satan proposes first that Jesus turn stones into bread, but Milton develops this enticement by having Satan then present Jesus with a large, gorgeous feast—"A table richly spread, in regal mode, / With dishes piled" (Book 2, lines 340–41)—replete with gentle music, fragrant flowers, and seductive boys and nymphs. Satan's third try is another offer of material comfort, in this case heaps of riches and treasure, the things that are, he proposes, the best means to power, to "honor, friends, conquest, and realms" (Book 2, line 422).

Jesus naturally rejects all of these attempts. The devil's "pompous delicacies" (Book 2, line 390), the Son explains, are less important than spiritual strength and insight. It is at this point that Milton might have been thinking specifically of the restoration of Charles II and the need to resist the rewards that could come with supporting the new monarch: Jesus calls out the legitimacy of all earthly kings and insists that all people should instead reign over themselves. "A crown / Golden in show," he adds, "is but a wreath of thorns, / Brings dangers, troubles, cares, and sleepless nights" (Book 2, lines 458–60). This description clearly recalls

Charles I's presentation as a martyr in *Eikon Basilike* (on that book's frontispiece, the late king appears on his knees, clutching a crown of thorns), but after the Restoration, Jesus's words also seem a veiled warning to the new resident of the Palace of Whitehall. Charles II, Milton implies, should anticipate his own dangers and trials.

Satan, though, is not a quick learner. Soon after the Son champions the idea of self-rule instead of worldly power, the devil tries to tempt him with the "blaze of fame, / The people's praise" (Book 3, lines 47–48). Jesus's sharp rejection of popularity comes with a stinging condemnation of the people—"a herd confused, / A miscellaneous rabble, who extol / Things vulgar, and well weighed, scarce worth the praise" (Book 3, lines 49–51). This seems in part an expression of Milton's own exasperation with recent events and his anger and frustration with the multitude of English men and women who had lined the streets of London and eagerly welcomed back a monarch. When the Son adds, "Of whom to be dispraised were no small praise" (Book 3, line 56), how could Milton not have been thinking of his own low esteem after the Restoration? Instead of seeking fame, says the Son, the truly righteous person "dares be singularly good" (Book 3, line 57) and—despite being derided by many people—steadfastly pursues not his own but God's glory.

When Satan then brings Jesus to the top of a mountain and shows him the great Roman empire stretching below—its ornate gates, golden spires, and gilded parapets—he offers the Son the spoils of a bloodless coup: Jesus needs only bow down to the devil to rule Rome in place of the Emperor Tiberius. Jesus has already refused Satan's offer of military power—what he rejects as the "cumbersome / Luggage of war" (Book 3, lines 400–401)—and he now sounds just as contemptuous of Rome's "civility of manners, arts, and arms" (Book 4, line 83). The Romans, Jesus argues, deserve to be vassals to a bad ruler such as Tiberius because they chose to enslave themselves. Just as the Son's rejection of armed combat could reflect Milton's own disillusionment with warfare after England's failed revolution, Jesus's disdain for Roman arts and culture could suggest Milton's anger with his fellow citizens for agreeing to have their rights under the commonwealth stripped away by the new monarch. Jesus

FIGURE 32. Illustration by J.M.W. Turner, *The Temptation on the Mountain*, from *The Poetical Works of John Milton*, 3 vols. (London: John Macrone, 1835)

Source: Robert J. Wickenheiser Collection of John Milton, Irvin Department of Rare Books and Special Collections, University of South Carolina Libraries, Columbia, S.C.

emphasizes instead his spiritual kingship, and he promises one day to destroy all earthly monarchies, a pledge that must have sounded especially threatening just ten years after England had again become a kingdom.

One of the things that sets Jesus apart in *Paradise Regained* is his profound self-knowledge. As he withstands the devil's repeated assails, he cannot recall his existence before the incarnation, and when he ventures into the wilderness, he is still "Musing and much revolving in his breast, / How best the mighty work he might begin / Of savior to mankind" (Book 1, lines 185–87). But even at the start of his self-imposed exile Jesus comprehends a great deal about himself: he has perused Hebrew scriptures, he has been taught about his birth by his mother, and he realizes that he will have to overcome many obstacles. He is ready to act on his preparation—to "publish his Godlike office now mature" (Book 1, line 188)—but, as he tells himself in his opening soliloquy, he knows his "way must lie / Through many a hard assay even to the death" (Book 1, lines 263–64), and he will have to withstand "whate'er may tempt, whate'er seduce, / Allure, or terrify, or undermine" (Book 1, line 178–79).

Satan, in contrast, lacks the Son's self-possession, and he does not understand who Jesus is. The devil's mistake is that he repeatedly looks to the outside world as a source of happiness and power instead of searching within for the poise and strength that Jesus embodies. Near the end of *Paradise Regained*, the devil is still trying to puzzle out what the title "Son" means:

> The son of God I also am, or was,
> And if I was, I am; relation stands;
> All men are sons of God; yet thee I thought
> In some respect far higher so declared. (Book 4,
>   lines 518–21)

Satan admits that he might be overmatched after first meeting Jesus, and he quickly senses that seducing the Son will be far more difficult than what he experienced when he brought down Adam and Eve. But Satan does not recognize that Jesus is the Son and does not realize that they previously faced each other in the war in heaven. The repetition and choppy syntax in the above passage—the pauses after each *am* and *was*—enact Satan's confusion. He cannot get beyond the fact that all people and angels are created by God. What makes the Son special, he has no idea.

Part of the answer is the Son's commitment to "matchless deeds" and the "public good" (Book I, lines 204, 233). Jesus had previously considered resorting to violence, but before heading into the wilderness he settles instead on words as the best way to regain a lost paradise. The Son decides that it is "more humane, more heavenly, first / By winning words to conquer willing hearts, / And make persuasion do the work of fear" (Book I, lines 221–23). Again, Milton sounds as if he were thinking about himself and his own circumstances. Disenchanted with war after the Restoration, he was reaffirming his belief in the power of language and devoting himself full-time to working as a writer. In the poem's first edition, Jesus had resolved "the stubborn only to destroy" (Book I, line 226), but Milton even reconsidered this concession, and in a list of "Errata" appended at the back of the book, he asks readers to replace *destroy* with the less violent-sounding *subdue*.[22] Milton might be down after the Restoration, his cause might seem defeated, but resisting patiently was the surest way to victory. He is reminding himself and his readers about the right way to deal with defeat and failure. As God in *Paradise Regained* proclaims encouragingly about the Son, "By humiliation and strong sufferance: / His weakness shall o'ercome Satanic strength / And all the world, and mass of sinful flesh" (Book I, lines 160–62).

For Milton, though, the most personal aspect of *Paradise Regained* was probably the devil's attempt to seduce Jesus with learning. All of Satan's other propositions derive loosely from the trials that Jesus endures in the Bible, but Satan's offer of the sum of Greek art and literature is a temptation original to Milton's poem. The devil catalogues the ancients' grand achievements in drama, rhetoric, philosophy, and verse—and Jesus refuses all of it:

> he who receives
> Light from above, from the fountain of light,
> No other doctrine needs, though granted true;

But these are false, or little else but dreams,
Conjectures, fancies, built on nothing firm. (Book 4,
       lines 288–92)

Jesus sounds almost angry as he rejects the potential value of such knowledge and dismisses all classical writers because they lacked true wisdom. He goes on to list Socrates, Plato, and Epicurus along with two schools, the Skeptics and Peripatetics, and sums up all of them as fakery, an "empty cloud" (Book 4, line 321). All of the ancient writers mislead, he explains, because they did not have self-knowledge; they did not understand their own characters and the things that they should most value. As he succinctly puts it, they were "ignorant of themselves, of God much more" (Book 4, line 310).

Such a thoroughgoing denial of antiquity is, of course, a surprise, as it comes from an author who so loved classical literature that he often borrowed ancient modes and models, and frequently alluded to individual passages and figures from works by a wide range of pre-Christian writers. In *Paradise Lost*, Milton had found a way to incorporate antiquity, in part by explaining that pagan gods were in fact the rebel angels, devils whom descendants of Adam and Eve would one day wrongly adore as deities. Even in Milton's early ode, "On the Morning of Christ's Nativity," he had described the infant in the manger supplanting all previous religions, but he had let go of the ancients almost reluctantly, cataloguing the ranks of disempowered gods at length—watching them troop to hell, the "infernal jail" (line 233)—but mourning with a "loud lament" (line 183) the loss of Greek and Roman deities. How could Milton, who aspired to compete with Homer and Virgil, ostensibly renounce antiquity altogether?

On one level, Jesus has to refuse classical culture in *Paradise Regained* because Satan taints everything he touches. The devil's easy presentation of ancient learning as a means to power undermines the hard work that is needed for obtaining the knowledge that he offers the Son.[23] But Milton in this temptation may have also been admitting to himself one of his own weaknesses. Unlike the perfect Son who can resist all of Satan's trials, Milton was especially vulnerable to the allure of classical literature and learning. After his release from custody in late 1660, he must have been

tempted to go back into hiding and indulge in his favorite books and authors instead of directly confronting the fallout from an unpopular war
and the return of a king. In *Paradise Regained*—which he published at
age sixty-two, just three years before his death—he seems to be acknowledging the mistake of taking pleasure in learning for learning's sake and
extolling instead Jesus's more ambitious and more difficult task of seeking
spiritual insights that can be applied in the real world.

Jesus goes on to qualify his outright rejection of antiquity—but only
slightly. He accepts that reading beyond the Bible can be worthwhile, but
he advocates a specific type of study:

> who reads
> Incessantly, and to his reading brings not
> A spirit and judgment equal or superior,
> (And what he brings, what needs he elsewhere seek)
> Uncertain and unsettled still remains,
> Deep-versed in books and shallow in himself,
> Crude or intoxicate, collecting toys,
> And trifles for choice matters, worth a sponge;
> As children gathering pebbles on the shore. (Book 4,
>   lines 322–30)

These lines again capture the risk that Milton knew an enthusiasm for
learning could entail. Years earlier in 1632, after graduating with an MA
from Cambridge, he had returned to his parents' home and avidly continued to pursue his studies. Milton had long been planning to enter the
priesthood. It was the career that his parents intended for him, that his
friends had encouraged, and that he had personally felt inclined to embrace.[24] But when he saw that dishonest bishops had seized control of the
English church, he could not in good conscience take final orders and
pledge allegiance to the king. Milton was (in his words) "church-outed
by the Prelates" (YP I: 823)—he felt compelled to give up his plans to
become a minister because of the corrupt episcopal clergy.

But Milton in deciding to forgo the priesthood did not then retreat into a life of bookish seclusion. Living with his parents outside of
London, he began searching for a different career that would still center

on public service, and he committed himself to a program of assiduous reading as a means of preparing himself. When he maps out his plans in one of his tracts against the bishops, he announces that he has decided to write something great—"to be an interpreter & relater of the best and sagest things" (YP I: 811)—but he realizes that he first needs to do more work—to read diligently, pray devoutly, and observe keenly.

In the same way, after the Restoration, Milton was again outed from public office, this time not by choice but because of the return of monarchy. But again the author remained committed to staying active and engaged, to writing works that would challenge, inform, and inspire his fellow citizens. He resisted the temptation of retreating from public life and turned instead to long poetry as the best means of meditating on the lost revolution, of helping his nation and instilling in readers the "seeds of virtue, and public civility" (YP I: 816).

Paradise Regained concludes with a breathtaking scene high in the air as a frustrated Satan grabs Jesus, flies with him to the top of an alabaster temple, and sets him on the highest, golden pinnacle. With the towered city of Jerusalem and the surrounding plains extending for miles below them, the devil taunts Jesus one last time. He dares him either to stand upright or, if he is truly the Son of God, to throw himself safely to the ground.[25] This temptation comes directly from Luke (4:9–13) and Matthew (4:5–7). In both passages, as in Milton's poem, Jesus responds by reminding Satan, "It is written, 'Thou shalt not tempt the Lord thy God'" (Luke 4:12).

But in *Paradise Regained*, Milton has Jesus renounce the devil's either-or logic. Jesus will stand, *and* he will reveal himself to be the Son of God:

> To whom thus Jesus: "Also it is written,
> 'Tempt not the Lord thy God,'" he said and stood.
> But Satan smitten with amazement fell
> As when Earth's son Antaeus (to compare
> Small things with greatest) in Irassa strove

FIGURE 33. Illustration by J.M.W. Turner, *The Temptation on the Pinnacle*, from *The Poetical Works of John Milton*, 3 vols. (London: John Macrone, 1835)

With Jove's Alcides, and oft foiled still rose,
Receiving from his mother Earth new strength,
Fresh from his fall, and fiercer grapple joined,
Throttled at length in the air, expired and fell;
So after many a foil the tempter proud,
Renewing fresh assaults, amidst his pride
Fell whence he stood to see his victor fall. (Book 4,
    lines 560–71)

After all of the devil's temptations and blandishments, after all of the
Son's rebuttals and refusals, this sudden reversal is striking and tonic.
Milton has found a way to make stasis compelling, and in a single line—
"Fell whence he stood to see his victor fall"—he compresses the poem's
entire narrative of Satan's failure and the Son's triumph. The devil's fu-
tility is underscored by the repetition of "fell . . . fall," like the echoing
sound of something hitting the ground from a great height. In contrast,
Jesus takes a stand, literally standing on the pinnacle and figuratively
remaining steadfast against all worldly seductions. Instead, it is Satan,
amazed and anguished, who suddenly falls, like the giant Antaeus, who is
strangled in midair by the demigod Hercules so that he cannot continue
to draw strength from contact with his mother, the earth. Jesus's victory
over Satan, though, is expressly nonviolent, and rather than relying on
God's intervention, he saves himself by remaining upright, just as Satan
damns himself, falling freely from the pinnacle instead of being shoved or
even touched.

At the end of *Paradise Regained*, the Son is rewarded for his heroic
fortitude. A band of bright angels flies up to meet him on the pinnacle
and receive him softly on their wings. They set him gently in a flowered
valley, where, on a grassy hill, he finds a table laid with heavenly fruits and
drinks. The angels then break out in song to celebrate Jesus's resilience:

            now thou hast avenged
    Supplanted Adam, and by vanquishing
    Temptation, hast regained lost Paradise,

And frustrated the conquest fraudulent:
He never more henceforth will dare set foot
In Paradise to tempt; his snares are broke:
For though that seat of earthly bliss be failed,
A fairer Paradise is founded now
For Adam and his chosen sons, whom thou
A savior art come down to reinstall. (Book 4,
   lines 606–15)

One final time, Milton reminds his readers and himself that even when life is precarious, even when they seem on the verge of caving in or falling off, they can still triumph and count themselves among Adam's "chosen sons," if they resist temptation and stand fast. The rewards will exceed their expectations, and their enemies will defeat themselves.

In the closing lines of *Paradise Regained*, Jesus returns quietly to his mother's house, a humble, almost anticlimactic resolution after his resounding victory over the devil's many temptations. But, like Milton after being released from custody—and like Milton, years earlier, after deciding not to become a minister—the Son is not retiring, and he is not giving up. He is continuing to get ready so that he can fulfill his role as the savior of humankind. Milton in the 1660s was also readying himself to make a stand, to overcome his blindness, his dwindling health, and his many personal hardships. In writing *Paradise Lost*, then *Paradise Regained*, he was still attempting, like the Son, "by winning words to conquer willing hearts."

NINE

Doubt

"Strenuous liberty"

AROUND THE SAME TIME THAT Milton had married for the third time and was still at work on *Paradise Lost*, probably near age fifty-five, he suffered his first attack of gout, an acute type of arthritis that causes swelling and redness in the joints of the hands and feet. Attacks are sudden and agonizing, sometimes lasting up to twelve hours; the residual discomfort can linger for days. Sufferers compare the pain to having their limbs set on fire or being chewed by a dog.[1] Milton's disease was so far advanced by his early sixties that he had difficulty walking, and his hands had become gnarled, his fingers swollen and misshapen, like gingerroot.

The poet, though, remained cheerful, even when the attacks grew more frequent. So reports his brother Christopher, his daughter Deborah, a former student, and the early biographer Aubrey.[2] Even Milton's former maidservant, Elizabeth Fisher, who would later testify that he and his daughters had a poor relationship, recalled that the author suffered from gout but was still "very merry and not in any passion or angry humour."[3] On sunny days, Milton would sit in his grey coat outside his home in

Artillery Walk, listening to passersby and enjoying the fresh air. He grew paler in his later years, but he still had good color in his cheeks—"ruddy to the very last," according to one contemporary writer.[4] His hair was still light brown, and his blindness was not immediately obvious. His blue eyes remained clear and bright—"without a cloud," he wrote, "as the eyes of men who see most keenly" (YP IV: 583).

Milton also continued to enjoy walking for hours at a time. Even when his joints began to stiffen from his ailment, he could be seen ambling along the city's winding streets on the arm of his young wife or one of his friends, such as the bookseller Edward Millington. Before Milton lost his sight, he

FIGURE 34. Illustration by Richard Westall, *Milton Composing "Paradise Lost"*

Source: Robert J. Wickenheiser Collection of John Milton, Irvin Department of Rare Books and Special Collections, University of South Carolina Libraries, Columbia, S.C.

had worn a sword and is said to have handled it with skill and dexterity.[5] But in his later years, his chief physical activity was walking. On rainy days, or when the pain grew too intense, he took exercise by playing the organ that he and his wife owned; the couple also had set up a rudimentary exercise machine in their home, "a Pully to swing and keep him in motion."[6]

Still, after the civil wars, after the initial shock of the return of monarchy, Milton must have also been grappling with a profound sense of disappointment that the nation's hard-won liberty had been given up so easily.[7] As he lamented in one of his prose works, "the blood of so many thousand faithful and valiant *English* men" had been spilled (YP VII: 423–24). And for what? On 30 January 1661, the anniversary of Charles I's execution, the bodies of three of the revolution's leaders—Oliver Cromwell (who had died in 1658), Henry Ireton (who had died in 1651), and John Bradshaw (who had died in 1659)—were pulled out of their coffins, hanged in effigy, and then decapitated. Their heads were set on poles on the top of Westminster Hall. The bodies were later tossed in an unmarked grave.[8]

It is no surprise, then, that Milton has Jesus thoroughly reject Satan's temptation of warfare as a means to power in *Paradise Regained*. And in *Paradise Lost*, when Milton depicts the war in heaven—fought with a mixture of swords, rocks, and cannons—the first two days of battle accomplish almost nothing. On the third day, shortly before sanctioning the Son to drive out the bad angels and end the conflict, God sums up evenly, "War wearied hath performed what war can do" (Book 6, line 695). God's pronouncement probably reflects Milton's own view of military conflict after the Restoration. He had witnessed "what war can do," and like many other English men and women, he must have been wearied.

———

This sense of disappointment is expressed most intensely in *Samson Agonistes*, which was published in 1671, three years before Milton died. It is likely the last poem that he ever composed and seems to be one of his most personal works.[9] Yet, he took the basic story from the Book of Judges, which would have been familiar to his contemporary readers: Samson's tremendous strength resides in his hair, Dalila badgers him to reveal his secret, and he is blinded and imprisoned. Later, when Samson is led into the Philistines' temple, he has his revenge, shaking the pillars and causing the roof to collapse on the Philistines.

In Milton's version, Samson has already regained his strength, but he has given up on violent resistance. The former champion dwells instead on the physical nature of his suffering:

> Thoughts of my tormentors armed with deadly stings
> Mangle my apprehensive tenderest parts,
> Exasperate, exulcerate, and raise
> Dire inflammation which no cooling herb
> Or med'cinal liquor can assuage,
> Nor breath of vernal air from snowy alp. (lines 623–28)

Samson is here describing his inner turmoil to his father, but the account of his torment seems to capture Milton's own corporeal affliction. Samson also compares his "griefs" to a "ling'ring disease" with "wounds" that "rankle, and fester" (lines 617–21).

Surely Milton, who had lost his sight almost twenty years earlier, felt an instinctive connection to his blind protagonist. He depicts Samson's struggling just to accept that his blindness is permanent:

> my thoughts portend,
> That these dark orbs no more shall treat with light,
> Nor th'other light of life continues long,
> But yield to double darkness nigh at hand:
> So much I feel my genial spirits droop,
> My hopes all flat, nature within me seems
> In all her functions weary of herself;
> My race of glory run, and race of shame,
> And I shall shortly be with them that rest. (lines 590–98)

How can readers not see such speeches as a thinly veiled version of Milton's own darkest thoughts? Milton was not, of course, writing directly about himself in the poem. But in the immediate aftermath of the Restoration— living with painful gout, coping with blindness, having been imprisoned by his enemies, only barely evading worse punishment—his own hopes must have been "flat," and he must have sometimes felt, like the Hebrew champion, old and exhausted.

Even Samson's friends, who come to visit him in prison in the hope of offering counsel or consolation, quickly grow less sanguine. They are struck by how defeated the former hero looks—spread out carelessly on the ground, wearing soiled and ill-fitting rags, his head drooping: "Can this be he, / That heroic, that renowned, / Irresistible Samson?" (lines 124–26). His friends complain about the inadequacy of the many adages that extoll patience in face of hardship. They wonder how God can suddenly desert the "solemnly elected," his earthly ministers (line 678), and they deplore how he

> throw'st them lower than [he] didst exalt them high,
> Unseemly falls in human eye,
> Too grievous for the trespass or omission,
> Oft leav'st them to the hostile sword
> Of heathen and profane, their carcasses
> To dogs and fowls a prey, or else captíved:
> Or to th' unjust tribunals, under change of times,
> And condemnation of the ingrateful multitude.
>   (lines 689–96)

Like Samson and his friends, Milton after the return of the king must at times have felt shaken and dispirited. If in these lines he were reflecting on England under Charles II, perhaps even thinking about himself as among the "solemnly elected"—and the topical imagery of tribunals and hostile swords suggests that he was—it is notable that Samson's friends present such a reversal of fortune, when it occurs, as unremitting. The only solution is to beg God for mercy and to hope to "feel within / Some course of consolation" (lines 663–64).

———

And yet, in depicting Samson's suffering, Milton follows Hebrew scriptures and concludes his poem with another reversal: Samson in the end takes decisive action and mows down his captors. After dramatizing the Son's repeated resistance to the devil in *Paradise Regained*, Milton was entertaining in *Samson Agonistes* one last, powerful temptation: What if his hero's enemies could be defeated? What if, with one fell swoop, he could exact revenge?

Paradise Regained and *Samson Agonistes* were originally published together as a double book, so that readers turned immediately from the Son's sublime imperviousness to Milton's portrayal of the Old Testament strongman. Given the almost casual phrasing on the original title page— *"Paradise Regain'd* . . . To which is added *Samson Agonistes"*—Milton may not have conceived of the two poems as one cohesive statement. But the joining of the Son's perfection with Samson's fallibility suggests that Milton was of at least two minds after the Restoration. He could admire and celebrate Jesus's self-possession but still acknowledge the appeal of Samson's vengeance.

Samson had been among the list of possible subjects that Milton had jotted down twenty years earlier as he ruminated on writing something great and lasting: "Samson pursophorus or Hybristes, or Samson marrying or in Ramath-Lechi."[10] The first two phrases mean "Samson the Firebrand" and "Samson the Violent"; the final phrase, "Ramath-Lechi," refers to the site where Samson allegedly slew a thousand Philistines by wielding an ass's jawbone (Judges 15:15–17). But now, near the end of Milton's life, after sacrificing his sight and writing repeatedly in support of a failed revolution, the author settled on the title *Samson Agonistes*, the latter word (from the Greek) describing not a conquering hero but a combatant at public games who exerts both body and mind, a champion who struggles. Milton's Samson has to contend with his guilt for having succumbed to Dalila, with the moral dilemma of performing for the Philistines, and with his ongoing desire to serve God and fulfill the angel's prophecy.

In *Samson Agonistes*, as in the Bible, an angel had twice foretold Samson's birth and promised his parents that their son would free his people, the Israelites, from their enslavement by the Philistines (Judges 13:3–5, 10–20). When Milton's poem opens, Samson seems to have failed utterly. He has been enslaved and put to work, grinding daily in a mill, chained and humiliated. Samson fears that he will not get another opportunity to help his people. He does not know what to do next.

Readers of Milton have not known what to do with *Samson Agonistes*. The poem is a curious hybrid, crossing the story of a controversial figure from Hebrew scriptures with the form of a classical drama. It reads like an ancient tragedy by Euripides or Sophocles, not like a play by Shakespeare or Christopher Marlowe. Instead of a large cast of characters and a sequence of varied scenes, the story occurs in one place and depicts one continuous action. Milton wrote in the preface that he never intended for it to be performed, but did he mean that literally? Maybe he was just dissatisfied with the state of the theater after the Restoration and did not think his dramatic poem could be staged.

Readers have argued about almost all aspects of *Samson*—its structure, genre, imagery, and date of composition.[11] Mostly, though, they have disagreed about the way that Milton depicts Samson's final action when he leans against two massive pillars and slaughters hundreds of Philistines. Is Milton glorifying or condemning Samson's destruction? Is Samson the Old Testament counterpart of Jesus's righteousness, or is he a counterexample of Jesus's enlightened piety? Is Samson a hero or a terrorist?

Milton in writing in support of the revolution during the 1640s had not hesitated to see violence as a means to an end. He supported the execution of King Charles I, and in his sonnet to Oliver Cromwell, he had praised the Lord General's wartime deeds—he imagines the River Darwen "imbrued" with "blood of Scots" (line 7)—while emphasizing the more difficult and pressing political challenges facing the new leader. Even in the first of Milton's prose tracts for the commonwealth government, he seems to have condoned violent action, laying the groundwork for Cromwell's brutal military offensive in Ireland. In *Observations on the Articles of Peace*, Milton seems blinkered, unable to recognize that the Irish rebellion was a war of national liberation. He does not go as far as some polemical tracts from this period in slandering the Irish as cannibals and seeking their destruction.[12] But his remarks are still repugnant: he disparages the Irish Confederates for having supported the Royalist cause, calling them "Barbarians" and "Malignants" (YP III: 308, 334).

In the years after the war, though, after the failure of the republic, Milton grew disillusioned with not just warfare but all violent action. In a letter to Richard Jones, Milton wrote that his friend and former student should not praise matters "in which force is of most avail" and should learn to discern "great characters not by force and animal strength, but by justice and temperance."[13] Later, near the end of *Paradise Lost*, the angel Michael instructs Adam about the consequences of human sin and explains that some of Adam's offspring will be "styled great conquerors." Instead, Michael says, these descendants should be "destroyers rightlier called and plagues of men" (Book 11, lines 695, 697).

In 1659, around the same time that Milton began working intently on his epic, he also published a treatise in which he argued more plainly and at greater length that force should never be used in matters of religion. Violence, Milton insisted, was more harmful than helpful; it does not promote God's glory or foster spiritual goodness. A magistrate who makes people "do that whereof they cannot be persuaded" compels them to contradict their conscience, which is a sin: "He forces them to do evil" (YP VII: 266). Above all, Milton argues, each person's "liberty . . . is the certain and the sacred gift of God" (YP VII: 267). It can "can neither be won nor lost by arms" but must be achieved within by living virtuously; only then will it "put down the deepest and most far-reaching roots in your souls" (YP IV: 680).

Writing against censorship fifteen years earlier in *Areopagitica*, Milton had already foreseen the problem with trying to enforce conformity through violent punishments. As a Christian writer, he should have believed that religion was a truth revealed by God, a truth that everyone should accept and share across the world, including with nonbelievers. False beliefs are not to be tolerated. But in *Areopagitica*, he concedes that truth "may have more shapes than one" (YP II: 563). And in other places in the same tract he holds out an ideal of toleration and religious liberty:

I conceive therefore, that when God did enlarge the universal diet of man's body, saving ever the rules of temperance, he then also . . . left arbitrary the dieting and repasting of our minds; as wherein every mature man might have to exercise his own leading capacity . . . God commits the managing so great a trust, without particular Law or prescription, wholly to the demeanor of every grown man. (YP II: 513)

Instead of being coerced, each person has to work individually to discern truth—through study, reflection, and prayer—and then should share these insights with other people so that, through collaboration, a more complete and higher understanding can be reached. This is the argument that anticipates the emphasis on free will in both *Paradise Lost* and Milton's unfinished theological treatise. In *Areopagitica*, Milton specifically objects to prepublication censorship as a type of violence against writers, readers, and books: he calls it a "persecution . . . against the living labours of public men, . . . a kind of homicide, . . . sometimes a martyrdom, and if it extend to the whole impression, a kind of massacre" (YP II: 493). When Milton imagines lifting Parliament's restrictions on the press, he compares England to a regenerate Samson, "a noble and puissant Nation rousing herself like a strong man after sleep, and shaking her invincible locks" (YP II: 558).

As apparently Milton's last word on the use of outward force, *Samson Agonistes* offers a more measured answer to the question of whether violence can ever be righteous. At the end of the poem, after learning of Samson's death and destruction, his father and friends try to overcome their shock, and they rationalize that Samson's vengeful act was justified. But Milton has raised enough doubts along the way that the friends' conclusions are not entirely persuasive. In his final years, reflecting on all that had happened—the civil wars, the death of the king, the restoration of monarchy—Milton now seems to suggest that some situations are morally ambiguous. In *Samson*, he strikes a cautionary note. Doing the right thing and discerning God's will are not easy, but violence, even when it is a powerful temptation, is always self-defeating.

———

When *Samson Agonistes* opens, the Philistines are celebrating a holiday dedicated to their deity Dagon (half-man, half-fish), so they allow Samson a temporary reprieve from his hard labor. The blind former champion asks to be led to a quiet bank to enjoy the breeze—the "breath of heav'n fresh-blowing, pure and sweet," as he describes it (line 10). Here he sits, meditating on the many bad choices that led to his blindness and captivity. God had "motioned" Samson to begin Israel's deliverance by marrying his first wife, a Philistine woman whom Milton, like the Book of Judges, identifies only by her hometown of Timnah (line 222). When this wife was killed by her own countrymen—they set her on fire as retribution for Samson's burning the Philistines' grain and orchards—Samson reasoned that he should marry Dalila. He explains, "I thought it lawful from my former act" (line 231), and this logic is compelling: if God wanted

FIGURE 35. *Samson in Chains* from *The Poetical Works of John Milton*, 3 vols., ed. William Hayley (London, 1794–1797)

Source: Robert J. Wickenheiser Collection of John Milton, Irvin Department of Rare Books and Special Collections, University of South Carolina Libraries, Columbia, S.C.

Samson to marry a Philistine woman to help free his people, then why shouldn't Samson marry a second time for the same purpose?

But Milton never confirms Samson's reasoning, and this omission foregrounds the poem's moral ambiguity. "What do you make of Samson's marital choice?" Milton seems to be asking at the start—and he then steps back, inviting readers to reach their own decisions. The Bible in this regard is no help: based on the few details in the Book of Judges, many biblical commentators conclude that Dalila was a concubine and never Samson's wife. The poem's readers—along with Milton's Samson—must determine on their own whether his marriage to Dalila was a terrible mistake, a missed opportunity, or a fortuitous decision that brings him to the place where he will strike down his enemies.

Milton, even more so than in *Paradise Lost* and *Paradise Regained*, is playing fast and loose with his biblical source text. He distills chapters 13–16 from the Book of Judges into a single day (into, more exactly, about seven hours) while dramatizing a scene entirely of his own invention.[14] He depicts Samson in captivity, receiving three visitors—his father, his wife Dalila, and a rowdy giant named Harapha—before being called by an officer to perform for the Philistines. Samson's friends, who have come to comfort him, arrive before everyone else and linger on stage for the duration of the poem; Milton calls them "the Chorus" after the commentators who speak and move in unison in ancient Greek drama. But the other three visitors in *Samson*—each with a different viewpoint and motive—take turns, entering successively, speaking with the former hero, then departing.

Samson's father Manoa comes first, white-haired, walking with great care. He has been working to free his son and negotiating with the Philistines to pay a ransom. But he almost does not recognize Samson in his fallen state, "Ensnared, assaulted, overcome, led bound" (line 365). Manoa recalls how his son in his glory had single-handedly "Dueled their armies . . . / Himself an army" (lines 345–46), and he cannot square that memory with the abject figure sitting on the ground outside the prison. He tells Samson to be contrite, but not too contrite. He does not want him to be a martyr, to be "self-rigorous" (line 513) and to die in captivity because, he hopes, Samson may still be able to return home: "Perhaps / God will relent, and quit thee all his debt" (lines 508–09). The "perhaps," set off by a hard line-break, underscores how tenuous the father's wish is.

Samson's second visitor is his wife, and with Dalila Milton has created something astonishing. In the Book of Judges, she plays a small but crucial role: she browbeats Samson to divulge the secret of his physical strength. As he rests with his head on her lap, she has his locks shaved. She awakens him with a final mocking taunt, announcing with feigned surprise the Philistines' assault—and then disappears entirely from scriptures (Judges 16:19–20).

But whereas Dalila's reason for betraying Samson in the Book of Judges is straightforward and base—the Philistine lords offer her 1,100 pieces of silver (Judges 16:5)—Milton boldly reimagines a Dalila moti-

FIGURE 36. *Samson and Delilah* (1609–1610) by Peter Paul Rubens. Oil on panel.
Source: Cincinnati Art Museum.

vated by love, who comes to see Samson in prison so that she can explain herself and beg his forgiveness. Dalila enters the poem like a yacht, trim and richly decorated—"Sails filled, and streamers waving, / Courted by all the winds," as Samson's friends describe her (lines 718–19). The pungent scent of her perfume announces her approach, and in her wake glides a group of confidants, a train of young unmarried women, also presumably bedecked and ornate. Dalila says she never meant to cause Samson any harm, and she did not betray him for money. She was worried that he might leave her, as he had his first wife, and she was assured that he would not be hurt:

> Hear what assaults I had, what snares besides,
> What sieges girt me round, ere I consented;
> Which might have awed the best resolved of men,
> The constantest to have yielded without blame.
> It was not gold, as to my charge thou lay'st,
> That wrought with me: thou know'st the magistrates
> And princes of my country came in person,
> Solicited, commanded, threatened, urged,
> Adjured by all the bonds of civil duty
> And of religion, pressed how just it was,
> How honorable, how glorious to entrap
> A common enemy, who had destroyed
> Such numbers of our nation: and the priest
> Was not behind, but ever at my ear,
> Preaching how meritorious with the gods
> It would be to ensnare an irreligious
> Dishonorer of Dagon: what had I
> To oppose against such powerful arguments?
> (lines 845–62)

Certainly, this defense sounds reasonable. Milton in developing the brief sketch of Dalila in Judges rebuts the long misogynist tradition of treating her as a malevolent temptress. Instead, he has conceived a well-intentioned but misguided figure who elicits readers' sympathy, not contempt. How could Dalila have resisted the commands and appeals of her country's priest, princes, and magistrates? Naturally, she still loves her husband, and naturally she feels terrible about what her government has done to him. Dalila offers to intercede with the Philistine lords on Samson's behalf. Maybe she can get him released. Maybe he can come to live with her, "where my redoubled love and care / With nursing diligence, to me glad office, / May ever tend about thee to old age" (lines 923–25).

Samson refuses her entirely. He is convinced that Dalila is motivated by malice, not repentance. If she had loved him, he says, she would have known that her betrayal would inspire his infinite hatred. She should have put her affection for him above her country, even though he himself had married her for political reasons. Yes, he admits, he was weak, and he is to blame for revealing the secret of his strength, for giving up his "fort of silence" (line 236). But, he insists, she was weak, too, for not putting first her love for him and the obligations of matrimony.

Dalila, abashed and disheartened, asks Samson if she can approach and just touch his hand. After all of her explanations and pleading, after trying and failing repeatedly to persuade him of her abiding affection, she just wants the slightest contact—less than a kiss, less than an embrace, even less than a handclasp. But Samson is enraged, and he lashes out: "Not for thy life, lest fierce remembrance wake / My sudden rage to tear thee joint by joint" (lines 952–53). If Dalila in her final, humble request sounds genuine and caring, Samson in his refusal sounds cruel and savage.

Maybe, though, Dalila cannot be trusted. She responds to Samson's angry repulse with an outburst of her own, condemning Samson and taking comfort in the fame that she has earned among her own people: "In my country where I most desire, / In Ecron, Gaza, Asdod, and in Gath / I shall be named among the famousest / Of women, sung at solemn festivals" (lines 980–83). Readers must decide whether Dalila's parting tirade exposes what she had been thinking all along, or whether she lays into Samson because she feels lost and manipulated, and he so badly embarrasses her.

The Chorus believes that this, at last, is the real Dalila and that her earlier appeals were a façade, that she came to gloat about her victory.

"She's gone," they tell Samson, "a manifest serpent by her sting / Discovered in the end, till now concealed" (lines 997–98). This view of Dalila would certainly fit with the brief account of her in Judges and Milton's own most reprehensible ideas about a hierarchy of the sexes that seep elsewhere into his writings. Yet Samson's misogynistic friends are hardly objective. They often sound unreliable, in part because they speak in such ungainly verse:

> It is not virtue, wisdom, valor, wit,
> Strength, comeliness of shape, or amplest merit
> That woman's love can win or long inherit;
> But what it is, hard is to say,
> Harder to hit,
> (Which way soever men refer it)
> Much like thy riddle, Samson, in one day
> Or seven, though one should musing sit. (lines 1010–17)

Samson's friends are saying here that women are as mysterious as the riddle he posed at his first wedding, which would have been difficult to answer regardless of whether a person had "one day / Or seven." But these are some of the least musical lines that Milton ever wrote. And the dogged rhyme of *wit, merit, inherit, hit, it,* and *sit*—interrupted by *say-day*—makes the speech sound even clumsier, an unlikely lumbering form for Milton to convey his personal feelings. By the time he wrote *Paradise Lost,* Milton had grown disenchanted with the "jingling sound of like endings" and the "troublesome . . . bondage of rhyming"; it is doubtful that he would now resort to rhyme—and such poor rhymes and meter—to express himself through the Chorus.[15]

But Milton again refuses to offer a straightforward moral judgment about the Chorus or Dalila as she exits. He seems to convey the perhaps frustrating point that the truth is not always clear-cut and that knowledge is sometimes partial—that is, both incomplete and biased. Of course, Milton sided with Samson's God over the Philistines' Dagon, but who is to say whether Samson or Dalila is wholly right in their exchange? During the civil wars, Milton had believed that God was on the side of the commonwealth—that the monarchy was corrupt and that his republican cause was righteous—but then Cromwell had become Lord Protector, the revolution had foundered, and Charles II had returned to England. Milton, like Samson, must have wondered at times why God had abandoned him, and his confidence in his own actions must have wavered. If in *Areopagitica* he compared England with Samson, perhaps near the end of his life he was also still thinking of the Hebrew hero as a national symbol. Maybe he and the commonwealth government had, like Samson, also shown poor judgment and now they, too, were being punished.

———

This sense of doubt is nowhere more conspicuous than at the end of the poem. Blind and in chains, Samson is led into a spacious, semicircular theater. The choice of an amphitheater for the setting of Samson's final act is another of Milton's innovations; in the Bible, it is merely a "house," sometimes glossed as a "temple" (Judges 16:27–30). In Milton's poem, the theater is open on one side, with tiers of covered seats facing the stage. There sit hundreds of Philistines, according to their rank—"Lords, ladies, captains, counsellors, or priests, / Their choice nobility and flower" (lines 1653–54). Behind the stage are banks and benches, under the open sky, for the poorer spectators.[16]

Samson is newly humiliated, having been made to don a Philistine uniform, and his captors are taking no chances: he is brought onto the stage by armed guards, part of a grand military procession. Musicians play pipes and bang on tambourines, accompanied by archers, spearsmen, and mounted and armored soldiers. The spectacle resembles the kind that Charles II enjoyed upon his return to England, as if Milton after the Restoration were allying the Philistines with the king's party and associating the captive Samson with the Good Old Cause, the name given retrospectively to the lost revolution. The court of Charles II embraced just such displays and entertainments. In good weather and especially on summer evenings, the court processed or rode in their carriages through St. James Park, or dined in their barges as they floated along the River Thames, accompanied by musicians and other professional performers.[17]

As Samson enters the theater, the Philistines erupt in cheers, delighted to see "their dreadful enemy their thrall" (line 1622), and they praise Dagon for their victory. Samson performs a series of demeaning feats— "To heave, pull, draw, or break . . . / All with incredible, stupendious force" (lines 1626–27)—as his captors sit entranced. The ladies and lords cheer and clap. The great hero has been reduced into a carnival show.

It is during the intermission that Samson has his revenge, and it is both tragic and spectacular. Samson says he feels overtired and asks to lean against the main pillars holding up the theater's arched roof. He stands for awhile, maybe catching his breath or collecting his thoughts, staring down, his head bowed—"as one who prayed, / Or some great matter in his mind revolved" (lines 1637–38). But again Milton does not tip his hand: he never explains whether Samson was actually praying to God or merely standing in a prayerful pose. Earlier, when Samson was being led in to the theater, he told his friends that he began to "feel / Some rousing motions in me which dispose / To something extraordinary my thoughts" (lines 1381–83), but he added, "The last of me or no I cannot warrant" (line 1426). Clearly, Samson himself was uncertain; he did not know beforehand that he would pull down the theater and kill himself. Even his reference to "rousing motions" is vague; whether they were inspired by God or merely mark a change in Samson's outlook, Milton never says.

Now, as the former champion stands between the pillars and puts a hand on each, he speaks his final words:

> Hitherto, lords, what your commands imposed
> I have performed, as reason was, obeying,
> Not without wonder or delight beheld.
> Now of my own accord such other trial
> I mean to show you of my strength, yet greater.
>   (lines 1640–44)

All of these details are relayed secondhand by a messenger who survives the collapse and subsequently reports to Manoa and the Chorus; Milton denies readers direct access to Samson's final moments so that his specific thoughts and hopes must remain uncertain. The phrase "of my own accord" distinguishes Samson's act of killing his enemies from the feats of wonder that he just performed at the command of the Philistines. But the phrase could also mean that Samson murdered the Philistines in the theater on his own, without divine prompting. Milton is directly confronting the moral ambiguity of such acts of destruction. Certainly freeing the enslaved Israelites was righteous, but should freedom be purchased at such a high price? Would a just god ever condone large-scale destruction?

Milton after the Restoration seems unsure. That he continued to defend free will and personal liberty in his poetry and prose indicates that he was, like Samson, still ready for a fight, still willing to take up the charge and support the Good Old Cause. Just before this scene, while Samson is imprisoned, his third visitor rushes in to the poem like a storm—the giant Harapha, a character of Milton's own creation—and Samson quickly turns bilious. Harapha has come to gawk at and ridicule the former champion; he wishes, he says, that he could have met Samson on the battlefield, but he now disdains fighting him because he is enslaved and blind. Samson dares the giant to step closer. He is ready to meet Harapha's challenge and wants to pit his god against the giant's. "Go baffled coward," Samson taunts, as Harapha slinks away, "lest I run upon thee" and "with one buffet lay thy structure low, / Or swing thee in the air, then dash thee down / To the hazard of thy brains and shattered sides" (lines 1237–41).

This type of combativeness must have sounded appealing to Milton and many of his readers in 1671 as they continued to adapt to life under a restored monarchy and mourned the loss of the commonwealth. Even enslaved and in prison, Samson remains defiant, exposing the emptiness of Harapha's bluster and refusing to despair and blame God. Like Milton himself in his later years—blind, in poor health, but writing some of his greatest works—Samson "Revives, reflourishes, then vigorous most / When most unactive deemed" (lines 1704–5).

But Milton near the end of his life also seems to have been skeptical of Samson's belligerence. He amplifies the scale of Samson's violence from the Book of Judges, adding a list of the groups who perished, exempting

only the crowd of common people who stood outside. Everyone else—
including, presumably, Dalila and the giant Harapha—is crushed:

> He tugged, he shook, till down they came and drew
> The whole roof after them, with burst of thunder
> Upon the heads of all who sat beneath,
> Lords, ladies, captains, counsellors, or priests,
> Their choice nobility and flower, not only
> Of this but each Philistian city round,
> Met from all parts to solemnize this feast. (lines 1650–56)

Milton in the scene underscores both the potency and tragedy of
Samson's "horrible convulsion" as the Nazarite topples the theater's roof
and kills hundreds of people (line 1649). Manoa's initial reaction seems
apt; he describes Samson's final action as "dreadful" (line 1591). Even
as Samson's father and friends try to rally and to look at his death more
hopefully—the Chorus ultimately concludes that it is "dearly-bought . . .
yet glorious" (line 1660)—Milton lingers on their pain and sorrow. When
Manoa asks Samson's friends to help him find his son's body among the
ruins and "wash off / The clotted gore" (lines 1727–28), it hardly sounds
heroic.

Decades earlier, while still a teenager, Milton in "On the Death of a
Fair Infant" had compared a child's passing to being kissed by winter.
At the end of *Samson Agonistes*, he again resorts to seasonal imagery,
but now it is a parent's fragile hope for his child that has been destroyed
by the cold fact of his son's death: Manoa's "windy joy" for his son's release from prison "proves / Abortive as the first-born bloom of spring /
Nipped with the lagging rear of winter's frost" (lines 1574–77). Samson's
father puts on a brave face and tries to rationalize his son's sacrifice, but
Milton understood the father's inconsolable ache. Manoa in the poem's
final lines insists on finding Samson's body. He wants to take his son with
him, to bring him

> Home to his father's house: there will I build him
> A monument, and plant it round with shade

FIGURE 37. *Samson in Dagon's Temple* (1866). Illustration by Gustave Doré.

> Of laurel ever green, and branching palm,
>
> With all his trophies hung, and acts enrolled
>
> In copious legend, or sweet lyric song. (lines 1733–37)

Here Manoa seems to seek comfort in both the ritual of burial and the act of writing, but his emphasis on ownership along with the emotional distance he tries in vain to insert by using the third person—not just "home" but "home to his father's house"—hints at the pain and deep-seated love of a parent trying to cope with the loss of a child.

If Samson's final act of destruction symbolizes the violent revival of England's revolution—and it is sometimes read that way—Milton's dramatic poem is not a straightforward celebration of revenge and resistance. If Milton meant to endorse Manoa and the Chorus's hopeful spin on Samson last act, the poet's heart just was not in it. "Milton Agonistes" seems an accurate gloss on the text, as he, too, was grappling with doubt, with the difficulty of knowing God's will and determining the right thing to do. The author seems both repulsed and fascinated by his poem's protagonist.

———

After Samson's death and the destruction of the Philistines, *Samson Agonistes* concludes quietly, not triumphantly. The eloquent meditation at the end of the poem resonates in part because it comprised, so far as we know, Milton's final words in his final poem. Here, in a fourteen-line speech that teeters on the brink of a sonnet, Samson's friends reassert their faith in God while stressing both the mystery of divine power and the doubt that God's unsearchableness provokes:

> All is best, though we oft doubt,
>
> What th' unsearchable dispose
>
> Of highest wisdom brings about,
>
> And ever best found in the close.
>
> Oft he seems to hide his face,
>
> But unexpectedly returns

And to his faithful champion hath in place
Bore witness gloriously; whence Gaza mourns
And all that band them to resist
His uncontrollable intent;
His servants he with new acquist
Of true experience from this great event
With peace and consolation hath dismissed,
And calm of mind, all passion spent. (lines 1745–58)

Recalling Aristotle's ancient theory of tragedy, the Chorus claims to have achieved release from their emotions—to have obtained a *catharsis*—and to have acquired "true experience" from the "great event" of Samson's destruction. The final description of "With peace and consolation . . . / And calm of mind, all passion spent" is a beautiful phrase that might describe both the effect of great art and the acceptance of mortality. But these lines, as with the bulk of the poem, are also ambiguous: Is the Chorus emphasizing the doubt that comes with an aloof and unknowable God—whose intent is "uncontrollable" and who "oft . . . seems to hide his face"? Or does the Chorus's willful conclusion convincingly reassure readers that "all is best" and that God always returns gloriously?

Regardless of how the poem's concluding speech is interpreted, any new understanding that Samson's friends and father achieve was necessarily short-lived. As Milton's readers would have known, Samson's final act was ultimately a failure: the Israelites were not freed by his destruction of the theater and the death of so many Philistines. Saul would subsequently be crowned king of Israel and continue the same battle, and as part of this war David would famously fight and defeat Harapha's son, the Philistine giant Goliath.

Earlier in the poem, Samson had recalled how, long ago, the Israelites did not take advantage of his victory at Ramath-Lechi; they refused to seize the strategic opportunity that his military achievement gave them, and so they failed to overthrow their captors. His people, he explains, had grown corrupt in their servitude and had begun to "love bondage more than liberty, / Bondage with ease than strenuous liberty" (lines 270–71). Milton in the 1660s and 1670s must have regretted that his own people also lacked the courage to hold on to the liberty that had been briefly won in the war years. They, too, had apparently come to love the bondage that came with absolute monarchy. On the eve of the Restoration, he passionately implored his country not to revert to kingship, which he described as "a Lent of Servitude" and a "common enemy, gaping at present to devour us" (YP VII: 408, 331).

———

This is also the message at the heart of Milton's *The History of Britain*, a more than 300-page prose narrative of his country's ancient past that he published in 1670, the year before *Paradise Regained* and *Samson Agonistes*. Milton probably began researching and writing his history more than twenty years earlier, shortly before the start of the Second Civil War, when Charles I was handed over to Parliament for custody. But the responsibility of serving as Secretary for Foreign Tongues temporarily forced Milton to lay the book aside, and he only took it up again in the final years of the commonwealth, completing it a decade later, after Charles II assumed the throne and Milton suddenly found himself with more time on his hands.

The *History* begins with Britain's mythic past, the founding of the nation as a new Troy by the Trojan Brutus, and it then progresses through the line of British monarchs who descended from King Arthur. It concludes with the Battle of Hastings, the conflict in 1066 in which the Norman Army defeated the Anglo-Saxons. But far from a straightforward, objective account of ancient British history, Milton's book—like *Samson Agonistes*—clearly reflects his nation's recent political upheaval. In a telling digression on Parliament—redacted in 1670 and first published separately eleven years later—Milton bemoans the legislature's failure to hold on to the liberty gained during the civil war. It is a topical complaint that highlights how many of the other episodes in his narrative of antiquity also focus on the themes of incompetent monarchs, corrupt clerics, and decadent aristocrats.[18] He concludes the book somewhat abruptly, unwilling (he says) to detail more about the "misery and thralldom" of his ancestors and with a warning against "like Vices" and "like Calamities" (YP III: 403).

One year later in *Samson Agonistes* Milton was sorely tempted to solve his nation's backsliding by resorting to violence, and he chose to write a story of a blind former champion who rallies yet once more, who remains defiant and tries to do something heroic, even if it means enacting whole-sale slaughter and sacrificing his own life.

Readers of *Samson Agonistes* in 1671, would have turned to the end of the book and discovered one last challenge. There on the last page is a standard list of "Errata," the minor printing mistakes discovered after the text had been typeset. But on the opposite page, on the penultimate leaf, is something that occurs in no other seventeenth-century book: an "Omissa," with new material conceived after the book's printing had started.[19] Here Milton adds ten extra lines of verse along with detailed instructions for readers to insert the new text in the scene where Manoa and Samson's friends listen, unaware, to the terrible sounds of Samson, offstage, murdering the Philistines.[20] Before the messenger arrives and explains what has happened, Samson's friends in the poem's extra lines now wonder whether Samson has miraculously regained his sight. Maybe he is "dealing dole among his foes, / And over heaps of slaughter'd walk his way." They remind Manoa that God "wrought things as incredible / For his people of old" and, they add, "to *Israels* God / Nothing is hard."

Manoa, though, is of two minds in the added text: God "can I know, but doubt to think he will; / Yet Hope would fain subscribe, and tempts Belief." Here is Milton one last time entertaining an alternative ending— for his poem, for his nation, and for himself. What if Samson could regain his sight, defeat his enemies, and walk away? For a blind poet in his sixties, for a writer suffering from gout who now found it difficult just to walk around his beloved city, this more satisfying vision of revenge and power remains doubtful but tempting, both bracketed off as an afterthought at the end of the poem and yet more prominent because it appears here sep-arately. And once again Milton invites his readers to read actively and to make their own decisions. This final violent vision can be realized only if readers lend their guiding hands, insert the missing lines, and help com-plete Milton's last poem.

TEN

Surviving Disaster
"By small / Accomplishing great things"

MILTON MIGHT HAVE BEEN PUTTING the final touches on his epic in the summer of 1666 when some 436 square acres of London were desolated by fire. He probably wrote the bulk of *Paradise Lost* earlier, between 1658—shortly after the death of his second wife, as the revolution was collapsing around him—and 1665, five years after the restoration of the king, when he gave a draft of the poem to his friend and former pupil Thomas Ellwood.[1] But Milton did not obtain a publisher and sign a contract until two years later, in April 1667, and he must have been tinkering with his long poem in the many intervening months. We know that he continued to make small changes in Book 1 between the surviving manuscript—the copy given to the printers—and the first publication, and he revised the poem again for a reprint of the first edition, then revised it again for the second edition.

Milton spent only half of his time during these years writing the epic. Family and other projects demanded his attention, and of course blindness and poor health slowed his progress. He also struggled mightily to

meet his own exacting standards. He said he felt most inspired between
the autumnal and vernal equinoxes, in the fall, winter, and spring. It was
then, he told his nephew, that "his Vein . . . happily flow'd."[2] It is not
surprising that within the epic he would imagine Paradise as not having
summer. Only as part of the punishment for Adam and Eve's sin does God
create "decrepit winter" and "scorching heat" (Book 10, lines 655, 691).

The summer of 1666 had been especially punishing and hot. While
Milton would have been anticipating the renewed poetic creativity that
usually came to him in late September, most Londoners were just waiting
for cooler temperatures and the rain that they would surely bring.[3] The
city's lack of rain also meant that its wells and springs were dangerously
low, so that when a fire broke out on Sunday, 2 September, around 2:00
a.m.—a blaze that spread rapidly through London's dried-out, timbered
structures and became known as the Great Fire—attempts to douse the
flames were initially hobbled.

The fire began modestly, in a bakery in a narrow street called Pudding
Lane, lined mostly with basket makers and butcher shops.[4] The baker's
neighbors, suddenly awake and standing in small groups to watch the
spectacle, took the precaution of removing prized possessions from their
homes and piling them carefully along the opposite side of the road. But
there was no need to panic; these fires were not uncommon, and they
were typically short-lived. Only when the roof of the baker's house collapsed, sending up a shower of sparks and blazing timber, did the horror
of the situation become manifest. The wind sent burning debris into the
yard and stables of Star Inn, directly behind the bakery, and within less
than a minute, all of the hay had ignited, and the beautiful wooden structure was also ablaze. Throughout the crisis, the insistent wind blowing
from the east—the poet John Dryden called it "a Belgian wind"[5]—fanned
the fire across the city.

London would burn for four days. Witnesses described a thick, suf-
focating smoke, forming a gray arch across the sky, like a rainbow. It
extended to the western horizon and turned the sun red and faint. In the
end, the Great Fire destroyed more than eighty-seven churches, St. Paul's
Cathedral (at one time, the tallest church in Europe), most city govern-

FIGURE 38. The Great Fire of London, 1666

Source: *Cassell's Illustrated History of England* (London: Cassell, Petter, and Galpin, 1865), volume 3.

Photograph by Lori Howard, Georgia State University.

ment offices, four bridges across the Thames, and 13,000 houses and buildings, including Milton's boyhood home in Bread Street, the only property that he then owned.[6]

What made the fire's devastation even more distressing was that the city had not yet fully recovered from a virulent outbreak of the plague that occurred in the previous year. How much suffering could the people abide? It was well known that cases of the plague tended to come in waves, surging in the summer months, but the year before the Great Fire, the disease had reached epidemic proportions: almost 57,000 Londoners had died from the plague, about one-fifth of the population. Infected homes were sealed off and painted with a red cross, often dooming whole households to exposure, while people with means migrated to residences in the country until the worst of the sickness passed. Victims could be easily identified by the black, blister-like sores or buboes that erupted all over their bodies. Usually, a person died from plague within eight days.[7]

By June 1665, the year before the Great Fire, as the number of dead climbed in the weekly bills of plague, one of the city's mass graves—a large "plague pit"—was dug in Bunhill Fields near Milton's home. The novelist Daniel Defoe recalled that some people "that were infected and near their end, and delirious also, would run . . . , wrapt in blankets or rugs, and throw themselves in."[8] Milton knew he had to take prompt action. He called on his young friend Ellwood, who found Milton and his family a charming timbered cottage outside the city, in Chalfont St. Giles. It is the only one of Milton's homes that still stands today. There, twenty-three miles from London, in an unassuming village with an inn, a duck pond, a church, and a few rows of antique houses, the poet continued to write.[9]

Still, however much Milton appreciated his time in the country, he was by nature and by habit a city dweller, and the following year, in 1666, probably in February or March, he moved back to London, back to his home in Artillery Walk in the parish of St. Giles Cripplegate.[10] The Great Fire reached this neighborhood on the fourth day, its flames burning up to the city's wall and destroying Sion College and three guild halls.

It was also to Cripplegate that Charles II repaired on 5 September to lend a hand in extinguishing the Great Fire.[11] Did Milton know at the

FIGURE 39. Milton's Cottage by David Short
Source: Reproduced with the photographer's permission.

time of the crisis that he was so close to the son of the monarch whom he
had publicly castigated and whose execution he had defended at length?
The presence of Charles II was no doubt political—he wanted to assure
Londoners that he took the fire seriously—but the king also tried to make
a real difference, not just encouraging townsfolk and handing out silver
sovereigns, but carrying buckets of water and helping to destroy homes
and market stalls to create firebreaks.[12] In the latter case, a barrel of gunpowder was ignited so that wooden structures, instead of burning, fell in
on themselves, denying the flames further fuel. Surely Milton, if he knew,
would have appreciated the irony that the machinery of war, having rent
the nation in two during the preceding decade, was now being used by his
enemies to save the nation's capital.

Milton never directly recorded his thoughts about the 1665 outbreak of
plague or the Great Fire that followed, but to explain the catastrophe of the
Restoration, he resorted naturally to the language of disease. He blamed

an "epidemic madness" and "strange degenerate contagion" for inciting his fellow citizens to give up their liberty and rush back to kingship (YP VII: 422, 463). And in *Paradise Lost*, the angel Raphael similarly describes Satan's "perfidious fraud" as a "contagion spread" among the devil's followers (Book 5, line 880). When the angel Michael then catalogues a long list of literal maladies that will afflict humanity as a result of Adam and Eve's sin, he lingers on an overcrowded hospital—"sad, noisome, dark"— wherein "were laid / Numbers of all diseased" (Book 11, lines 478–80). Milton at least in this latter case was likely drawing on his firsthand observation of London's strained attempt to cope with the plague, what he calls in the poem a "wide-wasting pestilence" (Book 11, line 487).

The Great Fire, in turn, may have influenced some of the epic's incendiary imagery, especially hell's "whirlwinds of tempestuous fire" or its "ever-burning sulfur unconsumed" (Book 1, lines 69, 77). Although much of the poem would have been written before 1666, Milton's recollection of the noise and panic over those four days could have also swayed his depiction of Satan's flight through chaos, a "universal hubbub wild / Of stunning sounds and voices all confused" (Book 2, lines 951–52). Other images of wind and flame that occur when Satan enters chaos and spreads his wings "in the surging smoke" (line 928)—or when, near the end of the poem, Sin and Death witness the gates of hell "belching outrageous flame" (Book 10, line 232)—could have evoked the city's recent conflagration for the epic's first audience.

But even if Milton did not specifically have in mind any of London's tragedies as he wrote *Paradise Lost*, all three of his long poems focus to varying degrees on disasters. In many of his earlier works, he had written about individual loss—most notably, the deaths of his best friend Charles Diodati and his university classmate Edward King—but in Milton's later poems he more often turned to large-scale destruction. No doubt this choice was due to his grand ambition: he wanted to write about graver subjects, to create poems with more at stake, and he wanted to try his hand at epic and tragedy. He also wanted to emulate Virgil and Homer who had chosen oversized themes for their greatest works—the founding of Rome, the wanderings of Odysseus, and the wrath of Achilles.

Milton, though, was also shaped by his times, and having lived through war, fire, and plague, he must have come to appreciate how hardship can either wear people down or inspire individual acts of bravery. He had no interest in portraying traditional heroic subjects—

> races and games,
> Or tilting furniture, emblazoned shields,
> Impresses quaint, caparisons and steeds;
> Bases and tinsel trappings, gorgeous knights
> At joust and tournaments. (Book 9, lines 33–37)

The emphasis on the fussiness of the equipment—"quaint," "gorgeous," and "tinsel"—suggests Milton's contemptuous tone. Instead, he wished to celebrate and explore "patience and heroic martyrdom" (Book 9, line 32), by which he presumably meant the brand of heroism that the Son evinces when he volunteers to become mortal and sacrifice himself to save humanity. But Milton himself had repeatedly shown tremendous patience in the face of suffering, and he must have witnessed this same trait in many of his fellow citizens as they, too, confronted disaster and found a way to endure.

Paradise Lost is Milton's most fully developed depiction of a calamity. *Paradise Regained* is about a disaster averted, about the Son's adamant refusal to submit to Satan, and *Samson Agonistes* focuses on the uncertainty of Samson's final act but acknowledges the act's disastrous consequences: the Philistines are left with "years of mourning, / And lamentation" (lines 1712–13). *Paradise Lost* tells an even more capacious tragic narrative. When Eve reaches out and plucks the Forbidden Fruit, the whole world is made worse: "Earth felt the wound, and Nature from her seat / Sighing through all her works gave signs of woe, / That all was lost" (Book 9, lines 782–84). The same thing happens when Adam, too, disobeys God and bites into the fruit:

> Earth trembled from her entrails, as again
> In pangs, and Nature gave a second groan;
> Sky loured, and muttering Thunder, some sad drops

Wept at completing of the mortal sin
Original. (Book 9, lines 1000–1004)

The practice of transferring human emotions or qualities onto nature was a common trope in the seventeenth century—it became known as a *pathetic fallacy*[13]—but Milton seems to be describing a literal connection between humanity and the natural world. The first couple's mistake of eating the Forbidden Fruit is not just a death sentence, as God had forewarned; it is a catastrophe. Milton portrays a god who systematically lays waste to the cosmos, realigning the planets, resetting the winds to create ruinous weather—snow, hail, storms, and thunder—and recasting the sea and land to produce earthquakes, tidal waves, and volcanoes. He then turns to the animals, who had previously lived in happy concord, and mutates some of them into wild carnivores. They now devour each other and either flee from Adam and Eve or glare threateningly at the first couple.

God also allows Sin and Death to build a bridge of rock from hell to Earth, fastening it with pins and chains, as they darken the planets and dim the stars that they pass. Sin and Death think that they are erecting a monument to evil so that bad angels will have an easier route for creating waste and havoc. But God explains that he is using these "hell-hounds" to deal with the carrion and other refuse that are another consequence of the Fall—"to lick up the draff and filth / Which man's polluting sin with taint hath shed / On what was pure" (Book 10, lines 630–32).

For some readers, the extent of this tragedy surely seems extreme: it is Adam and Eve who transgress God's sole command, so why punish their descendants, ruin the natural world, and ravage the solar system?[14] Milton does not shy away from this question; he had set out to "justify the ways of God to men" (Book 1, line 26), and he has his deity announce early on that because of Adam and Eve's disobedience all of humanity must suffer and die—not just the first parents but also their "faithless progeny" (Book 3, line 96). Such a far-reaching punishment is not, strictly speaking, spelled out in Genesis; there Adam and Eve's work becomes laborious, childbirth will now be painful, and Adam will now rule over Eve (Genesis 3:16–19). But commentators traditionally gloss these verses as also applying to future generations, based in part on the Hebrew Bible, where *adam* can mean "humankind"; based on other passages in the Bible that describe human sin (such as Romans 3:23 and 5:12); and, most simply, based on the fact that we no longer live in Paradise.

Still, Milton was freely extrapolating from Genesis in describing a fallen world and debased cosmos, as if he wanted to underscore both the enormity of Adam and Eve's sin and the magnanimity of God's grace. The scale of the disaster is what Adam initially struggles to understand. He accepts that his own punishment is right and just, but he asks God, "Why hast thou added / The sense of endless woes? Inexplicable / Thy justice seems" (Book 10, lines 753–55). Adam knows that he consented to God's terms when he was created, and he reasons that he enjoyed the rewards of Paradise, so he should now accept the punishment. But, like any good father, he cannot help worrying about his children:

> Ah, why should all mankind
> For one man's fault thus guiltless be condemned,
> If guiltless? But from me what can proceed,
> But all corrupt, both mind and will depraved,
> Not to do only, but to will the same
> With me? How can they then acquitted stand
> In sight of God? (Book 10, lines 822–28)

It is here, the moment when Adam admits "*if* guiltless," that he begins to comprehend that he and Eve will now infect all of their descendants, like parents unwittingly passing along a fatal genetic anomaly. He has become one with death so all of his offspring must be "depraved" and "corrupt," not just in "mind" but also in "will." Milton does not endorse Calvin's concept of total depravity, the doctrine that individuals cannot be good unless God predestines them to be so. Instead, Milton believed in a "prevenient grace" (Book 11, line 3), as discussed in chapter 7: divine favor comes before human action and can be either freely rejected or freely embraced. Adam is reasoning that his children will refuse this grace; the first sin will contaminate all future generations, and these descendants will choose to disobey God, like their parents had.

As Adam and Eve gradually fathom the scale of these consequences, they naturally are shattered. For the first time, they feel terrible, as if the Fall has also affected them physically:

> highs winds worse within
> Began to rise, high passions, anger, hate,
> Mistrust, suspicion, discord, and shook sore
> Their inward state of mind, calm region once
> And full of peace, now tossed and turbulent. (Book 9,
>   lines 1122–26)

Of course, the couple squabbles. Adam says that Eve should not have wanted to garden alone; Eve says that he should have commanded her to stay; Adam reminds her that he just gave up immortal bliss to be with her; she says that he would have been tricked by the serpent if it had approached him. Milton offers an all too realistic portrait of two people facing a tragedy of their own making.

How to overcome such a disaster? Part of the answer for Milton was, as we have already seen, forgiveness. Adam and Eve need to stop bickering, repent, and actively seek God's grace. But the other part of Milton's answer is, more simply, persistence. The poem's final image of the couple's going forth, hand in hand, as the world stretches before them, encapsulates this ideal. They choose to go on, resolute and wiser, even though they and their world are diminished. A chastened Adam and Eve depart Paradise, not dwelling on their disobedience and all they have lost. Instead, the poem's final image is of a couple looking to the future. "With thee to go, / Is to stay here," Eve tells Adam after they have reconciled (Book 12, lines 615–16). She means that as long as they go on together they will still have paradise, regardless of where they live and regardless of the many hardships they must now face.[15] Paradise after the Fall is no longer a fixed place but, more important, it has now become associated with motion, with going onward.

The angel Michael, sent by God to remove the pair from hallowed ground and instruct them about what will now happen to their offspring, also imparts this larger lesson of happiness through perseverance. The angel looks fierce: he holds a spear, wears a purple cuirass with a sword, and strides toward the couple with a majestic gait. But Michael is more compassionate than commentators often acknowledge. He accommodates Adam and Eve's fallen, diminished capacity, forgoing "his shape celestial" and greeting the sorrowful pair in the form of a man (Book 11, line 239). He also acts with tenderness toward Adam, responding with "sweet new speech" when the first man's sight falters under the strain of the angel's foreknowledge (Book 12, line 5). Michael kindly switches from providing direct visions of the future to narrating and explaining what will occur. He summarizes more than 2,000 years of biblical history, beginning with Cain and Abel, then continuing through Noah, Nimrod, Abraham, and Moses.

The angel finally offers a hopeful vision for the newly fearful humans. Near the end of his lesson and overview, he anticipates the day when a savior—the "one greater man" from the very start of the poem (Book 1, line 4)—will purge the heavens and earth of all perversions.[16] Mostly, though, the angel emphasizes what the couple and their children must do now, in the meantime. Even as they can look forward to their ultimate salvation, they must go on, step by step, year by year, and generation by generation. In this way, they can help to effect the restoration of paradise—in part, as Eve stresses in her final lines, because their savior will be one of their descendants. But their abiding is itself the way to achieve future happiness. They must learn "true patience" and strive for a new balance, accepting that they can still experience good even though they will now also suffer. As the angel puts it, they must learn to "temper joy with fear / And pious sorrow, equally inured / By moderation either state to bear, / Prosperous or adverse" (Book 11, lines 361–64).

Michael underscores the humility of this new path for Adam, Eve, and their descendants. They should not embrace worldly values and try to become rich or powerful. Instead, they can overcome their disastrous loss through persistent small acts of virtue or kindness—or, to quote the angel again, "one bad act with many deeds well done / May'st cover" (Book 11, lines 256–57). It is a message that Adam quickly accepts, reassuring Eve that they can still achieve peace and happiness after the disaster of the Fall:

> by small
> Accomplishing great things, by things deemed weak
> Subverting worldly strong, and worldly wise
> By simply meek; that suffering for truth's sake
> Is fortitude to highest victory,
> And, to the faithful, death the gate of life. (Book 12,
>   lines 566–71)

Adam concludes these lines with a glance at the afterlife, as had Michael, but the key for humankind in the final books of *Paradise Lost* seems to be endurance—accomplishing many "small things" in the face of devastating loss—and the recognition that even these small steps represent great strides. It is an uncanny echo of Milton's own poetic enterprise in his later years, attempting (as he repeatedly put it) "to set forth / Great things by small": he wished to capture the scale and grandeur of his epic subject by describing celestial events and characters in terms of the familiar or more mundane.[17] And just as Milton found himself out of step with political and poetic fashion in his later years—a republican after the Restoration, writing an epic that did not rhyme—so Adam and Eve and their descendants should not judge their accomplishments by the world's changing standards of "strong" and "wise."

Michael makes clear the scale of the injustice that will have to be endured because Adam and Eve allowed their passions to overrule their reason. Whenever a man

> permits
> Within himself unworthy powers to reign
> Over free reason, God in judgment just
> Subjects him from without to violent lords;
> Who oft as undeservedly enthrall
> His outward freedom: tyranny must be,
> Though to the tyrant thereby no excuse.
> Yet sometimes nations will decline so low
> From virtue, which is reason, that no wrong,

But justice, and some fatal curse annexed
Deprives them of their outward liberty,
Their inward lost. (Book 12, lines 90–101)

Milton was, of course, attempting to reverse-engineer the various social
ills that he saw around him and to trace them back to the original sin in
the garden. Why are there tyrants? Milton blames the same thing that
undid the first parents: a lack of good sense. He does not justify autocratic
leaders in these lines ("to the tyrant thereby *no* excuse"), but he lays out
in stark terms the potential political consequences of obscuring or not
obeying reason: people will lose their liberty and subject themselves to
"violent lords." Milton is close here to endorsing his learned opponent
from the civil war years, Salmasius, who had denounced the trial and execution of Charles I by insisting that God has complete authority to punish
bad nations with bad rulers. Milton is offering a similar but more nuanced
argument: if people give up their reason, if they become distracted by the
pursuit of pleasure—if, say, they relinquish their civil rights by allowing
the return of monarchy or by choosing a morally bankrupt head of state—
then God's harsh judgment is "just," and the nation deserves to forfeit its
"outward liberty."

More disturbing, Milton might also be offering a divine rationale for
slavery. As Michael enumerates the consequences of the Fall, he refers
to Noah's curse, which was sometimes used as a biblical justification of
chattel slavery:

witness th' irreverent son
Of him who built the ark, who for the shame
Done to his father, heard this heavy curse,
"Servant of servants," on his vicious race. (Book 12,
    lines 101–104)

The "irreverent son" here is Ham, cursed by his father Noah after the
Flood for having looked at him drunk and naked. Noah reacts angrily,
"Cursed be Canaan [one of Ham's sons]; a servant of servants shall he
be unto his brethren" (Genesis 9:25). This curse was used to justify spe-

cifically the Canaanites' enslavement by the ancient Hebrews and, while "race" during Milton's time meant only descendants or tribe—it did not obtain its modern meaning until the eighteenth century—the curse was also used more broadly to explain the slavery of Black people, as Ham and another of his sons, Cush, were thought to be the progenitors of Black Africans.

What makes this passage so troubling is that Milton lets it pass without comment. In such an ambitious and imaginative poem, why not at least specify that Noah was referring only to the Canaanites, as did some of Milton's contemporaries who cited the same biblical text?[18] Of course, even better would have been for Michael in his exchange with Adam to condemn slavery and racism outright. But for all of Milton's interest in personal liberty—his defending divorce, free speech, religious freedom, and a more representative government than monarchy—he never published a tract or poem about racial justice, and in all of his works he says nothing directly about the horrors of enslaving and owning people as property. Thinking outside one's own customs and circumstances is admittedly difficult, but it seems reasonable to expect a great thinker such as Milton to have been more far-reaching in his sense of liberty and justice.

Instead, as a white, educated man living in seventeenth-century Europe, Milton appears to have assumed that his white identity was the norm against which other people were to be seen and measured.[19] In an early prose work about the corruption of the bishops, he makes a passing reference that seems to equate "slaves and Negro's" (YP I: 617), and within *Paradise Lost*, when he refers to indigenous people of the Americas, he uses them to describe Adam and Eve's shameful fig leaves after the Fall: "Such of late / Columbus found th' American so girt / With feathered cincture [meaning, a belt], naked else and wild / Among the trees on isles and woody shores" (Book 9, lines 1115–18). Some of Milton's contemporaries assumed that indigenous people were innocent, but Milton treats all of Adam and Eve's descendants as already fallen. Here he cannot untangle himself from European colonialism and so envisions cultural difference as a form of sinfulness.[20]

Milton's failure in such passages is all the more striking because in the final books of his epic he is charting a way for coping with humanity's most abhorrent practices, including tyranny, slavery, and colonialism. The angel Michael stresses to Adam and Eve that they and their descendants will need to work hard to combat all forms of injustice—and they will be on their own. They will have to undertake their various struggles and try to overcome all that they have lost by taking individual action, without depending on a church or other spiritual leaders for guidance. Corrupt clerics will contort and taint organized religion for "their own vile advantages" of "lucre and ambition" (Book 12, lines 510–11); Michael calls these priests "grievous wolves" (Book 12, line 508), a common metaphor in Milton's time for corrupt clergy and perhaps a jab at the Jesuits, whose society is identified by a lupine seal. As this dishonesty spreads, the angel explains, Adam and Eve's children will need to foster patience and self-reliance—to "persevere / Of Spirit and Truth," even in the face of "heavy persecution" (Book 12, lines 531–33).

This was the lesson that Milton himself had learned in taking controversial positions—in developing his own heterodox theology and eschewing English church doctrine. It was also the lesson that he learned in challenging the bishops, defending divorce, and arguing against censorship. And he learned it again after the Restoration, as he fell into disfavor, his writings were burned, and (for a time) he feared for his life.

But here at the end of *Paradise Lost* Milton was not just rehearsing a version of his own perseverance. In writing the epic, he was telling the origin story of needing to stay strong in the face of adversity. The final two books of the poem conclude with the angel Michael describing the long legacy of pain and suffering that Adam and Eve's descendants—that we—must now accept. It cannot be avoided, but it can be endured, and ultimately through virtue, patience, faith, and love it will be vanquished.

———

Decades earlier, in *A Masque Presented at Ludlow Castle*, Milton had first celebrated this same ideal of persistent virtue and virtuous persistence to commemorate the Earl of Bridgewater's installation as Lord President of the Council of Wales. The Spirit who helps to rescue the earl's three children who are lost in the dark woods praises their faith, patience, and truth; they must pass through "hard assays" to triumph over "sensual

FIGURE 40. *The Gates of Eden Open to Expel Adam and Eve* (1805).
By Moses Haughton after Johann Heinrich Fuseli.

folly and intemperance" (lines 972, 975). The Lady and her two brothers need assistance—from both the Spirit and the water deity Sabrina—but their victory is primarily one of forbearance: the Lady refuses to give in to the demon Comus and drink from his enchanted cup, and the brothers remain steadfast in their belief in their sister and themselves. "This I hold firm," the Elder Brother tells his younger sibling,

> Virtue may be assailed, but never hurt,
> Surprised by unjust force, but not enthralled,
> Yea even that which mischief meant most harm,
> Shall in the happy trial prove most glory.
> But evil on itself shall back recoil,
> And mix no more with goodness, when at last
> Gathered like scum, and settled to itself,
> It shall be in eternal restless change
> Self-fed and self-consumed; if this fail
> The pillared firmament is rottenness,
> And earth's base built on stubble. (lines 588–99)

So wrote Milton at age twenty-five, and so Milton continued to believe at the end of his life—even after blindness, war, plague, and fire. This is part of the moral of *Paradise Lost* as Satan's evil recoils on itself: he is punished when he returns to hell and is changed into the form of the serpent that he had tried to use to destroy humankind. Adam and Eve instead walk away, assaulted but not enthralled. They have fallen, but they get up and are free to live another day, making their solitary way with providence their guide, just as the Lady and her brothers in *A Masque* avoid calamity and walk on, out of the woods and into their parents' arms so that they can continue their moral and spiritual preparation.

Persistence is again the source of consolation in Milton's sonnet about a disaster that occurred just as he was beginning to undertake his epic. Sonnet 18 "On the Late Massacre in Piedmont" focuses on the slaughter in 1655 of a Christian sect living in the Italian Alps. The Waldensians (named after their founder, Peter Waldo) had brokered a treaty with the Duke of Savoy in 1561 to build a community in the Piedmont Valley, a region in northwest Italy that borders Switzerland and France. When the duke's successor, Charles Emmanuel II, attempted to force the sect's members to convert to Catholicism, they refused, moving instead to nearby villages in the region's upper valley not covered by the treaty. The new duke's response was ruthless and swift. He deployed the army, and on 24 April his men killed some 1,700 members of the sect. They were butchered—impaled, mutilated, burned alive, or thrown to their death from cliffs. As Cromwell and his republican government scrambled to respond—providing aid to survivors, seeking an international alliance, calling for a national fast as a show of support[21]—Milton turned to verse, his own small attempt to accomplish something great. His fury is there at the start of poem in a vivid image of brutal murder—the Duke's soldiers, "the bloody Piemontese," rolling "mother with infant down the rocks" (lines 7–8). Quickly, though, Milton's response evolves from a call for retributive action—"Avenge O Lord thy slaughtered saints" (line 1)—to a simple need for remembrance: he exhorts both God and his readers to "forget not" and "in thy book record their groans" (line 5). All of these demands melt away by the end of the sonnet as he expresses (most simply) a desire for survival and continuation. He concludes the poem anticipating the Waldensians' future descendants and trusting "that these may grow / A hundredfold" (lines 12–13).

Many of Milton's other poems end with a similar depiction of endurance and expectation, of a hope for overcoming something horrible or difficult—of surviving disaster or loss—and going onward with fortitude and patience. At the end of *Samson*, the champion's father and friends try to make sense of Samson's death and his dearly bought revenge as they make plans for his funeral and predict a monument being built to his valor and sacrifice. Samson's father, Manoa, imagines how "all the valiant youth" will visit and be inspired by his son's grave and how "virgins also" will come on feast days to deck the tomb with flowers (lines 1738, 1741). *Paradise Regained* also ends with a description of ongoing preparation, as the Son defeats Satan, steps out of the wilderness, and—like Adam and Eve, and like the descendants of the Waldensians and the three children in *A Masque*—continues to ready himself for the enormous tasks ahead. "Lycidas," too, which Milton had written on the death of his university classmate, ends with an image of continuity. In the final verse, Milton portrays his shepherd lad accepting at last the loss of his friend, as he faces the chill of evening and heads off to new pastures and a new day.

It is fitting that Milton's earliest masterpiece, "On the Morning of Christ's Nativity," also ends with a sense of continuation and greater things to come. There is no disaster in the ode, although Milton passingly anticipates the Passion and Crucifixion. Instead, after the newborn messiah sends all of the false gods to hell, his virgin mother lays the infant to sleep in his swaddling bands. The ode's final image is of the quiet manger as "all about the courtly stable, / Bright-harnassed angels sit in order serviceable" (lines 243–44). Even this poem, which concludes with the peaceful image of a dozing baby, pans back to disclose a throng of angels, clad in dazzling armor, prepared to act on their god's command, and eager to leap into action.

Milton in a sonnet on his blindness summed up the fortitude needed to survive disaster, whether widespread or more personal. Affectionately addressing his friend and former student Cyriack Skinner, he insists in Sonnet 22 that, despite having lost his sight three years prior, he does not "bate a jot / Of heart or hope"—meaning, he has not lost courage or confidence since going blind (lines 7–8). On the contrary, he says, he will "still bear up and steer / Right onward" (lines 8–9). This is the crucial combination that Milton repeatedly idealizes in his poetry and prose, patiently enduring and actively navigating, always pushing forward, striving to go on, and pursuing wisdom, love, and justice.

That is the lesson the angel Michael finally presents at the end of *Paradise Lost* after explaining the horrible, far-reaching consequences of Adam and Eve's disobedience. "This having learnt, thou hast attained the sum / Of wisdom," the angel says,

> only add
> Deeds to thy knowledge answerable, add faith,
> Add virtue, patience, temperance, add love,
> By name to come called charity, the soul
> Of all the rest. (Book 12, lines 575–76, 581–85)

The couple, like Milton's readers, must put into action what they have learned, but their future happiness will depend, above all, on love—"By name to come called charity," or in Latin *caritas* and in Greek *agape*. Eve is absent during this lesson, but when Adam returns to her and expects to explain what he has heard, he is surprised to find that she is awake. She tells him that she has had her own vision and already understands what Adam is going to say: "Whence thou return'st, and whither went'st, I know," she says (Book 12, line 610), and the emphatic final iamb claps the line shut, highlighting her authority and preventing Adam from voicing any objections or doubts. Compared to Adam, Eve is largely offstage in the epic's final books, but of the two, she gets the last word in the poem. She emphasizes the joys of marriage and adds the "further consolation" that, as the mother of humankind, she will play a preeminent role: "By me the promised seed shall all restore" (Book 12, lines 620, 623).

After Michael's long list of misdeeds and miscreants in Books 11 and 12, Eve's assertive and hopeful tone at the end is heartening, as if she has already accepted the angel's concluding prescription of "deeds . . . faith / . . . virtue, patience, temperance, . . . love." Milton in compiling this list of desirable traits was working closely from 2 Peter 1:5–7. But the addition of "deeds"—set off by a hard line-break and in place of Peter's "godliness" and "brotherly kindness"—is all Milton.[22] The poet is emphasizing yet once more the need to act. The pursuit of "a paradise within thee, happier far"—also an idea original to Milton—begins with consciously doing something outward (Book 12, line 587). This is how to survive disaster, and it depends ultimately on love—a universal, unconditional goodwill, affection, and commitment toward the well-being of others. It is this, as the angel says, that is the foundation of everything.

Epilogue

IN 1667, FOURTEEN MONTHS AFTER the Great Fire of London, *Paradise Lost* was published, probably in the first week of November. Milton was almost fifty-nine. That month the royalist John Denham burst into the House of Commons, grasping a sheet of paper still wet from the press. Denham was not held in the highest regard by his fellow legislators. Grey eyed, double-chinned, with long wavy hair and a small goatee—he had been appointed to oversee the building of royal residences after the Restoration, but he knew little about architecture. Also, he had recently suffered a nervous breakdown, attributed by many to his wife's death.[1]

On that autumn morning Denham must have caused a minor stir as he rushed into Parliament's gilded chamber, loping with his characteristic bent shoulders. "What have you there, Sir John?" reportedly inquired George Hungerford, Denham's fellow MP, twenty years his junior. Denham may have been ill-suited to oversee the king's new castles, but he was a writer himself, and he could readily recognize great poetry. Milton's regicide politics did not matter; his controversial position on divorce was immaterial. Denham could see at once the scale and depth of Milton's achievement. He did not hesitate, "Part of the Noblest Poem that ever was Wrote in Any Language, or in Any Age."[2]

Three Poets, *in three distant* Ages *born,*
Greece, Italy, *and* England *did adorn.*
The First *in loftiness of thought Surpass'd*
The Next *in* Majesty; *in both the* Last.
The force of Nature *coud no farther goe:*
To make a Third *she joynd the former two.*

FIGURE 41. Milton's frontispiece portrait in *Paradise Lost:*
A Poem in Twelve Books, 4th ed. (London, 1688)

Within a few years *Paradise Lost* would become a bestseller. According to the author's contract with the Stationer Samuel Simmons, Milton was to be paid £5 upfront for the epic's initial publication and an additional £5 at the end of each of the first three editions.[3] Karl Marx would later single out the terms of Milton's agreement to illustrate the concept of "unproductive labour." As part of his critique of capitalism, Marx was trying to highlight the apparent inefficiency of Milton's enormous effort and modest remuneration.[4] But Milton's payment was no small sum: about £7 in the seventeenth century could buy a good horse, and the total of £20 would have been a sizeable payout. A skilled tradesman might need the better part of a year to earn as much.[5]

More importantly, Milton's contract in itself was a major advance in the history of authors' rights and intellectual property. The agreement is the earliest one of its kind in England. Decades before Britain's first copyright law in 1709, Milton was to be compensated as the ongoing owner of his own writing.

The contract for *Paradise Lost* was signed on 27 April 1667, and (based on typical rates of production) Simmons probably finished the forty-three sheets that were needed for the first edition in November, around the same time that Denham hurried into the House of Commons regaling his colleagues and touting Milton's triumph. All of these books—some 1,300 copies—must have then sold out in just sixteen months because on 26 April 1669, in keeping with the terms of the original agreement, Simmons paid Milton a second £5 for the second edition.[6]

But it was only after Milton died that he began to achieve the poetic success that had been anticipated some thirty years earlier when, as a freshly minted graduate from Cambridge, he made such an impression in Rome and Florence. Even in his final years, he could not resist fine-tuning his masterpiece, and he published a slightly revised second edition of *Paradise Lost* in 1674, the year of his death. For this edition—the version used in all modern texts—Milton restructured his poem's ten books into twelve. He divided the original Book 7 (containing the story of creation) into Books 7 and 8, and he divided the original Book 10 (containing Michael's vision of life after the Fall) into Books 11 and 12. Why did he make these changes? Perhaps he was trying to emulate Virgil's twelve-book *Aeneid* instead of Lucan's ten-book *De Bello Civili* because the latter classical epic had become associated with royalist poems by William Davenant and Abraham Cowley.[7]

The second edition of *Paradise Lost* also included for the first time commendatory poems by Milton's friend Andrew Marvell and a physician-poet named Samuel Barrow, who both praised the epic for its scope and gravity. Marvell in his poem also sounds defensive, as if he were targeting skeptical readers, standing in a bookseller's stall and skimming the book's front pages at arm's length. Even more than a decade after the Restoration, he knew that some readers would hold a grudge against Milton for his vociferous defense of regicide. Marvell admits that he himself "misdoubt[ed]" the "intent" and that he "liked" Milton's "project, the success did fear" (lines 6, 12).[8] But, he reassures readers, Milton had treated his divine subject with the requisite respect: he "hast not missed one thought that could be fit, / And all that was improper dost omit" (lines 27–28). Marvell adds that Milton should be commended for being in his "own sense secure" and writing in blank verse—what Marvell calls a "sublime" form—instead of (like himself) following the "fashion" of trying to allure readers with "tinkling rhyme," which he compares to a pack horse laden with bells (lines 46, 50, 53).

A few years later, no less than John Dryden, England's first Poet Laureate, joined his voice to this growing chorus and penned an epigraph for the first illustrated edition of Milton's poem. Sometime in the early 1670s, Dryden had visited the blind author in Artillery Walk, at his small home with the large garden. Dryden wanted permission to adapt *Paradise Lost* into rhyme for the stage. Milton easily agreed—although, he reportedly added (with either great irony or profound humility), some of his verses were now "so Awkward and Old Fashion'd" that Dryden might not want to bother with them.[9] Published in 1674 but never performed during Milton's or Dryden's lifetime, *The State of Innocence and the Fall of Man* distills the epic's more than 10,000 lines into five acts, focusing on the drama between Adam and Eve, and removing (among other things) Satan's journey to Earth, the war in heaven, and the story of the creation.

Now, in 1688, Dryden amplified his admiration for Milton's poem. In the first illustrated edition of *Paradise Lost*, he added a brief but emphatic encomium that appeared on the book's frontispiece, directly beneath a portrait of the blind poet in his later years:

Three poets, in three distant ages born,
Greece, Italy, and England did adorn.
The first in loftiness of thought surpassed;
The next in majesty; in both the last.
The force of nature could no further go;
To make a third, she joined the former two.[10]

Surely such a tribute would have thrilled Milton, if he had been alive to read it. To think that he had not just competed with Homer and Virgil but that he might have bested them! This new edition (the epic's fourth) was signed by more than 500 members of the nobility and gentry, men of high regard who helped to finance the printing and whose names were listed at the back of the book—a conspicuous and overwhelming endorsement of Milton's accomplishment.[11]

Who could doubt the late author's growing stature? Eight biographies appeared within sixty years of his death, and both *Miltonic* and *Miltonian* entered the language within forty years of his passing. In 1737, a monument to Milton was added to the Poets' Corner in Westminster Abbey, his bust joining an already crowded choir of marble luminaries, including Chaucer and Shakespeare. In the late 1700s, street vendors in London were selling strands of hair of various hues that, they claimed, belonged to the great John Milton.[12]

But if today we find fault with Milton for his biases and arrogance, for his assumption at times that he was the smartest person in the room, some English readers in the years after his death were troubled instead by the moral tenor of his writings, by his insistent calls for toleration and personal freedom. They also questioned his audacity in rewriting scripture and disdained his affront to the sanctity of monarchy and matrimony. Even the influential eighteenth-century critic, Samuel Johnson, one of Milton's most discerning readers, loved the poetry but not the poet.

Unlike Denham and Dryden, Johnson could not see beyond Milton's rev-
olutionary politics and wrote that he found Milton to be "acrimonious,"
"surly," and "sullen."[13]

Johnson was probably reacting in part to the strength of Milton's personality. On the page, as in life, Milton was above all a teacher, striving to
instill in his readers both virtue and insight. And Milton is deeply present
in almost all of his writings, forcefully expressing his personal convictions.
He dared to imagine Adam and Eve in the garden of Eden and to portray
Satan's conflicted motives, Samson's last day in prison, and Jesus's exile
in the wilderness—but always in the service of what he believed to be the
truth. Throughout his life Milton demonstrated the power of language—
for overcoming loss, dealing with physical affliction, combating injustice,
resisting temptation, surviving disaster, and affecting political change.
And he staked his own life on this ideal: blind, in poor health, in solitude
and neglect in his later years, he aspired to transcend his own limitations,
defeats, and prejudices, continuing to work tirelessly and trying to "build
the lofty rhyme" (as he put it), to help humankind reach new understanding, and to help his readers to live freely and righteously.[14]

This book has tried to show how Milton's approach to his art was in-
timately connected to his life. He came of age in a period of deep political
divisions, and they left their mark. It was an age that required reason and
fortitude, righteous leadership and individual virtue. It was not a time
for breezy verses about a romantic dalliance, but for ethical, civic-minded
poetry and prose that would help people cope with their hardships and
regain the freedoms that were lost under Charles I's and Charles II's re-
pressive governments.

Over the ensuing centuries, Milton's legacy has been as a poet for
troubled times. He was adored by both generations of the revolution-
minded Romantics—by the likes of William Blake, Mary Shelley, William
Wordsworth, and John Keats. Shelley turned to Milton to critique the ex-
cesses of her generation. In *Frankenstein*, her young, overambitious protagonist assembles and animates a creature out of parts of cadavers only
to discover the folly of daring to defy nature's laws; Victor Frankenstein is
a combination of both Milton's God and his Satan, able to create life but

undone by vaunting pride.[15] Wordsworth also insisted on Milton's time-lessness and timeliness. He begins one of his sonnets shouting: "Milton! thou shouldst be living at this hour: / England hath need of thee: she is a fen / Of stagnant waters." Writing near the start of the nineteenth century, he saw Milton as a moral hero and called on the author of *Paradise Lost* to rescue England from its corruption and vanity, to "give us manners, virtue, freedom, power."[16]

Decades later, the novelist Mary Ann Evans (under her pen name, George Eliot) praised the continuing value of Milton's writings on education and marriage, and a few other eighteenth- and nineteenth-century women writers—Hannah More, Margaret Fuller, Margaret Collier, Phillis Wheatley—felt inspired by Milton's works and found support in his poetry for rethinking patriarchal assumptions.[17] In the twentieth century, Malcolm X first read Milton in prison. He used Milton's Satan to deprecate the evils of European imperialism: "So Milton and Mr. Elijah Muhammad," he wrote, "were actually saying the same thing."[18]

Milton's was also an important voice during the American Civil War, providing in his works the language and indignation needed for attacking the Southern revolt. Abraham Lincoln is said to have heard the rhetoric of Milton's Satan in utterances by Jefferson Davis, and Ralph Waldo Emerson praised Milton as an "apostle of freedom," launching "formidable bolts against the enemies of liberty."[19] During the tumultuous years of World War II, Milton was again ardently embraced, this time as a bastion of Christian humanism. The publication of newly annotated, scholarly editions of his complete works represented a renewed argument for individual freedom in the face of encroaching tyranny.[20] Milton has, over time, been championed especially in America and Canada as an intellectual founding father—in particular, a patron saint of the American Constitution and, perhaps, a direct influence on that document's authors.

What would Milton have thought of his status today? He despised pedantry and had special contempt when writers—such as, most notoriously, William Prynne—overstuffed the margins of their books with obscure annotations and references.[21] But certainly Milton would not have objected to the serious attention, scholarly and otherwise, that has been given to his works over the past few centuries. Translations of his prose and poetry have been published in almost every national language, including Arabic, Chinese, Farsi, Hebrew, Portuguese, Serbo-Croatian, and Urdu. He is a mainstay of university curricula, even as the canon of British writers has aptly expanded and diversified over the past decades. New books and essays continue to apply new methods to his life and writings. In the past seventy-five years, he has been historicized, psychoanalyzed, ecologized, feminized, formalized, materialized, nationalized, deconstructed, queered, postmodernized, and examined bibliographically.

Milton would have bristled, though, at some of the personal criticisms that have been leveled at him. Whenever he was attacked personally in print, he responded in kind, meeting invective with invective, derision with derision. And he had little patience with readers who utterly misconstrued his meaning. When his defense of divorce was misread as a call for licentiousness, he wrote two angry sonnets, satirizing hostile critics. Years later, he would conclude that he should have probably avoided the controversy by publishing his argument on marriage in Latin (YP IV: 610).

But Milton also thoroughly revised his first treatise on divorce after it was attacked—not changing but bolstering his position—and he published three more tracts on the same subject, all in the English vernacular, all with the hope that he could clarify his ideas and avoid future misunderstanding. Years later, he did the same thing with *The Tenure of Kings and Magistrates* and *Eikonoklastes*, publishing augmented versions shortly after the first editions. Milton could be prickly, his humor cruel, and his patience short. But he kept trying to explain himself, he kept writing and aspiring to reach—and to teach and to uplift—even an unwilling audience.

Milton also championed the right of readers to interpret books freely. This was one of the reasons that he argued for a free press: the government's interference would lead to the "dis-exercising and blunting" of people's intelligence and the "hindering and cropping" of truth and knowledge (YP II: 491–92). In his response to Charles I's *Eikon Basilike*, Milton claimed that readers should have the final say over what a writer wrote, especially the claims of their political leaders. Milton justified his own reading of Charles I's book by arguing that "in words which admit of various sense, the liberty is ours to choose that interpretation which may best mind us of what our restless enemies endeavor, and what we are timely to prevent" (YP III: 342). The year before he died, he was still urging his readers to peruse books critically, to think independently, and to "examine their Teachers themselves" (YP VIII: 435).

———

John Milton passed away at home, by all accounts peacefully, on 9 or 10 November 1674, most likely from kidney failure associated with the painful fits of gout that had been troubling him for years. Near the end, when the pain became intolerable, he tried to distract himself by singing.[22] Apothecaries did not sell pain relievers during the seventeenth century. Many people thought pain was a spiritual experience, not a physical sensation. The most widely accepted remedy was prayer.

Little is known about Milton's funeral, but many of his friends apparently attended, along with a "friendly concourse" of fellow Londoners.[23] Funerals at that time usually occurred at night, perhaps to convey an added sense of solemnity.[24] Friends and family members would have held wax torches as they rode in carriages or walked behind the cart that carried the coffin—a wavering trail of lights to accompany the soul in its ascent to the firmament.

Milton's widow had his body buried near his father's grave in St. Giles, a parish church in Cripplegate. The neighborhood still had affluent sections but had not fully recovered from nine years earlier when it was hit hard by plague.[25] Because of London's overcrowding, graves often held multiple bodies. Milton, though, had a separate site. He also was laid to rest inside the church's vault, a more sought-after—and more expensive—location than the churchyard. The service would have concluded as mourners watched his body being interred, face up so that he was ready to awaken to glorification on the Last Judgment.

Milton is no longer as revered as he had been by the Romantics, and no longer as reviled as he had been by supporters of King Charles. But he was never determined to become as famous as the Latin and Greek authors whom he so admired. In "Lycidas," he called fame "that last infirmity of noble mind" (line 71), and in his epitaph to Charles Diodati he conceded that one person should not hope for all things. Despite his abiding self-concern, he says that he could be satisfied if he were only appreciated in his own country: "Let me be forever unknown and utterly without fame in the outside world" ("sim ignotus in aevum / Tum licet, externo penitusque inglorius orbi," lines 173–74). The ideal that he held out in *Paradise Lost* was a "fit audience . . . though few" (Book 7, line 31). The word *fit* during the seventeenth century meant a well-suited group of readers, but also implied one that was adroit and intelligent.[26] Just as Milton described marriage as an apt and cheerful conversation between two spouses, and just as he hoped for a republican government that answered to its people, he wanted a reciprocal relation between an author and readers.

John Milton wrote some of the finest prose and poetry ever composed in English. His description early on of great writing as "where more is meant than meets the ear" ("Il Penseroso," line 120) was an apt prediction of his own poems' sweep and subtlety, and the impact of his writing continues to be felt in the works of both other authors and other artists. *Paradise Lost* in particular has become so deeply embedded in Western thought that when readers today try to imagine Satan or the Garden of Eden, they are likely envisioning—without even knowing it—some version of Milton's epic poem.

One of the primary lessons that Milton can still teach us is his unshakeable belief in free will and personal responsibility. At the core of so many of his works is this principle, a radical argument for self-determination. He combined this belief with a commitment to a collaborative social contract on which subsequent, more inclusive calls for liberty have been based. Milton himself, as we have seen, was a flawed person. But he repeatedly tried to embrace in his daily life the religious and political ideals that he wrote about. He worked hard, sacrificed much, and never backed down from controversial ideas or his devotion to written expression, rendered with both passion and precision. He hoped for nothing less than the same unfailing dedication from us.

ACKNOWLEDGMENTS

I AM ESPECIALLY GRATEFUL TO Erica Wetter, who showed faith in this book early on, and I am indebted to the entire team at Stanford, in particular Caroline McKusick, Gigi Mark, and Catherine Mallon. I also must thank Pete Simon, who first encouraged me to pursue this project when we met on a bright January afternoon at a conference in Vancouver.

In the field of Milton and early modern studies, I have benefited from the insights of a wide range of scholars, many of whose works I cite directly in the preceding pages and many more whom I am pleased to count as friends. A necessarily incomplete list includes Sharon Achinstein, Cedric Brown, Gordon Campbell, Gregory Chaplin, Thomas Corns, Karen Edwards, Stephen Fallon, Stanley Fish, Wendy Furman-Adams, John Hale, Edward Jones, Jason Kerr, Laura Knoppers, John Leonard, David Loewenstein, Nicholas McDowell, Catherine Gimelli Martin, Joad Raymond, Elizabeth Sauer, William Shullenberger, Nigel Smith, Paul Stevens, and Joseph Wittreich.

I am grateful to Dennis Danielson for reading an early draft of the proposal for this book and for offering enthusiastic support and sage advice. In the later stages, I benefited from the comments of two anonymous readers, whose questions and observations helped me to make significant improvements. I am also fortunate to teach and work in a supportive department at Georgia State University. I am thankful for colleagues, past and present, whose contributions have helped to refine my thinking and writing. In particular, Randy Malamud and Paul Schmidt graciously read several chapters and made keen suggestions.

My largest intellectual debt remains to John Rumrich, with whom I first studied Milton more than twenty years ago at the University of Texas in Austin and who has since become a great friend.

The research for this book was conducted over many years at the Harry Ransom Center, the British Library, and the New York Public Library. I am grateful to the staffs for their kindness and expertise. For the book's illustrations, I repeatedly relied on the generosity and practical assistance of several people, most notably, Ming Aguilar and Lisa Caprino of the Huntington Art Museum; Lori Howard of Georgia State University; Susanna Coit of the Perkins School for the Blind; and especially Elizabeth Sudduth of the Irvin Department of Rare Books and Special Collections at the University of South Carolina. When one image proved troublesome, Thomas Corns, Gordon Campbell, John Hale, and Jason Kerr quickly came to my aid.

Finally, I wish to thank my wife Shannon, who read this book many times in its various stages over the years. She offered wise advice, asked smart questions, and offered timely reassurance. She glimpsed before I did what the book might become. I am also grateful to our daughter Audrey for the countless intangible ways that she has contributed to the joy of writing this book. She has been listening to and thinking about Milton her whole life.

NOTES

CPEP   *The Complete Poetry and Essential Prose of John Milton*, ed. William Kerrigan, John Rumrich, and Stephen M. Fallon (New York: Modern Library, 2007).

Campbell and Corns Gordon Campbell and Thomas N. Corns, *John Milton: Life, Works, and Thought* (Oxford: Oxford University Press, 2008).

Chronology   Gordon Campbell, *A Milton Chronology* (New York: St. Martin's, 1997).

CIM   Stephen B. Dobranski, *The Cambridge Introduction to Milton* (Cambridge: Cambridge University Press, 2012).

Context   *Milton in Context*, ed. Stephen B. Dobranski (Cambridge: Cambridge University Press, 2010; rpt. 2015).

DDC   *Milton's De Doctrina Christiana* (*On Christian Doctrine*) in vol. VIII of *The Complete Works of John Milton*, ed. John K. Hale and J. Donald Cullington (Oxford: Oxford University Press, 2012).

EL   *The Early Lives of Milton*, ed. Helen Darbishire (London: Constable, 1932).

ELR   *English Literary Renaissance* (journal)

ELH   *English Literary History* (journal)

Lewalski, *Life*   Barbara K. Lewalski, *The Life of John Milton: A Critical Biography* (Oxford: Blackwell, 2000).

LR   J. Milton French, ed., *The Life Records of John Milton*, 5 vols. (New Brunswick, NJ: Rutgers University Press, 1949–1958).

Masson, *Life*   David Masson, *The Life of John Milton*, 7 vols. (1877–1896; New York: Peter Smith, 1946).

ODNB   *Oxford Dictionary of National Biography* (Oxford: Oxford University Press, 2016).

OED   *Oxford English Dictionary*, 3rd ed.

Parker, *Biography* William Riley Parker, *Milton: A Biography*, ed. Gordon Campbell, 2 vols., 2nd ed. (1968; Oxford: Clarendon Press, 1996).

PMLA   *Publication of the Modern Language Association* (journal)

ϒP   *The Complete Prose Works of John Milton*, gen. ed. Don M. Wolfe, 8 vols. (New Haven, CT: Yale University Press, 1953–1982).

WJM   *The Works of John Milton*, 18 vols. in 21, ed. Frank Allen Patterson (New York: Columbia University Press, 1931–1938).

INTRODUCTION

1. Aubrey in *EL* 4.

2. Alfred Tennyson, "Milton (Alcaics)," in *Alfred Tennyson*, ed. Adam Roberts (Oxford: Oxford University Press, 2000), 375.

3. Ralph Waldo Emerson, *Journals and Miscellaneous Notebooks of Ralph Waldo Emerson*, ed. William H. Gilman et al., 16 vols. (Cambridge: Belknap Press, 1960), II: 107; Margaret Fuller, *Papers on Literature and Art* (New York: Wiley and Putnam, 1846), I: 36.

4. Plato, *Laches*, in *Plato*, 10 vols., trans. W.R.M. Lamb (Cambridge, MA: Harvard University Press, 1952), IV: 46–83 (191a–201c); and see Aristotle, *Nichomachean Ethics*, trans. H. Rackham (Cambridge, MA: Harvard University Press, 1947), Book III, sections 6–9.

5. Sonnet 22, lines 8–9. All quotations of Milton's poetry, unless otherwise indicated, are taken from *CPEP*.

6. Michael Braddick, *God's Fury, England's Fire* (London and New York: Allen Lane, 2008), xxii, 389.

7. *The Parliamentary or Constitutional History of England*, ed. William Cobbett et al., 2nd ed., 24 vols. (London, 1761–1763), vol. IV, column 162.

8. Parker, *Biography*, II: 1089, n43.

9. *Paradise Lost*, Book 7, line 25.

10. *A Masque Presented at Ludlow Castle*, lines 221–22.

CHAPTER ONE: THE POWER OF LANGUAGE

1. *Remarkable Passages, or, A Perfect Diurnall of the Weekly Proceedings in Both Houses of Parliament*, 5–12 Sept. 1642, A2v-A3r.

2. Lawson Nagel, "'A Great Bouncing at Every Man's Door': The Struggle for London's Militia in 1642," in *London and the Civil War*, ed. Stephen Porter (London: Macmillan; New York: St. Martin's, 1996), 65–88.

3. See the facsimile of the Trinity College Manuscript in vol. 1 of Harris Francis Fletcher, ed., *John Milton's Complete Poetical Works*, 4 vols. (Urbana: University of Illinois Press, 1943–1948), 396. The second note in the manuscript has been struck through for some reason.

4. Phillips in *EL* 62.

5. *The Complete Prose Works of John Milton*, 8 vols., ed. Don M. Wolfe et al. (New Haven, CT: Yale University Press, 1953–1982), I: 821; hereafter cited as YP (for "Yale Prose"). I have modernized the spelling in Milton's prose.

6. Peter Berresford Ellis, *The Great Fire of London* (London: New English Library, 1976), 16.

7. Archer, "London," *Context*, 363.

8. Phillips in *EL* 62.

9. Neil Hanson, *The Great Fire of London in That Apocalyptic Year, 1666* (Hoboken, NJ: Wiley, 2002), 13.

10. John Earle, *Micro-cosmographie* (London, 1628), I6r-K1r.

11. Ellis, *The Great Fire of London*, 16.

12. Walter Thornbury, *Old and New London*, vol. 1 (London: Cassell, Petter and Galpin, 1878), 32–53.

13. Phillips in *EL* 60.

14. Aubrey in *EL* 12; Phillips in *EL* 60.

15. Phillips in *EL* 72; Parker, *Biography*, 259.

16. Phillips in *EL* 68.

17. Joseph Moxon, *Mechanick Exercises of the Whole Art of Printing (1683–4)*,

ed. Herbert Davies and Harry Carter, 2nd ed. (London: Oxford University Press, 1962), 13; and Marjorie Plant, *The English Book Trade: An Economic History of the Making and Sale of Books*, 2nd ed. (London: Allen and Unwin, 1965), 248–49.

18. Campbell and Corns 20.

19. *WJM* 12: 18–19.

20. Aubrey in *EL* 10.

21. "Educating Shakespeare: School Life in Elizabethan England," The Guild School Assoc., Stratford-upon-Avon, 2005 (www.likesnail.org.uk/educating/kings.htm).

22. Elegy 1, line 51.

23. Aubrey in *EL* 2.

24. YP I: 810–12.

25. Thomas W. Ross, "Expenses for Ben Jonson's 'The Masque of Beauty,'" *The Bulletin of the Rocky Mountain Modern Language Association* 23.4 (1969): 169–73.

26. It is also possible that Milton's father put in a good word for his son. Milton senior, an investor in Blackfriars Theater, would have moved in some of the same circles as Lawes, and he could have recommended his precocious middle child, promising that his son could certainly write an enchanting musical drama.

27. Masson, *Life*, I: 608. The performance of Milton's masque took place in the castle's great hall where, 150 years earlier, the young Prince of Wales had been crowned Edward V before embarking on his fateful journey to London that ended with the murder of him and his brother in the Tower of London—perhaps by their treacherous uncle, Richard III.

28. Harry Ransom Center, shelfmark Pforz. 714.

29. I use "English church" and "Church of England" interchangeably to describe the national religion during Milton's life. "Anglican" was used to refer to the church in the sixteenth century, but it did not become common usage until 300 years later.

30. See YP I: 283.

31. Aubrey in *EL* 6.

CHAPTER TWO: PERSONAL LOSS

1. The upper-case *S* in Scrivener signifies that Milton's father was not just a practicing scrivener but a formal member of the livery guild, the Worshipful Company of Scriveners.

2. *Camdeni insignia* (London, 1624).

3. Quoted in Masson, *Life* I: 163.

4. *WJM* XII: 21.

5. Quoted in Masson, *Life* I: 162, 163.

6. *WJM* XII: 25.

7. Gregory Chaplin, "The End of Friendship," in *Political Turmoil: Early Modern British Literature in Transition, 1623–1660*, ed. Stephen B. Dobranski (Cambridge: Cambridge University Press, 2019), 253–70.

8. Elegiacs are couplets consisting of a line of hexameter and a line of pentameter. Here "elegy" describes only the meter; it does not mean that the poems were sad.

9. Stow, *A Survey of London*, ed. Charles Lethbridge, 3 vols. (Oxford: Clarendon Press, 1908–1927).

10. The residents included a girdle maker, a milliner, and a maker of lace. See Campbell and Corns 8.

11. At the time of his death, Charles was living with his sister in the district of Blackfriars, a fashionable residential part of London's inner city most famous for the theater of the same name where a young Shakespeare had written and performed. See "Diodati, Charles," in *ODNB*; and Masson, *Life* II: 82–83.

12. Quoted in Masson, *Life* I: 163.

13. Phillips in *EL* 62. In his nephew's more formal phrasing, Milton would "drop into the Society of some Young Sparks of his Acquaintance" with whom "he would so far make bold with his Body, as now and then to keep a Gawdy-day" (that is, a holiday).

14. Richardson in *EL* 229; and Wotton's letter to Milton in the 1645 *Poems*, E4r-E5r.

15. See Milton's letter to Lukas Holste, 30 March 1639, in YP I: 333–36; Edward Chaney, *The Evolution of the Grand Tour: Anglo-Italian Cultural Relations Since the Renaissance* (London: Frank Cass, 1998); and Estelle Haan, "England, Neo-Latin, and the Continental Journey," in *Political Turmoil: Early Modern British Literature in Transition, 1623–1660*, ed. Stephen B. Dobranski (Cambridge: Cambridge University Press, 2019), 322–38.

16. YP I: 333–36; and Margaret Byard, "'Adventrous Song': Milton and the Music of Rome," in *Milton in Italy: Contexts, Images, Contradictions*, ed. Mario A. Di Cesare (Binghamton: NY: Medieval and Renaissance Texts and Studies, 1991), 305–28 (316).

17. *Paradise Lost*, Book 5, lines 261–66. No documents survive to corroborate Milton's visit with the famed astronomer. Much has been written on Galileo's presence in *Paradise Lost*; see, for example, Dennis Danielson, *"Paradise Lost" and the Cosmological Revolution* (Cambridge: Cambridge University Press, 2014).

18. *Epitaphium Damonis*, Argument (*CPEP* 233).

19. John P. Rumrich, "The Erotic Milton," *Texas Studies in Literature and Language* 41.2 (1999): 128–41 (139).

20. Rumrich, "Erotic Milton," 135.

21. *CPEP* 233.

22. Lucinda M. Becker, *Death and the Early Modern Englishwoman* (Aldershot: Ashgate, 2003), 44.

23. E. A. Wrigley, R. S. Davies, J. E. Oeppen, and R. S. Schofield, *English Population History from Family Reconstitution, 1580–1837* (Cambridge: Cambridge University Press, 1997), 206–9, 307–22, 328.

24. In a companion poem offhandedly named "Another on the Same," Milton again finds humor in the carrier's death—"Ease was his chief dis-ease," he continues to pun (line 21)—but near the end of the verse he momentarily treats Hobson's passing more seriously. He imagines how the postman could have achieved immortality through his service, "his fate / Linked to the mutual flowing of the seas" (lines 30–31), if he had lived longer and continued his weekly route.

25. See Parker, *Biography*, 5.

26. Leo Miller, "On the So-Called 'Portrait' of Sara Milton," *Milton Quarterly* 15.4 (1981): 113–16.

27. Aubrey in *EL* 5. Sara Milton began wearing glasses at age thirty.

28. For information about King, I have relied on Norman Postlethwaite and Gordon Campbell, eds., "Edward King, Milton's *Lycidas*: Poems and Documents," *Milton Quarterly* 28.4 (1994): 77–111; "King, Edward," in *ODNB*; and Scott Elledge, ed., *Milton's "Lycidas"* (New York and London: Harper and Row, 1966).

29. A string of stone watchtowers had been built along the coast of north Wales; at the first sign of trouble, a fire would be lit at the top in a metal cage, and because each tower could be seen from the next, the alarm traveled quickly up and down the coast. Six years earlier, on 20 June 1631, the Irish village of Baltimore had been attacked by pirates from Turkey and Algeria, and more than 100 men, women, and children were shackled and sold into slavery. Claire Jowitt, *Pirates? The Politics of Plunder, 1550–1650* (New York: Palgrave Macmillan, 2007); and Des Ekin, *The Stolen Village: Baltimore and the Barbary Pirates* (New York: Fall River, 2008).

30. See John Pullen's poem in *Justa Edouardo King* (Cambridge, 1638), C2r-C3r.

31. Phillips in *EL* 54, 55; and see YP I: 884.

32. YP I: 314. The poem might have been the Latin verse "*Naturam non Pati Senium*" ("That nature does not suffer from old age"); no copies of the printing survive.

33. This event, which may have occurred even later, in 1631, was a *salting*, a long-standing ritual that included much drinking and joke-telling, as upper-classmen formally inducted freshmen into their ranks. If a student's humor was deemed sufficiently funny, he was rewarded with a cup of caudle, a drink made of ale, gruel, and eggs; if his wit was thought to be weak—not "salty" enough—he had to drink beer that had literally been salted. See Campbell and Corns 58–59; John Howard Marsden, *College Life in the Times of James the First* (London, 1851), 14; and Roslyn Richek, "Thomas Randolph's Salting (1627), its Text, and John Milton's Sixth Prolusion as Another Salting," *ELR* 12 (1982): 102–31.

34. See Ann Baynes Coiro, "Anonymous Milton, or, *A Maske* Masked," *ELH* 71 (2004): 615.

35. In the same year, Ben Jonson's university friends from Oxford published *Jonsonus Virbius, or the Memorie of Ben Johnson Revived by the Friends of the Muses*, and John Donne's posthumous *Poems, By J. D.* (1633) concludes with thirteen elegies by his friends and admirers. Even Milton's poems for the mail carrier are part of a rash of verses composed about Hobson's death, perhaps intended for an omnibus edition.

36. *Justa Edouardo King* (Cambridge, 1638; STC 14964), sig. I2r.

37. See Hebrews 12:26–27.

38. The quotation is taken from the headnote that Milton added to "Lycidas" when the pastoral elegy was reprinted in 1645 in his first collection of poetry.

39. See *Paradise Lost*, Book 5, lines 493–503. God later tells the Son that humankind will live on Earth, not in Heaven, "till by degrees of merit raised / They open to themselves at length the way / Up hither, under long obedience tried, / And Earth be chang'd to Heav'n, and Heav'n to Earth" (Book 7, lines 157–60). But God could also be describing the fate of a fallen humanity that will one day reside in Heaven.

40. William Winstanley, *Lives of the Most Famous English Poets* (London, 1687), O2r.

41. See Phillips, "To the Reader," in *Letters of State* (London, 1694), A2r-A3v.

CHAPTER THREE: COMBATING INJUSTICE

1. King Charles, *His Speech Made upon the Scaffold*, A3v.

2. King Charles, *His Speech Made upon the Scaffold*, A3v.

3. See *Diaries and Letters of Philip Henry, M.A.*, ed. Matthew Henry Lee (London: Kegan Paul, Trench, 1882), 12.

4. *The Secret History of the Court and Reign of Charles the Second*, 2 vols. (London, 1792), I: b4v; and Thomas Fuller, *The Church History of Britain*, 3 vols. (London, 1837), III: 189.

5. John Ruskin, *Sesame and Lilies* (New York: John B. Alden, 1883), 28.

6. Also, during these years, 30 Protestants died in prison, and 800 more fled England and went into exile. See Eamon Duffy, *Fires of Faith: Catholic England under Mary Tudor* (New Haven, CT: Yale University Press, 2009), 79.

7. For the account of Charles I and the civil wars in this chapter, I am drawing on "Charles I," in *ODNB*; Charles Carlton, *Charles I: The Personal Monarch*, 2nd ed. (London and New York: Routledge, 1995); Michael Braddick, *God's Fury, England's Fire: A New History of the English Civil Wars* (London: Allen Lane, 2008); Robert Ashton, *The English Civil War: Conservatism and Revolution 1603–1649*, 2nd ed. (London: Weidenfeld and Nicolson, 1989); Martyn Bennett, *The English Civil War, 1640–1649* (London: Longman, 1995); David Plant, "British Civil Wars. Commonwealth, and Protectorate, 1638–60," 2001–2009 (http://www.british-civil-wars.co.uk); and Cornelius Brown, *A History of Newark-on-Trent, Being the Life Story of an Ancient Town*, vol. II (Newark: S. Whiles, 1907).

8. Keith Thomas, *Religion and the Decline of Magic* (New York: Charles Scribner's Sons, 1971), 192; and David J. Sturdy, *The Royal Touch in England. European Monarchy: Its Evolution and Practice from Roman Antiquity to Modern Times* (Stuttgart: Franz Steiner Verlag, 1992), 190.

9. Years earlier, Charles had spent his honeymoon at Hampton Court. During the war, he was held there for almost three months.

10. Samuel R. Gardiner, *History of the Great Civil War, 1642–1649*, 4 vols. (London: Longmans, Green, 1894), IV: 14–19.

11. *The Moderate Intelligencer* (23–30 November 1648), 1754.

12. *Mercurius Pragmaticus* (9–16 November 1648), 65.

13. Phillips in *EL* 26.

14. The National Archives (New, Richmond, Surrey, 2018), http://www.nationalarchives.gov.uk/currency-converter/#.

15. See YP III: 150.

16. Francis F. Madan, *A New Bibliography of the "Eikon Basilike" of King Charles I*, vol. 3 of the Oxford Bibliographical Society Series (Oxford: Oxford University Press, 1950).

17. David Cressy, *Literacy and the Social Order: Reading and Writing in Tudor and Stuart England* (Cambridge: Cambridge University Press, 1980); and Gregory Clark, *A Farewell to Alms: A Brief Economic History of the World* (Princeton, NJ: Princeton University Press, 2008).

18. Quoted in Masson, *Life*, IV: 167.

19. Quoted in Masson, *Life*, IV: 167.

20. Quoted in Masson, *Life*, IV: 167–69.

21. Masson, *Life*, IV: 164.

22. Masson, *Life*, IV: 164.

23. Phillips in *EL* 70.

24. Phillips in *EL* 70.

CHAPTER FOUR: PHYSICAL SUFFERING

1. See YP IV: 307.

2. For the letter to Philaras, see YP IV: 869.

3. *CPEP* 780.

4. Excerpts of *Regii Sanguinis Clamor* are translated in YP IV: 1036–81, these quotations IV: 1048, 1049; and Masson, *Life*, IV: 456–57.

5. *Regii Sanguinis Clamor*, in Masson, *Life*, IV: 457.

6. The members were, in order, Stephen Marshall, Edmund Calamy, Thomas Young (Milton's former tutor), Matthew Newcomen, and William Spurstowe. The letter W in the seventeenth century was sometimes printed with two consecutive U's, thus "Smectymnuus" and not "Smectymnws."

7. *Regii Sanguinis Clamor*, in YP IV: 1050–51.

8. Phillips in *EL* 71.

9. Milton never names his wife in the sonnet, and he might have alternatively written it about his second wife, Katherine Woodcock.

10. *CPEP* 780.

11. John Rumrich, "The Cause and Effect of Milton's Blindness," *Texas Studies in Literature and Language* 61.2 (2019): 95–115.

12. See George B. Bartley, "The Blindness of John Milton," *Mayo Clinic Proceedings* 68.4 (1993): 395–99; John J. Ross, *Shakespeare's Tremor and Orwell's Cough: The Medical Lives of Great Writers* (New York: St. Martin's, 2012); and Eleanor G. Brown, *Milton's Blindness* (New York: Columbia University Press, 1934). Another widely held belief is that Milton's blindness may have been caused by the onset of chronic glaucoma, but the symptoms he described in his letter to Philaras do not fit this diagnosis. An inventory of Milton's widow dated 26 August 1727 includes "2 Pair Spectables [*sic*]," but it is unknown whether they had been Milton's. See *LR* V: 133.

13. Parker, *Biography*, 992–93.

14. The sonnet is most often read biographically, but "light" could also refer not to vision but to the speaker's "divine light," as in Matthew 5:15–16. See Dayton Haskin, *Milton's Burden of Interpretation* (Philadelphia: University of Pennsylvania Press, 1994).

15. The first institution in England for the education of the blind was founded in Liverpool more than 100 years later, in 1790 or 1791. See Richard Slayton

French, *From Homer to Helen Keller* (New York: American Foundation for the Blind, 1932), 99.

16. *A Full and True Narrative of One Elizabeth Middleton* (London, 1679), A4r; Keith Thomas, *Religion and the Decline of Magic*, (New York: Charles Scribner's Sons, 1971), 79–112; and Moshe Barasch, *Blindness: A History of a Mental Image in Western Thought* (New York and London: Routledge, 2001), 140–45.

17. Thomas Ellwood, *The History of the Life of Thomas Ellwood*, ed. S. Graveson, with an intro. by W. H. Summers (1714; London: Headley Brothers, 1906), 199–200.

18. Ellwood, *The History of the Life of Thomas Ellwood*, 199–200. Earlier critics, committed to the idea of the poet as a solitary genius, tried to discredit Ellwood, but there is no reason to doubt the young Quaker's account.

19. Simmons added an explanatory note in some versions of the epic's reissue: "*Courteous Reader*, There was no Argument at first intended to the Book, but for the satisfaction of many that have desired it, I have procur'd it, and withal a reason of that which stumbled many others, why the Poem Rimes not. *S. Simmons*" (A2r). Some copies omit Simmons's note, and some contain a shorter version. See Harris Francis Fletcher, ed., *John Milton's Complete Poetical Works Reproduced in Photographic Facsimile*, 4 vols. (Urbana: University of Illinois Press, 1945), II: 178–79.

20. Aubrey in *EL* 6; Jonathan Richardson in *EL* 291; and Cyriack Skinner in *EL* 33.

21. Phillips in *EL* 73.

22. "An Historical and Critical Account of the Life and Writings of Mr. John Milton," in *A Complete Collection of the Historical, Political, and Miscellaneous Works of Mr. John Milton*, 2 vols., ed. Thomas Birch (London, 1738), I: lxii.

23. See, for example, YP II: 249.

24. *The Gentleman's Magazine*, 2 (Jan. 1732), 556.

25. *Aubrey's Brief Lives*, ed. Oliver Lawson Dick (1949; rpt. Ann Arbor: University of Michigan Press, 1965), xxxi–xxxiii.

26. Hannah Woolley, *The Gentlewomans Companion; or A Guide to the Female Sex* (London, 1673), H6.

27. One recent critic has hypothesized that Milton's daughters exaggerated their father's flaws. In the years after he died, biographers sought out the three girls and eagerly hoped to light on new anecdotes or gossip about the great poet. Perhaps, according to this theory, the girls caved in to the pressure and stretched the truth about their relationship with Milton in an attempt to please these writers. See Lewalski, *Life* 399.

28. Phillips in *EL* 77.

29. Masson, *Life* V: 382; Phillips in *EL* 71, 77; and Lewalski, *Life* 320.

30. Aubrey in *EL* 3; Lewalski, *Life* 410–11.

31. See, for example, Lewalski, *Life* 408.

32. Thomas Keightley in his 1855 biography of the poet thus concluded that Milton did not neglect his daughters' education. See Aubrey in *EL* 2; and Thomas Keightley, *An Account of the Life, Opinions, and Writings of John Milton* (London, 1855), 85–91. The novelist Mary Ann Evans (whose pen name was George Eliot) was also convinced of Milton's goodwill toward the girls. She wrote that he had been "vindicated . . . from the charge of ill-conduct towards his children." See *The Westminster Review* 64 (1 Oct. 1855), 602, 603; and "Life and Opinions of Milton," in *Essays of George Eliot*, ed. Thomas Pinney (New York: Columbia University Press; London: Routledge and Kegan Paul, 1963), 154–57.

33. Richardson in *EL* 229.

34. Anne Manning, *The Maiden & Married Life of Mary Powell, Afterwards Mistress Milton* (New York: Dodd and Mead, 1899), 256, 268.

35. In one of Milton's early prose works against the bishops, he also credits the "ceaseless diligence and care of my father" as the basis for his learning and later accomplishments (YP I: 808).

36. Phillips in *EL* 78.

CHAPTER FIVE: FREE SPEECH

1. See Leo Miller, *John Milton and the Oldenburg Safeguard* (New York: Lowenthal Press, 1985), 214–15; and *LR* IV: 133.

2. On 30 May 1649, to take a single one-month period as an example, the council ordered Milton to review thoroughly the papers found on a man named John Lee; on 11 June, it ordered Milton and the Sergeant-at-Arms Edward Dendy to go through the papers of a Mr. Small and confiscate any they deemed politically incriminating; and again on 23 June, the council ordered Milton to examine and report back on more captured papers, this time belonging to Marchamont Nedham, the author and publisher of a royalist periodical, *Mercurius Pragmaticus*. All references to the proceedings of the Council of State are taken from the *Calendar of State Papers, Domestic Series*, 13 vols., ed. Mary Anne Everett Green (London, 1874–1886). (Public Records Office: Draft Order Books, SP 25/1–61; Fair Order Books, SP 25/62–79.)

3. See Keith Thomas, *Religion and the Decline of Magic* (New York: Charles Scribner's Sons, 1971), 152–53.

4. Milton's name shows up twice in the proceedings. The committee also examined "a Note under the Hand of Mr. *John Milton*" dated 10 August 1650 (now lost). *Journal of the House of Commons: Volume 7*, 113–14.

5. *LR* III: 206. A young Dutch ambassador named Lieuwe van Aitzema had arrived in London the day before Milton's hearing, and he recorded in his journal that Milton approved (*hadde gelicentieert*) the heretical book's printing. See also *Transcript of the Registers of the Worshipful Company*, I: 383.

6. Cyprian Blagden, *The Stationers' Company: A History, 1403–1959* (London: Allen and Unwin, 1960).

7. John Stow, *A Survey of London* (London, 1603), 175.

8. The term *items* here is deliberate because many of the printed texts were broadsheets and short pamphlets, not books. See D. F. McKenzie, "The Economies of Print, 1550–1750: Scales of Production and Conditions of Constraint," in *Producione e Commercio della Carta e del Libro secc. XIII–XVIII*, Istituto Internazionale di Storia Economica, "F. Datini" Prato, Serie II—Atti delle "Settimane di Studi" e altri Convegni 23 (Prato: Le Monnier, 1992), 389–425.

9. See "Stubbe, John," in *ODNB*.

10. William Camden, *Annales, or The True and Royall History of the Famous Empress*, 2nd ed. (London, 1625), Book III: C4r-v; and "Stubbe, John," in *ODNB*.

11. "Wightman, Edward," in *ODNB*; *Calendar of State Papers, Domestic Series*, 1611–1618; 1639–40; and "The Last Heretic," www.burton-on-trent.org.uk/1612-last-heretic.

12. David Cressy, "Book Burning in Tudor and Stuart England," *Sixteenth Century Journal* 36.2 (2005): 359–74 (372).

13. Mark Kishlansky, "A Whipper Whipped: The Sedition of William Prynne," *The Historical Journal* 56.3 (2013): 603–27 (604).

14. Strafford, Thomas Wentworth, Earl of, *The Earl of Strafforde's Letters and Dispatches*, 2 vols. (London, 1739), I: 261 (Xxx1r).

15. William Prynne, *A New Discovery of the Prelates Tyranny* (London, 1641), I3v-I4r.

16. *LR* III: 206.

17. D. F. McKenzie, "The London Book Trade in 1644," in *Making Meaning: "Printers of the Mind" and Other Essays*, ed. Peter D. McDonald and Michael F. Suarez (Amherst: University of Massachusetts Press, 2002), 126–43 (131).

18. John Toland in *EL* 180.

19. Parker, *Biography*, 387.

20. Parker, *Biography*, 420.

21. Masson, *Life*, IV: 531.

22. Milton seems to have taken this expression—and concept—from the work by the English scholar and jurist John Selden (1584–1654), *De Jure Naturali et Gentium* (1640). Milton refers favorably to Selden's book in both *The Doctrine and Discipline of Divorce* (YP II: 350) and *Areopagitica* (YP II: 513).

23. Stephen M. Fallon, *Milton's Peculiar Grace: Self-Representation and Authority* (Ithaca, NY: Cornell University Press, 2007), 124–32; and *CIM* 115.

24. See *CIM* 115.

25. *An Answer to a Book. Intituled, "The Doctrine and Discipline of Divorce"* (London, 1644), E2v. This was the critic whom Milton answered in *Colasterion*, which is mentioned in chapter 4.

26. Herbert Palmer, *The Glasse of Gods Providence towards His Faithfull Ones* (London, 1644), I1r; *Journal of the House of Commons: Volume 3: 1643–1644*, 606.

27. William Prynne, *Twelve Considerable Serious Questions Touching Church Government* (London, 1644); Parker, *Biography*, 275; and "Prynne, William," in *ODNB*. Milton would not soon forget Prynne's attack, and in an early draft of one of his sonnets, "On the New Forcers of Conscience," Milton included a cruel reference to the Puritan's cropped ears, but he then thought better of it and deleted the phrase.

28. Maurice Kelley, *This Great Argument: A Study of Milton's "De Doctrina Christiana" as a Gloss upon "Paradise Lost"* (Princeton, NJ: Princeton University Press, 1941); and Gordon Campbell, Thomas N. Corns, John K. Hale, and Fiona J. Tweedie, *Milton and the Manuscript of "De Doctrina Christiana"* (Oxford: Oxford University Press, 2007), 31–33.

29. *Arianism* should not be confused with *Aryanism*, an outdated term for describing people of European and West Asian descent, which is often associated with the Nazis' arguments for racial supremacy.

30. See, for example, *DDC* 1.5 [201–203].

31. *DDC*, Epistle [7]

32. Phillips in *EL* 61, 62; and Stephen B. Dobranski, *Milton, Authorship, and the Book Trade* (Cambridge: Cambridge University Press, 1999), 70.

33. *DDC* 1.30 [815].

34. *DDC*, Epistle [9].

35. Based on *DDC* 2.1 [907–909]. Milton uses *decalogo* here for the Ten Commandments.

36. *Journal of the House of Commons: Volume 7*, 113–14.

37. Marvell had to wait until 1657 to obtain his formal post in the government.

38. See Masson, *Life* V: 436.

39. Richard Baron, ed., *Eikonoklastes*, by Milton (London, 1756), A2v.

40. Parker, *Biography*, 661.

41. This institution was eventually replaced by the Public Record Office, which in 2004 subsequently became known as the National Archives. A lithograph of Lemon in the National Portrait Gallery reveals a genial-looking man.

42. See Keith W. F. Stavely, Preface, in *YP* VIII: 410–13.

CHAPTER SIX: ARROGANCE

1. According to seventeenth-century notions of great writing (based in part on Aristotle's poetic theory), the most significant literary genres were, in descending order, epic, tragedy, and an ode or hymn.

2. Oliver Cromwell allegedly appointed his eldest son as his successor on his deathbed.

3. YP IV: 537; and Parker, *Biography*, 518.

4. Masson, *Life* V: 574; Parker, *Biography*, 518.

5. Parker, *Biography*, 192.

6. On the likely date that Milton drafted the notes, see Masson, *Life*, V: 406–7.

7. Phillips in *EL* 71–72.

8. See *Paradise Lost*, Book 3, lines 372–82.

9. See *Paradise Lost*, Book 2, line 692; Book 5, line 710; and Book 6, line 156. Satan again exaggerates how many angels followed him in Book 1, line 633.

10. *A Collection of the State Papers of John Thurloe*, 7 vols. (London, 1742), II: 1.

11. *CIM* 166.

12. David Cressy, *Bonfires and Bells: National Memory and the Protestant Calendar in Elizabethan and Stuart England* (Berkeley and Los Angeles: University of California Press, 1989), 145–48.

13. "*In proditionem bombardicam,*" line 2.

14. See Job 1:6–12 and Job 2:1–7; and Matthew 4:1–11, Mark 1:12–13, and Luke 4:1–13.

15. On "begotten," see John 1:14, 1:18; John 3:16, 3:18; and 1 John 4:9.

16. *DDC* 1.2 [41].

17. See Edward Rogers, *Some Accounts of the Life and Opinions of a Fifth-Monarchy-Man. Chiefly Extracted from the Writings of John Rogers, Preacher* (London: Longmans, Green, Reader and Dyer, 1867), 13.

18. William Prynne, *Histriomastix* (London, 1633), Ggg*4r (part I, f. 556).

19. See Keith Thomas, *Religion and the Decline of Magic* (New York: Charles Scribner's Sons, 1971), 469–73.

20. David Lee Clark, ed., *Shelley's Prose; or, The Trumpet of a Prophecy* (Albuquerque: University of New Mexico Press, 1954), 267; and William Blake, "The Marriage of Heaven and Hell," in *Complete Writings*, ed. Geoffrey Keynes (London: Oxford University Press, 1972), 150. See also *CIM* 203–5.

21. C. S. Lewis, *A Preface to "Paradise Lost"* (1942; London: Oxford University Press, 1961), 92.

22. Lewis, *A Preface*, 130.

23. Stanley Fish, *Surprised by Sin: The Reader in "Paradise Lost,"* 2nd ed.

(1967; London: Macmillan, 1997). See John P. Rumrich, *Milton Unbound* (Cambridge: Cambridge University Press, 1996).

24. Fish, *Surprised by Sin*, 156–57; and see John Leonard, "There Is Such a Thing as Freedom in *Surprised by Sin*—and It's a Good Thing, Too," *Milton Quarterly* 52.4 (2019): 324–31.

25. See Rumrich, *Milton Unbound*, 18–22.

CHAPTER SEVEN: FORGIVENESS

1. See "Rouse, James" in *ODNB*.

2. Bodleian Library, shelfmark Arch.G.e.44.

3. "Some few of her nearest Relations," according to Milton's nephew Phillips in *EL* 63.

4. Phillips in *EL* 65.

5. Phillips in *EL* 65.

6. E. A. Wrigley, R. S. Davies, J. E. Oeppen, and R. S. Schofield, *English Population History from Family Reconstitution, 1580–1837* (Cambridge: Cambridge University Press, 1997), 128–39.

7. Aubrey in *EL* 14.

8. Milton at an early age defended divorce for ending a bad marriage. See his commonplace book, YP I: 414.

9. It is unclear what would have happened if Satan had repented after seducing the couple—if he had fallen to his knees, clasped his hands in prayer, and begged for God's mercy. Could the devil be saved? On this question, Milton equivocates. God in *Paradise Lost* announces that the bad angels sin on their own—"Self-tempted, self-depraved" (Book 3, line 130)—so they will not be saved. But he could mean that the bad angels will not find grace because he will never extend it to them or because they are so thoroughly debased that they will never seek it.

10. For the contrary view, see Augustine, *De civitate Dei*, XIV.26.

11. See Diane Kelsey McColley, *Milton's Eve* (Urbana: University of Illinois Press, 1983), 10–12.

12. Stephen B. Dobranski, *Milton's Visual Imagination: Imagery in "Paradise Lost"* (Cambridge: Cambridge University Press, 2015), 153–54.

13. Homer, *The Odyssey*, trans. Emily Wilson (New York: Norton, 2018), VI.230–31.

14. This idea can be traced back to Petrarch, *The Canzoniere*, trans. and ed. Mark Musa (Bloomington: Indiana University Press, 1996). In sonnet 197, for example, Petrarch refers to Laura's "golden hair" as his soul's "curly snare" (line 9), and in sonnet 198 he describes how "with her lovely eyes and hair she binds / my weary heart and lifts my vital spirits" (lines 3–4).

15. Edmund Spenser, *Amoretti*, in *"Amoretti" and "Epithalamion": A Critical Edition*, ed. Kenneth J. Larsen (Tempe, AZ: Medieval and Renaissance Texts and Studies, 1997), sonnet 73, lines 2–3; and sonnet 37.

16. *OED*, s.v. "wanton," defs. A.2, 7.b, 3.c.

17. Right before introducing Adam and Eve, Milton announces that "the fiend / Saw undelighted all delight" (Book 4, lines 285–86), and the scene concludes with a reminder of Satan's abiding presence: "Satan still in gaze, as first he stood" (Book 4, line 356). See Dobranski, *Milton's Visual Imagination* 163; and Irene Samuel, "*Paradise Lost* as Mimesis," in *Approaches to "Paradise Lost": The York Tercentenary Lectures*, ed. C. A. Patrides (London: Edward Arnold, 1968), 20.

18. So concludes Roland Mushat Frye from a survey of historical and mythical portraits. See *Milton's Imagery and the Visual Arts* (Princeton, NJ: Princeton University Press, 1978), 272. For Adam's "parted forelock," see *Paradise Lost*, Book 4, line 302.

19. Lewalski, *Life* 184.

20. Phillips in *EL* 66.

21. See Phillips in *EL* 66–67.

22. "House of John Milton, in Barbican," *Illustrated London News* (16 July 1864): 78+.

23. God had also repeated himself much earlier, when explaining to the Son that he would show mercy and "soften stony hearts / To pray, repent, and bring obedience due. / To prayer, repentance, and obedience due, / Though but endeavored with sincere intent, / Mine ear shall not be slow, mine eye not shut" (Book 3, lines 189–93). Again, the use of repetition illustrates the importance that Milton attaches to the act of seeking forgiveness and the fact that it is an activity.

CHAPTER EIGHT: RESISTING TEMPTATION

1. As stated in the introduction, some 62,000 soldiers were killed in the British civil wars. Close to 80,000 more men were imprisoned. See Michael Braddick, *God's Fury, England's Fire* (London and New York: Allen Lane, 2008), xxii, 389.

2. Samuel Pepys, *The Diary of Samuel Pepys*, ed. Robert Latham and William Matthews, 11 vols. (Berkeley and Los Angeles: University of California Press, 1970–1983), I: 158–59; Jenny Uglow, *A Gambling Man: Charles II's Restoration Game* (New York: Farrar, Straus, and Giroux, 2009), 40–41; and John Price, *A Letter Written from Dover* (London, 1660), A2.

3. Evelyn, *The Diary of John Evelyn*, ed. E. S. de Beer, 6 vols. (Oxford: Clarendon Press, 1955), III: 246.

4. *The Parliamentary or Constitutional History of England*, ed. William Cobbett et al., 2nd ed., 24 vols. (London, 1761–1763), vol. IV, column 162.

5. Skinner in *EL* 32; Wood in *EL* 48: and Phillips in *EL* 78.

6. "The Picture of the Good Old Cause Drawn to the Life" (London, 1660).

7. David Lloyd, *Eikon Basilike. Or, the True Pourtraicture of his Sacred Majesty Chalres the II in Three Books* (London, 1660), vol. II, sig, E2r.

8. Colonel Baker, *The Blazing-Star, Or Nolls Nose Newly Revived* (London, 1660), A4r.

9. G. S., *Britains Triumph* (London, 1660), C1r.

10. Ruth Spalding, ed., *The Diary of Bulstrode Whitelocke, 1605–1675* (Oxford: Oxford University Press, 1990), 606; Parker, *Biography* 574; and *LR* IV: 334.

11. Thirty-three of the regicides were still alive at the Restoration: they were tried as traitors and their estates were confiscated. All of them were sentenced to death, although some later had their sentences commuted to life imprisonment. That summer Parliament continued to debate almost daily who should be exempted from the new king's clemency. The members ultimately agreed that an additional twenty supporters of the republic were to be barred permanently from public office, and four other men were tried for their activities during the civil war years: three were executed, and one received life imprisonment. A fifth died in prison before being brought to trial. These five men were (in order) Hugh Peter, the chaplain to the Council of State; Archibald Campbell, the leader of the Scottish Covenanters; Henry Vane, a statesman and friend of Milton; John Lambert, an officer who led the army in its last resistance to the Restoration; and Arthur Hesilrige, a soldier and member of Parliament under the commonwealth. See David Plant, *The BCW Project: British Civil Wars, Commonwealth and Protectorate, 1638–1660* (2001–2015), http://bcw-project.org/.

12. Parker, *Biography* 1087; *Chronology* 193.

13. Various factions within Parliament had to be finessed without antagonizing some of the legislature's most powerful members, such as William Prynne, who continued to hold a grudge against Milton for his divorce pamphlets. See Masson, *Life* VI: 186–87.

14. *Britains Triumph*, C1r; and Lloyd, *Eikon Basilike*, vol. II, sig, E2r. Some twenty years later in 1681, Francis Turner, the future Bishop of Ely, was still singling out Milton in a fiery sermon delivered on the anniversary of Charles I's execution. Turner used Milton to underscore the martyred king's holiness. Milton was that "vile mercenary Satyrist" who had written "in justification of this prodigious Murder" and who "writ also upon *Divorce*, to make Adultery as well as Murder lawful in themselves, as they were delightful to him." See Francis Turner, *A Sermon Preached before the King on the 30 of January 1681* (London, 1681), 17–18.

15. Cyriack Sinner in *EL* 32; Richardson in *EL* 280; and Robert T. Fallon,

"John Milton and the Honorable Artillery Company," *Milton Quarterly* 9.2 (1975): 49–51.

16. Thomas Newton, "The Life of Milton," in *Paradise Lost: A Poem, in Twelve Books*, ed. Newton (London, 1770), xl, lxiv; and Richardson in *EL* 280.

17. Marcus Aurelius, *Meditations*, Book VIII.

18. Boethius, *Consolation of Philosophy*, trans. Samuel Fox (Cambridge, Ontario: Parentheses, 1999), 24–25 (chap. XI); and see Jackson Campbell Boswell, *Milton's Library* (New York: Garland Publishing, 1975), 37.

19. Also, according to the poet John Dryden, "Milton has acknowledged to me, that Spencer [*sic*] was his original." See Dryden, Preface, in *Fables Antient and Modern; Translated into Verse, from Homer, Ovid, Boccace and Chaucer*, vol. 1 (Glasgow: Robert and Andrew Foulis, 1771), B1v.

20. Phillips in *EL* 75.

21. *Poems* (London, 1645), B2r.

22. *Paradise Regain'd . . . To which is added Samson Agonistes* (London, 1671), P4r.

23. See Irene Samuel, "Milton on Learning and Wisdom," *PMLA* 64.4 (1949): 708–23; and *CIM* 183–84.

24. See YP I: 822–23.

25. See *Paradise Regained*, Book 4, line 555.

CHAPTER NINE: DOUBT

1. Edward A. Block, "Milton's Gout," *Bulletin of the History of Medicine* 28.3 (1954): 201–11. The swellings or lumps are called tophi or, informally, "chalk stones." On Milton's gout, see Richardson in *EL* 203. Other famous sufferers of gout include Leonardo da Vinci, Oliver Cromwell, Thomas Jefferson, Benjamin Franklin, Karl Marx, Henry James, Theodore Roosevelt, and Joseph Conrad.

2. Masson, *Life* VI: 728; Richardson in *EL* 229; Cyriack Skinner in *EL* 33; and Aubrey in *EL* 5. Sufferers of gout understandably can feel peevish and are often said to be short-tempered because of their extreme discomfort. See Block, "Milton's Gout," 211.

3. Masson, *Life* VI: 729.

4. Richardson in *EL* 202–03; Toland in *EL* 194.

5. Anthony à Wood in *EL* 48; and Toland in *EL* 194.

6. Toland in *EL* 194.

7. See YP VII: 481–82.

8. *Mercurius Publicus*, 24 Jan. to 31 Jan. 1661 (London, 1661), H4v.

9. Milton composed—or at least extensively revised—*Samson Agonistes* after the Restoration. See Blair Worden, "Milton, *Samson Agonistes*, and the Resto-

ration," in *Culture and Society in the Stuart Restoration*, ed. Gerald MacLean (Cambridge: Cambridge University Press, 1995), 111–36.

10. See the facsimile in vol. II of Harris Francis Fletcher, ed., *John Milton's Complete Poetical Works*, 4 vols. (Urbana: University of Illinois Press, 1943–1948), 19.

11. One of the oldest controversies surrounding the poem involves its structure. *Samson* seems to lack a sense of rising action; the concluding catastrophe does not directly grow out of the preceding events. This criticism began with Samuel Johnson, *The Rambler*, no. 139 (16 July 1751), in *Milton, 1732–1801: The Critical Heritage*, ed. John T. Shawcross (London and Boston: Routledge and Kegan Paul, 1972), 217–20.

12. See Joad Raymond, "Complications of Interest: Milton, Scotland, Ireland, and National Identity in 1649," *Review of English Studies*, new ser., 55.220 (2004): 315–45 (323).

13. *WJM* XII: 81.

14. Milton was also working from Josephus's first-century commentary on Judges in *Antiquities*, Book 5, chapter 8.

15. *CPEP* 291.

16. See David Masson, ed., *The Poetical Works of John Milton*, 3 vols., rev. ed. (London: Macmillan, 1890); and A. W. Verity, ed., *Milton's "Samson Agonistes"* (1892; Cambridge: Cambridge University Press, 1966).

17. See Jenny Uglow, *A Gambling Man: Charles II's Restoration Game* (New York: Farrar, Straus, and Giroux, 2009); and Ronald Hutton, *Charles the Second: King of England, Scotland, and Ireland* (Oxford: Clarendon Press, 1989).

18. Nicholas von Maltzhan, *Milton's History of Britain: Republican Historiography in the English Revolution* (Oxford: Clarendon Press, 1991).

19. *Paradise Regain'd . . . To which is added Samson Agonistes* (London, 1671), P3v.

20. The ten nonconsecutive lines of verse in the *Omissa* are not the result of a printing error. Through each step of the publication process, no member of a seventeenth-century printing house could have easily overlooked this text. See Dobranski, *Readers and Authorship in Early Modern England* (Cambridge: Cambridge University Press, 2005), 192–96. For the added lines, I am quoting *Paradise Regained . . . To which is added Samson Agonistes*, P3v.

CHAPTER TEN: SURVIVING DISASTER

1. Edward Phillips reportedly told John Aubrey that Milton began the poem "about 2 years before the King came in, and finished about 3 years after the King's Restoration." See Aubrey in *EL* 13.

2. Phillips in *EL* 73.

3. This account of the Great Fire is drawn largely from the following sources: Thomas Vincent, *God's Terrible Voice in the City* (London, 1668), D2v-E1r; J. P. Malcolm, vol. IV of *Londinium Redivivum, or An Ancient and Modern Description of London* (London: F. and C. Rivington, 1807); Peter Berresford Ellis, *The Great Fire of London* (London: New English Library, 1976); vol. III of Edward Hyde, *The Life of Edward Earl of Clarendon* (Oxford: Clarendon, 1759); Neil Hanson, *The Great Fire of London in That Apocalyptic Year, 1666* (Hoboken, NJ: Wiley, 2002); and Walter George Bell, *The Great Fire of London in 1666*, 3rd ed. (London: Bodley Head, 1951).

4. John Stow, *A Survey of London, Written in the Year 1598* (London, 1603), F8r.

5. John Dryden, *Annus Mirabilis* (London, 1667), quatrain 230.

6. Wood in *EL* 48.

7. Clare Gittings, "Sacred and Secular: 1558–1660," in *Death in England*, ed. Peter C. Jupp and Clare Gittings (New Brunswick, NJ: Rutgers University Press, 1999), 150.

8. Daniel Defoe, *A Journal of the Plague Year* (Philadelphia: John D. Morris, 1903), 68.

9. Masson, *Life*, VI: 490–98.

10. On Milton's changing residences in his later years, see Phillips in *EL* 75 and Lewalski, *Life* 411, 671–72.

11. Samuel Rolle, *Shilhavtiyah, or, The Burning of London in the Year 1666. Commemorated and Improved in CX. Discourses, Meditations, and Contemplations* (London, 1667), L2r-L3v.

12. Bell, *The Great Fire of London in 1666*, 113–14.

13. *OED*, 3rd ed., attributes the first use of this phrase to John Ruskin in 1856.

14. So objected one of Milton's most insightful twentieth-century readers, William Empson, who thought that the source of the poem's power was Milton's grappling with traditional Christian doctrine. See William Empson, *Milton's God*, rev. ed. (London: Chatto and Windus, 1965).

15. Eve's language here echoes the passage in the Bible where Ruth asks Naomi not to entreat her to leave (Ruth 1:16).

16. This does not mean that Adam and Eve are better off for having disobeyed God. Milton did not subscribe to the doctrine of the fortunate fall—in Latin, *felix culpa*—the idea that humanity's sin was actually a blessing because it allowed God to demonstrate his beneficence and to sacrifice his only Son. Milton's God plainly dismisses this notion, telling the angels that Adam was better off sinless: "Happier, had it sufficed him to have known / Good by itself, and evil not at all" (Book 11, lines 88–89).

17. Milton uses a similar phrase in three passages in *Paradise Lost*—Book 6, lines 310–11 (quoted here); Book 2, lines 921–22; and Book 10, line 306. He also uses the phrase in *Paradise Regained*, Book 4, lines 563–64. The originator of this type of metaphor is Virgil.

18. See Daniel Shore, "Was Milton White?," *Milton Studies* 62.2 (2020): 252–65 (256-57); and Mary Nyquist, *Arbitrary Rule: Slavery, Tyranny, and the Power of Life and Death* (Chicago: University of Chicago Press, 2013), 139–42.

19. See Shore, "Was Milton White?," 253–55.

20. See Paul Stevens, "*Paradise Lost* and the Colonial Imperative," *Milton Studies* 34 (1996): 3–21.

21. See *CPEP* 155.

22. On the biblical tradition of combining faith and works, see James 2:20.

EPILOGUE

1. The beautiful and much younger Margaret Brooke was thought to be a poor match for the stout Denham. She was widely known to be carrying on an affair with the Duke of York, Charles II's brother, the man who in some twenty years would be crowned King James II. When she passed away suddenly in January 1667, rumors began to swirl that Denham had murdered her out of jealousy. The specific story was that he had poisoned her with a tainted cup of the still new but very popular West Indian drink, chocolate. See "Denham, John" in *ODNB*; Pepys, *The Diary*, 19 August 1665, 26 September 1666, 8 and 13 October 1666, 10 November 1666, and 7 January 1667 (London, 1893), at Project Gutenberg (http://www.gutenberg.org/files/4200/4200-h/4200-h.htm); and Andrew Marvell, "The Last Instructions to a Painter," in *Collection of Poems on Affairs of State* (London, 1689), C2r (line 342).

2. The story occurs in Richardson in *EL* 295.

3. The contract is transcribed in *LR* 4: 429–31.

4. Karl Marx, *Capital: A Critique of Political Economy*, vol. 1, trans. Ben Fowkes (London: Vintage, 1990), 1044.

5. See the National Archives (Kew, Richmond, Surrey, 2018), http://www.nationalarchives.gov.uk/currency-converter/#.

6. The contract sets a limit of 1,500 copies for each edition but stipulates that Simmons was to pay Milton after 1,300 copies were sold. See *LR* 4: 448.

7. Milton also made a few, smaller changes for his epic's second edition: he added eight lines (Book 8, lines 1–3; and Book 12, lines 1–5), revised one line (Book 8, line 4), and appears to have made at least four other substantive revisions (in Books 1, 5, and 12) along with roughly thirty-seven other minor alterations.

8. Quotations of Marvell's "On *Paradise Lost*" are taken from Milton, *Paradise Lost*, ed. Stephen B. Dobranski (New York: W. W. Norton, 2022), 3-4.

9. See *The Monitor*, vol. 1, no. 17 (6–10 April 1713); and Masson, *Life*, VI: 483–84.

10. Milton, *Paradise Lost*, 4th ed. (London, 1688), πIv.

11. Milton, *Paradise Lost*, 4th ed., Zz2r-²Aa2v.

12. *The English Chronicle and Universal Evening Post* (7–9 Sept. 1790), 3 (column 4).

13. Samuel Johnson, *Lives of the English Poets*, ed. George Birkbeck Hill, 3 vols. (New York: Octagon, 1967), I: 191. 157, 183, 163. Many of Johnson's critical assessments are more memorable for their insolence than their insight. About *Paradise Lost*, he wrote, "None ever wished it longer than it is," and about "Lycidas," he opined, "Its form is that of a pastoral, easy, vulgar, and therefore disgusting."

14. "Lycidas," line 11.

15. The creature in *Frankenstein* is, in turn, a version of Milton's Adam. *Paradise Lost* is one of the three formative books that the creature studies as he struggles to comprehend his relationship with his absent creator. Shelley also chose a quotation from Milton's epic for her novel's epigraph: a fallen and defensive Adam asks, "Did I request thee, Maker, from my clay / To mold me man, did I solicit thee / From darkness to promote me?" (Book 10, lines 743–45). These are the same questions that Frankenstein's creature will ponder as he searches in vain for contentment and companionship.

16. William Wordsworth, "London, 1802," in *The Norton Anthology of English Literature: The Major Authors*, 8th ed., gen ed. Stephen Greenblatt (New York and London: Norton, 2006), 1549–50 (line 8).

17. Joseph A. Wittreich, *Feminist Milton* (Ithaca and London: Cornell University Press, 1987); and Diane McColley, review of *Feminist Milton*, in *Renaissance Quarterly* 42.3 (1989): 589–93. Some earlier twentieth-century feminist critics had argued that Milton inhibited female readers; they were working from Virginia Woolf's assertion that women writers should "look past Milton's bogey." But subsequent scholars such as Wittreich have not found historical support for this claim. See Virginia Woolf, *A Room of One's Own* (New York: Harcourt Brace, 1957), 125; and Sandra M. Gilbert, "Patriarchal Poetry and Women Readers: Reflections on Milton's Bogey," *PMLA* 93.3 (1978): 368–82 (368).

18. Malcolm X (with Alex Haley), *The Autobiography of Malcolm X* (New York: Ballantine Books, 1992), 203.

19. *The Diary of George Templeton Strong*, ed. Allan Nevins and Milton Halsey Thomas, 4 vols. (New York: Macmillan, 1952), III: 308; and Ralph Waldo Emerson, "Milton," *North American Review* 47 (1838): 69.

20. See Lewalski, *Life* 546.

21. See, for example, YP II: 724.

22. Aubrey in *EL* 5. For an alternative theory, that Milton died from a gastro-intestinal hemorrhage, see Campbell and Corns 374-75.

23. Toland in *EL* 193.

24. Clare Gittings, "Sacred and Secular: 1558–1660," in *Death in England*, ed. Peter C. Jupp and Clare Gittings (New Brunswick, NJ: Rutgers University Press, 1999), 162; and Maureen Waller, *1700: Scenes from London Life* (New York: Four Walls Eight Windows, 2000), 115–20.

25. Ian W. Archer, "London," in *Context*, 364.

26. *OED* s.v. *adj.* "fit," "feat."

INDEX

Egerton family, 22, 24, 123

Eikon Basilike, xii, xix, 80–83, 84, 202, 264–65

Eikonoklastes, xix, xxi, 81–83, 89–90, 132, 193, 264–65

elegies, Milton's, 35–36, 273

Elizabeth I, 63, 107, 116

Ellwood, Thomas, 101–102, 237, 240, 278

Emerson, Ralph Waldo, 3, 263

Empson, William, 288

epic, 3, 39, 40, 44, 109, 136–38, 155, 242–43, 266, 282

Epicurus, 206

episcopacy. *See* bishops

Epistolarum Familiarium (Familiar Letters), xxii. *See also* letters, Milton's

"Epitaphium Damonis" (Epitaph for Damon), xvi, 42–44, 48–49, 53, 56, 94, 242, 266. *See also* Diodati, Charles

"Epitaph on the Marchioness of Winchester, An," 46

Euripides, 11, 15, 219

Evans, Mary Ann (George Eliot), 263, 279

Ezekiel, 124

Fairfax, Thomas, xxiii, 182

Fallon, Stephen M., 269

felix culpa, 288

Fish, Stanley, 159–60

Fisher, Elizabeth, 105, 213

Foxe, John, 67

free expression, 6, 113–34

free will, 70–73, 124–26, 153, 158, 172–73, 178–82, 197, 220–21, 230, 245, 266. *See also* Arminians, Arminianism

French, J. Milton, 270

friendship, friends, 3, 5, 16, 19–20, 30, 33–36, 38, 41–44, 51, 54–56, 59, 88, 96–97, 100–103, 183, 193, 194–95, 197, 207, 220, 255, 265, 275. *See also the names of the poet's individual friends*

Frye, Roland Mushat, 284

Fuller, Margaret, 3, 263

Fuseli, Henry, xiii, xiv, 186, 252

Galileo Galilei, 39–40, 273

Gandhi, Mahatma, 130

Gill, Alexander Jr., 16, 101

Gouldman, Francis, 131

Great Fire of London, xiv, xxii, 237–42, 257

grit, 4, 5–7, 140–44, 162–63, 196–99, 250–56, 266. *See also* self-possession

Gunpowder Plot, 147–48, 151

Hale, John K., 269

Hall, Joseph, 66, 73, 89–90

Hammersmith, xvi, 49

Haughton, Moses, xiv, 252

Hayley, William, 107, 108, 186, 222

Henrietta Maria, Queen, 67, 77, 117

Henry VIII, 74, 123

Hesilrige, Arthur, 285

Hesiod, 15

History of Britain, The, xxii, xxiii, 235

Hobson, Thomas, xi, 46–48, 274, 275

Homer, 15, 37, 88, 136–37, 151, 153, 160, 187, 206, 261; *Iliad*, 137, 144, 161, 242; *Odyssey*, 24, 65, 137, 155, 173, 242

Horace, 15

Horton, xvi, 34, 49

Mill, John Stuart, *On Liberty*, 123

Millington, Edward, 214

Milton, Anne (poet's sister), 2, 46

Milton, Christopher (poet's brother), xv, 2, 16, 184, 213

Milton, John: blindness of, xvii, xix, xx, 3, 4, 5, 87–91, 95–100, 102–103, 109–11, 129, 214, 216–17, 218, 237, 277; composition practices of, 100–104, 109–11, 129, 137–38, 214, 237–38, 248; Continental journey (Grand Tour) of, xvi, 12, 37–41, 64, 137, 165, 259; death of, xxiii, 207, 215, 265, 291; and gout, 213–15, 216, 237, 286; imprisonment of, xxi, 5, 193–95, 206, 211, 216; nickname of, at college, 30–31; portraits of, xi, xii, xiv, 1–3, 30, 52, 108, 214, 258–59; as Secretary for Foreign Tongues (Latin Secretary), xix, xx, 62–63, 79–86, 114, 131, 133, 193, 235, 279, as teacher, 12–14, 84, 106, 137, 167, 262; and theology, 1, 12, 16–17, 69–73, 128–30, 220–21

Milton, John (poet's son), xix, 91–92

Milton, John, Senior (poet's father), xviii, 2–3, 17, 33, 107, 265, 272, 279. *See also* "Ad Patrem"

Milton, Sara (poet's mother), xi, xvi, 2–3, 49, 50

Minshull, Elizabeth (poet's third wife), xxii, 2, 106, 195, 213–14, 277

Montaigne, Michel de, 6

More, Alexander, xx

More, Hannah, 263

natural law, 126–27

"Naturam non Pati Senium" ("That nature does not suffer from old age"), 274

Nedham, Marchamont, 279

Newcomen, Matthew, 277

New Model Army, xviii, xx, 9–10, 31, 69, 73, 76, 88, 182–83

Observations on the Articles of Peace, xix, 219

Oedipus, 100

Of Education, xvii, xxii, 14, 198–99

Of Prelatical Episcopacy, xvii

Of Reformation, xvii, 250

Of True Religion, xxii, 134

"On Shakespeare," xv, xvi, 19, 46

"On the Death of a Fair Infant Dying of a Cough," 46, 48, 231

"On the Morning of Christ's Nativity" (the Nativity Ode), xv, 99, 110, 206, 255

"On the New Forcers of Conscience," 281

"On the University Carrier," 46–48, 275

Oxford, Oxford University, xvii, 2, 31, 33, 36, 73, 115, 132, 165–67, 182, 184, 193, 275

Ovid, 15, 37, 106

Page, William, 116, 117

Palmer, Herbert, 127

Paradise Lost, 18, 42, 55, 88, 223; Abdiel (angel) in, 99–100; Adam and Eve in, 6, 15, 57, 71–72, 168–78, 181–82, 200, 262, 275; Adam and Eve after the Fall in, 59, 162, 169, 171–72, 184–89, 243–48,

253, 255–56; Adam and Eve's
hair in, 171, 173–75, 182, 283,
284; Adam and Eve's hierarchy in,
73, 172–76, 184–86, 256, 284;
Adam's sin in, 181–82, 242, 243–
44; composition and publication
of, xx, xxii, 6, 86, 101–103, 113,
137–38, 194, 237–38, 257–61,
278, 287, 289; consequences of the
Fall in, 162, 171, 189, 198, 206,
220, 238, 242, 243–51, 255–56,
284, 288; contemporary context as
influence, 5, 111, 135–36, 138–39,
158, 160, 196, 211, 213, 241–43,
248; cosmos in, 39–40; creation
and matter in, 172; death in, 46,
56–59, 242, 244, 245; depiction
of God in, 71–72, 73, 139–40,
146, 149–50, 244–45, 275, 283,
284; Eve's temptation and sin in,
15, 29–30, 177, 178–81, 185, 242,
243; illustrations from, 58, 141,
143, 151, 156, 170, 179, 186, 188,
252; invocations (proems) in, 109–
11, 193; Michael (angel) in, 151,
189, 198, 220, 242, 246–51, 255–
56, 259; Raphael (angel) in, 39–40,
42, 59, 149, 153, 159, 172, 175,
177, 242; readers and readership
of, 18, 44, 102, 157–60, 257–66;
Satan in, 6, 15, 22, 29, 39–40, 57,
71–72, 99, 119–20, 125, 135–36,
138–63, 174, 178–81, 189, 200,
206, 242, 253, 262, 263, 266,
283, 284; the Son in, 71, 72, 138,
144, 149–53, 161, 168, 184, 200;
war in heaven in, 99–100, 149–53,
215
Paradise Regained, xiii, 6, 15, 102,

196, 254, 262; contemporary con-
text as influence, 201–204, 205,
207–208, 211; illustrations from,
203, 209; publication of, xxii, 205,
207, 215, 218, 235; temptations in,
199–211, 215, 217, 243
Parker, William Riley, 270
"Passion, The," 46, 200–201
pastoral, 42–44, 53–56, 109
Patterson, Frank Allen, 270
Payne, John, 47
Peter, Hugh, 285
Petrarch, Francesco, 38; *The Can-
zoniere*, 283
Philaras, Leonard, 88, 96–97
Phillips, Edward, xvi, 13, 38, 59, 85,
91, 103, 105, 108, 129, 166–67,
273, 287
Phillips, John, xvi, 13, 129
Phineus, 88
Pindar, 11
plague, xxii, 101, 240–42
Plato, 4, 35, 206
Poems (1645), xviii, 19, 29, 166
Poems, &c. (1673), xxii, 29, 198
Powell, Mary (poet's first wife), xvii,
xviii, xix, 80, 91, 93–94, 107, 113,
165–68, 182–84
Powell family, xvii, 166–67, 182–83
Presbyterians, Presbyterianism, 2, 69–
70, 74, 76, 101, 184
*Present Means . . . of a Free Common-
wealth, The*, xxi
Prolusions, 51
*Pro Populo Anglicano Defensio
(Defense of the English People* or
First Defense), xix, xx, xxi, 84–86,
88–89, 90, 103, 110, 123, 132,
137, 193